TIPIS | TEPEES | TEEPEES

TIPIS | TEPEES | TEEPEES

HISTORY AND DESIGN
OF THE
CLOTH TIPI

LINDA A. HOLLEY

Gibbs Smith, Publisher

TO ENRICH AND INSPIRE HUMANKIND

Salt Lake City | Charleston | Santa Fe | Santa Barbara

To all my "tipi slaves" and those who love a night and a day in a tipi.

First Edition
11 10 09 08 07   5 4 3 2 1

Published by
Gibbs Smith, Publisher
PO Box 667
Layton, Utah 84041

Orders: 1.800.835.4993
www.gibbs-smith.com

Designed by Kurt Wahlner
Printed and bound in the United States of America

Library of Congress Cataloging-in-Publication Data

Holley, Linda A.
   Tipis, tepees, teepees : history and design of the cloth
tipi / Linda Holley. — 1st ed.
      p. cm.
   Includes bibliographical references.
   ISBN-13: 978-1-58685-511-6
   ISBN-10: 1-58685-511-5
   1. Tipis—History. 2. Tipis—Design and construction. I. Title.

E98.D8H65 2007
796.54028—dc22

2006029424

Contents

Acknowledgments

I wish to thank all the members of Material Culture of the Prairie, Plains, and Plateau and Lodge Owners discussion Web site groups. The input of the following people—Bill Holmes, Benson Lanford, Jan Kristek, Billy Maxwell, Bill and Kathy Brewer, Bob Brewer, Peter Gibbs, Creig White, Georg Barth, "Jack in the Black Hills," Ted Asten, Mike Terry, David Sager, David Ansonia, Alexander Barber, Duane Alderman, Carolyn Corey, Mike Cowdrey, Allen Chronister, Ken Weidner, Curtis Carter, and the many others who helped by doing historic research, locating photos, e-mailing, and sending packages of information—has been invaluable. They made this book possible.

Thanks also to all of those wonderful people who kept my life sane during repeated computer crashes; three hurricanes (Francis, Ivan, and Jean) that left me with no electricity for weeks; surgery to fix my hand that was smashed during Hurricane Jean; and my knee replacement, which all my accidents with tipi poles contributed to. A special thanks to "Weird" Wayne McDowell who traveled from Illinois to Florida for the making of a 12-foot tipi. He took over five thousand pictures . . . and I only used about fifteen. "Tipi slaves" Bill Burns and Mike Ketchum endured a very intense week of filming and cutting and being yelled at by an unforgiving taskmaster. At least they got food and some money out of this and my gratitude. Thanks also to Jay Deen, my first tipi slave, who helped build many of the three hundred tipis that came from Alligator Trading Co., my tipi company.

Thanks to the tipi makers around the world (Richard Reese of Reese Tipis, Nomadics, Strinz Tipis, Spring Valley, R. K. Lodges, Wolf Glen Lodges of England/Scotland, Rainbow Tipis of Australia, Arrow Tipis of Canada, and others), who answered my phone calls and e-mails with a wealth of information in photos and personal tidbits, which they were not afraid to pass on to me. A big acknowledgment to Louis W. Jones and Doug Rodgers who kept me up late at night with questions and the inquisitiveness to go find the answers or the usual "when will the book be done?" And a special thanks to James E. Dudley and Ed De Torres who took the time to sit down with me and edit hundreds of pages of information into something readable.

Introduction

My interest in tipis began about 1971 when my husband and I saw a neighbor working on a set of tipi poles and we just had to dive in and help. That was it. Tipi fever hit us and we just had to have one. During the Christmas holidays of 1972, we ordered our first tipi, an 18-footer from Darry Wood. It arrived one night in the back of Darry's truck. I wanted to start painting it right away, but someone wisely advised me to wait a year, do some research, and then decorate. So, we began our research, finally settling on a beaded Cheyenne-style cover with a painted lining. We took that tipi everywhere—to rendezvous, powwows, and campouts.

When my husband and I "split the blanket" in 1977, I kept the tipi and continued to travel to events. In 1978, I accepted the challenge to make a tipi. With David Clayton, I headed down to south Florida to buy an industrial sewing machine. From 1978 to 1995, I sewed over three hundred lodges, sometimes with the assistance of "tipi slaves" (those foolish enough to volunteer to help me). During all of these years of making tipis, going to various gatherings, doing beadwork, and making tipi accoutrements, I was studying—doing research and listening to those knowledgeable about tipi life.

Like virtually all tipi lovers of my generation, I learned a lot from the classic work on tipis, *The Indian Tipi: Its History, Construction, and Use*, by Reginald and Gladys Laubin. This book, published in 1957 and still in print, proved to be a wellspring of knowledge and inspiration; it spread the lore of the tipi literally all over the world. In Europe, however, the tipi was already in use before the publication of the Laubins' book. In the early twentieth century, there were already American Indian hobbyists in Europe, especially in Germany, inspired by the works of novelist Karl May and the Wild West show of Buffalo Bill Cody. Even so, it is fair to say that "the Laubin book," as it is affectionately called by tipi lovers, stimulated newcomers to the tipi worldwide. Today tipis are made and camped in on every continent but Antarctica (but it might be possible to use them there as well!). The modern tipi lovers' debt to the Laubins is enormous.

It is time, however, to reassess. The Laubins wrote about the tipis they knew best, the tipis of the 1940s and 1950s. The tipis of that era represented a particular stage in the evolution of tipi design and construction. The cloth tipis, still popular at the time the Laubins' book was written, had replaced the early buffalo-hide tipis. Since then, tipi construction has evolved due to amazing developments in technology. So, focusing on the progress the tipi has undergone, this book will address three areas: first, the history and evolution of the tipi; second, a step-by-step process of acquiring or making your own tipi; and third, current uses of tipis, drawing on the experiences of tipi lovers all over the world.

Arapaho women sit by a buffalo-hide tipi in Ft. Sill, Indian Territory, Oklahoma. The tipi was created between 1869 and 1874.

Documenting the Historic Tipi

The nomadic dwelling structure of the American Indian is called several names by many different tribes. The Apsaroka, Apsáalooke, or Crow Native Americans call the tipi *ashé* (home) or *ashtáale* (real home). The Blackfoot call it *niitoy-yiss* (the tipi), and the Lakota call it *tipestola* (tipis) or what we now call all lodges.[i] In the last 175 years, the tipi has evolved in materials used, construction techniques, and usage. It has gone from buffalo and elk hides to cloth and now to the synthetic materials of the twenty-first century. The two important innovations in tipis were first the use of horses for transporting bigger poles and larger hide lodges. Then in the early nineteenth century came the introduction of cloth covers.

The information about the historic tipi and tipi camp of the early to late nineteenth century in this chapter is taken from historic ledger drawings, daguerreotypes (tin types), glass slides, photographs, and handwritten documentation. Many pieces of information come from diaries, observations of clergy and the military, trappers and rendezvous people, visitors to tribal camps, and trading post lists of materials. Secondhand material, not directly observed or experienced, was avoided in collecting this information. One main exception is the quoted material from the late James H. Creighton that follows in the next section. Since many books written in the mid-1800s were not published until later in the twentieth century, the bibliography in the back of the book lists the sources by the date they were originally written or when the major firsthand information was observed.

Historical References to the Tipi

My good friend the late James H. Creighton, who passed away in 2005, had a great love of the tipi and its construction. In honor of him, this special section on basic tipi history, which he wrote, is included:

> The stately conical lodges of the Great Plains, with their beautiful symmetry, adjustable smoke flaps and snug interiors are familiar to just about everyone. The tipi, a Sioux word, has come to immortalize the glamour of the Wild West, chiefly through Hollywood Westerns. Aside from a handful of movies, such as *Little Big Man* and *Dances with Wolves*, however, the tipi is rarely portrayed accurately. It is a comfortable dwelling that can be used in any weather year-round. It is perhaps the most perfectly designed tent structure that has ever been used and its history is long and detailed.
>
> The conical home is as old as man and has multiple origins worldwide. In this country, it was found in one form or another almost everywhere. It often acted as a 'mobile home' for hunting societies. With a series of slender poles arranged around a tripod or four-pole base, the structure was covered in whatever was available in a particular region. Birch bark or marsh grass matting in the Northeast, dressed caribou hides in the far north, buffalo or elk in the Midwest and Plains, and tulle mat covering in the Northwest were common. Today, the nomadic Laplanders still use reindeer-hide lodges very similar to the Plains tipi, as do indigenous tribal groups across Siberia and into Mongolia. In ancient Europe, I am sure that the tipi-style lodge was also used both as temporary hunting lodges as well as permanent homes. The classic Sioux tipi was a relative latecomer, but it was on the American prairies and Great Plains that it rose to its present form.
>
> In the 1530s the Spanish under Hernando de Soto tore a path from western Florida to Virginia, then turned west to the Mississippi, and traveled on into present-day Oklahoma. The Indians encountered were

already in a state of transition. Many were the remnants of the great Mound Builder societies that had centered on the Ohio River Basin. These overlapping cultures had once ruled networks of trade centers that spanned from the Atlantic to the Pacific and from Canada to Mexico. At that time, the Great Plains was not a center of population, although some groups had found their way to the Missouri River. Some appear to have been ancestors to the Pawnee and Arickara (Arikara), of the Caddoan language family. Farther upriver were transplanted Siouans, like the Mandan and Hidatsa, who had left their Ohio River homeland in prior centuries. In de Soto's time, other breakaway Siouan tribes, such as the Omaha, Ponca, Osage, Quapaw, and Kansa, were migrating west as they traveled. They took on traits learned from the groups already on the Missouri.

Western Algonquin groups had done the same over many centuries, leaving forest homes around the Great Lakes to enter the prairie country. Early breakaways included the Blackfeet bands that migrated west to Montana and the Canadian Rockies. The Algonquian Cheyenne, Arapaho, and Shutai joined the migrating Siouans at the Missouri, where they took on similar planting cultures to that of the Mandan and Arickara. These "river" tribes had developed an elaborate culture in which they lived in semipermanent earth lodge villages, traveling to the buffalo country to hunt. The "classic" tipi evolved, in part, from this transitional period.

Much of the cultural mixing between unrelated groups on the Missouri River occurred in the sixteenth and seventeenth centuries while the French were making rapid inroads to the Lakes region of the Midwest and beyond. Those that we refer to as Sioux were then more or less unified and lived in Wisconsin and Minnesota as "the Seven Council Fires." Linguistically they were of three main groups: the Dakota, or Eastern Sioux; the Nakota, or Middle Sioux; and the Lakota, or Western Sioux. Their culture also included earth lodges, especially among the eastern Dakota bands. These eastern bands, along with their Winnebago cousins also utilized the domed wigwam common to the Woodlands tribes, but it is probable that all used tipis as well. I suspect that the practice of fusing tribes was very old among the related Siouans that lived on the prairies' edge. Some of the Omaha (Dhe'giha) group and their related Iowa, Oto, and Missouri cousins (who with the Winnebago made up the Chiwere Siouans) built domed wigwams well into historic times.

Until the arrival of the horse on the Plains, the "Tipi People," wherever they were located, were forced to make small lodges that could be transported with dogs and by backpacking. Somewhere, a "three-pole" and a "four-pole" culture developed, but there does not seem to be a uniform tribal breakdown. The Crow, who broke away from their Hidatsa cousins, became four-pole people. The Omaha, learning from the Arickara, were four-pole people, but the Cheyenne, who also learned to make tipis from the Arickara, were three-pole people, as were the Sioux.

Innovative design alterations occurred as former woodland cultures adjusted to the windy, flat country. In former sheltered regions, a cone shape alone met their needs, with a separate flap possibly being pulled across the top opening in wet weather. On the Plains, where sudden wind gusts and tornados were common, attached smoke flaps were added to the tops of the lodges. With external poles, these flaps could be adjusted to prevent wind from blowing smoke back into the lodge. After horses became available, the "Holy Dogs" revolutionized the tipi culture to what it is today.

Horses became the symbol of wealth in this economy. The more horses to drag poles of ever lengthening size, the larger a lodge could become. Originally averaging 10 to 14 feet in pre-horse days, the "horse" tipis often stood 18 to 20 feet high. Some council lodges were much larger. Although individual tribal construction techniques varied, the basic hide tipi was fairly uniform from tribe to tribe. For an average family tipi, possibly 15 feet in diameter and height, fifteen spring-killed cow buffalo hides were sewn to make the cover and smoke flaps. The Cheyenne and Arapaho had women's sewing societies that specialized in tipi construction. Some survive to this day in Oklahoma. The finished product, always owned by the woman of the lodge, was snug and weather tight. The brain-tanned hide was soft as velvet, but heavy. Cooking indoors and constant wetting through the winters caused a tipi to become brittle and stained; the hide tipis were replaced at least every other year. When canvas became available in the early 1800s, many people replaced buffalo hide covers with the lighter army duck material. By 1875 the buffalo were all but gone and commercial canvas tipis became the norm." [ii]

The historic hide lodges are best shown in the early pictures and drawings by George Catlin, Karl Bodmer, Alfred Miller, Rudolph Kurz, and Mary Seth Eastman. After returning to the studios with their field sketches, some artists embellished their paintings, thereby showing far more detail than was originally observed. For the most part, these artists of the pre-1860 period did not show the existence of specifically cut smoke flaps, the large rectangular flaps or ropes from the bottom of the flaps to a pole out front. The lodges also appear circular or conical in shape, without formal door openings. Many lodges appear decorated while others are left plain. Few show some type of "streamer(s)" at the tips of the poles. Mayer, in his 1851 drawing, does show an undecorated Sioux lodge with the beginnings of smoke-flap extensions, but without a liner or formal door (Mayer 1932, 112). The pins at the bottom are pulled to open up the bottom of the door for easy access.

Buffalo-hide tipis were heavy, weighing about fifty to one hundred pounds on average. The skins were known for their translucence. They let in light, while still protecting the inhabitants from the weather. A big step in the evolution of tipi covers came around the late 1840s with the introduction of cloth to the western

Cowhide tipi.

trading market. The Native Americans started replacing hides with cloth because it was lightweight, materials to make it were readily available, it was easy to make, and it let more light inside the lodge.

Rudolph Friederich Kurz was a Swiss artist who spent the years from 1846 to 1852 at western trading posts on the Mississippi and upper Missouri Rivers. He recorded his experiences in his journals and drawings. His journal of the 1840s indicates a few wealthy Indians were experimenting with single-fill canvas that is similar to what is for sale today. As the hide trade accelerated and treaty annuities were collected, linen cloth and cotton canvas came into greater demand as they became more affordable. Also available were ticking material and striped awning cloth. Newspaper and magazine photographs and illustrations of the era show striped awning material used by the U.S. military and European visitors.

From the arrival of the first European explorers and settlers to North America, traders had been inviting the Indian Nations to trade their fur hides for guns, beads, cloth, needles, mirrors, or anything that might be of use or interest. The well-kept records of the trading companies (the Hudson Bay Company, Bent's Fort, Northwest Company, Astoria Inventories 1813, St. Louis Missouri Fur Company, the 1831 Manifest of Jedediah Smith's Trade Goods Santa Fe, and the Rocky Mountain Outfit of 1836, to name a few) have a wealth of information on the materials traded to the Indians in all parts of the country. For instance, steel needles were very popular along with kettles, pots, pans, vermilion, powder, and steel blades. The dates also show a healthy early trade at the turn of the nineteenth century in St. Louis, Santa Fe, and the Oregon territories. Wherever trading posts and early rendezvous were set up, the Indians came to exchange their furs and crafts.

George Ruxton describes the interior and exterior of a Sioux buffalo hide tipi in the later days of the mountain man. At this time, the fur trade days were ending and the trading posts were taking the place of the yearly Western Rendezvous held west of the Mississippi River. In his writings, "Life in the Far West" for *Blackwood's Magazine* and *Adventures in Mexico and the Rocky Mountains* (1847), he observes:

> The Sioux are very expert in making their lodges comfortable, taking more pains in their construction than most Indians. They are all of conical form: a framework of straight slender poles, resembling hop-poles, and from twenty to twenty-five feet long, is first erected, round which is stretched a sheeting of buffalo robes, softly dressed, and smoked to render them watertight. The apex, through which the ends of the poles protrude, is left open to allow the smoke to escape. A small opening, sufficient to permit the entrance of a man, is made on one side, over which is hung a door of buffalo hide. A lodge of the common size contains about twelve or fourteen skins, and contains comfortably a family of twelve in number. The fire is made in the centre immediately under the aperture in the roof, and a flap of the upper skins is closed or extended at pleasure, serving as a cowl or chimney-top to regulate the draught and permit the smoke to escape freely. Round the fire, with their feet towards it, the inmates sleep on skins and buffalo rugs, which are rolled up during the day, and stowed at the back of the lodge.
>
> In traveling, the lodge-poles are secured half on each side a horse, and the skins placed on transversal bars near the ends, which trail along the ground—two or three squaws or children mounted on the same horse, or the smallest of the latter borne in the dog travees (travois). A set of lodge-poles will last from three to seven years, unless the village is constantly on the move, when they are soon worn out in trailing over the gravelly prairie. They are usually of ash, which grows on many of the mountain creeks, and regular expeditions are undertaken when a supply is required, either for their own lodges, or for trading with those tribes

who inhabit the prairies at a great distance from the locality where the poles are procured.

A few years later, Mary Seth Eastman gave an account in her journals, *Dahcotah: Life and Legends of the Sioux* (1849), of the life of women and how they set up summer and winter lodges. This is one of the few accounts of the use of tipis and the more permanent lodges: "Her work is never done. She makes the summer and the winter house. . . . Visit her in her teepee, and the she willingly gives you what you need, if in her power: and with alacrity does what she can to promote your comfort. . . . The women plant the poles of their teepees firmly in the ground and cover them with a buffalo skin. A fire is made in the center and the corn put on to boil" (v, 60).

The eyewitness account of American artist Frank Blackwell, *With Pen and Pencil on the Frontier in 1851*, explores the structure and materials of the hide lodge. Mayer journeyed through the Minnesota frontier, recording his experiences and making sketches. His most memorable entries and sketches were made at Traverse des Sioux in the summer of 1851.

> The village is composed of two sorts of habitations winter houses and summer houses or Tipis a house, or Waykayas skin covering & Tipitonka's large house. [The Sioux word Tanka means 'large'; thus tipitanka may be translated as "large house." Mayer applies the term, variously spelled, to the summer house of the Sioux. The wakeya was the "skin tent," probably the same as the ordinary tipi . . . edited by Bertha L. Heilbron 1932.]
>
> The winter house is a tent made of furless buffalo hides tanned like buckskin & sewed together, supported on poles & hand held together at the seam by splints of wood, it being left open at the top to permit the smoke to escape & beneath is an aperture for egress & ingress—thus forming a circular conical edifice with the ends of the poles protruding from the top, the edges of the skin falling over & varying the colour & form. These are the winter habitations and are near ten feet in diameter generally. A fire is made in the center & the occupants repose around it. In warmer weather it is sometimes used. It is then thrown open, the aperture of entrance being enlarged & the portions of the slack skin supported on the sticks, thus giving rise to two graceful festoons from either side of the seam.
>
> [Teepees] . . . belonging to Indians of the plains are sometimes forty feet [in diameter]. The poles of tamarack are of large size . . . the protruding end of the tallest of which is suspended a horses tail, [an indication of] the residence of a principal warrior or a chief, the exterior being decorated with diagrams of his principal actions. I know not why, but there is home feeling about the interior of a teepee. As I have lounged on a buffalo robe by the light of a smoldering fire, it reminds me of my childish positions on the parlor rug in front of a hickory fire, during the winter evenings.

Sioux encampment, ca 1850.

The teepee is rendered very comfortable in the interior by piling straw around the exterior & strewing it within, & laying buffalo robes & furs upon it. Without, the snow soon accumulates about the straw leaving only the upper portion of the tent visible. Closing the entrance & building a fire it becomes a snug refuge from the inclement winters. Tepees last four or five years, but owing [to] the rotting of the lower portion of the skins decrease in size. The tipi or skin lodge is . . . peculiar to the western or Dacotah branch of the Indian races; the Algonquin having lived in bark-wigwams. . . . The summer house is similar in form to our log cabin, tho' more nearly approaching a square, & the roof reaching nearer to the ground .

It is seldom that the Indians congregate in villages during the winter. After the gathering of their crop of corn in the fall, they separate into parties of from one to three or four families, & with their tipis depart for the woods which afford shelter from the inclemency's of winter & brings them nearer to the game on which they subsist during that season (104–10).

Jedediah Smith's trade lists indicated that he carried a line of thousands of yards of linen cloth.[iii] This material as well as "heavy sheeting" was used in clothing

Home of Mrs. American Horse, 1891, showing a Sioux (Lakota) interior of a lodge with cooking pot and pole liner.

and wagon covers, and for tent making. Santa Fe was a major trading route and base for Smith in his travels of the Southwest and Great Plains area. None of this proves that the Native Americans traded or bought this material, but there are the records of this cloth offered for sale.

The earliest known photograph of canvas tipis was taken in 1852 when a Santee Dakota canvas/hide tipi was photographed near today's Bridge Square, Minnesota. The picture shows an encampment with several tipis. The tipis are randomly arranged, have no door poles or smoke flap ropes, and look conical in shape rather than having the steep-back tilt found in later tipis. Also notice the shorter lodge poles and the lack of streamers and decorations.

From an inventory of the Cheyenne and Sioux property destroyed by order of Major General W. S. Hancock in April 1867, we know that the Indians possessed diverse tools, cooking utensils, and other objects.[iv] Retaliations like this were for Indian raids on settlers camps, attacks by other native groups that were then misattributed to other tribes in the area or to materials and supplies from hostile tribes.

This list is a remarkable cross section of a nineteenth-century Plains Indian village. It gives insight into the lives of desperate people as they fled with their children, weapons, animals, and minimal personal belongings.

Cheyenne Camp

132 lodges
396 buffalo robes
57 saddles
120 travois
78 headmats
90 axes
58 kettles
125 fry pans
200 tin cups
130 wooden bowls
116 tin pans
103 whetstones
44 sacks—paint
57 sacks—medicines
40 hammers
63 water kegs
14 ovens
117 rubbing horns
42 coffee mills
150 rope lariats
100 chains
264 parfleches
70 coffee pots
50 hoes
120 fleshing irons
100 par-flesh sacks
200 horn spoons
42 crow bars
400 sacks feathers
200 tin plates
160 brass kettles
15 sets lodge-poles
17 stew pans
4 drawing knives
10 spades
2 bridles
93 hatchets
25 teakettles
250 spoons
157 knives
4 pickaxes

Sioux Camp

140 lodges
420 buffalo robes
226 saddles
150 travois
140 headmats
142 axes
138 kettles
40 frying pans
190 tin cups
146 tin pans
140 whetstones
70 sacks—paint
63 water kegs
6 ovens
280 rope lariats
140 chains
146 parfleches
50 curry combs
58 coffee pots
82 hoes
25 fleshing irons
40 horn spoons
14 crow bars
54 brass kettles
11 hammers
5 sets lodge-poles
4 stew pans
160 rubbing horns
3 pitchforks
3 teakettles
280 spoons
4 pickaxes
1 sword
1 extra scabbard
1 bayonet
1 mail bag
stone mallets
1 lance
9 drawing knives
2 spades
8 bridles
7 coffee mills

Father Peter J. Powell, a well-known and respected twentieth-century author on Cheyenne material and culture, sums up the loss of this way of life in his book *Sweet Medicine* (1969):

"Most of the old Northern Cheyenne material beauty died in the flames of Morning Star's camp. Two hundred tipis, nearly all of canvas, but some of buffalo hide, were destroyed. Among them were the elaborately decorated lodges of the military societies, their linings covered with vividly colored paintings, men and horses moving in battle. Exquisitely quilled and beaded clothing, the sacred shields, scalp shirts and war bonnets were carried off or burned" (166).

After the destruction of so many camps in the 1870s, and particularly on the southern plains as late as 1874, the U.S. government issued canvas for tipi covers to the bands that surrendered at Ft. Sill, Oklahoma. Records of the military supply offices and journal books show the distribution of supplies to the Indians.

Other historic visual evidence of tipis is in the sketchbook drawings of the Kiowa, Sioux, and Cheyenne. At first these drawings were not thought to be historic in detail or use, but they are now considered to be very accurate and rich with information on tipis, clothing, decorations of all types, manners, daily life, courting, and other customs (McCoy 1987, 51). Tipi sketches show detail paintings or beadwork on the outside covers, and how they were set up for cooking, sleeping, and meetings (Viola 1988, 44). They do not show smoke-flap ropes extending from the bottom of the flaps to a pole in the front. One good interior drawing depicts backrest, beds, and bags (Bad Heart Bull 1967, 299). Today the Internet is also a good place to find sketchbook drawings. Web sites are available for study and interpretation of these drawings.

From the late 1860s to the early 1900s, a few photographers came west to photograph and document the Indians. In the winter of 1872–73, William S. Soule took twelve photos of a Comanche camp showing buffalo-hide tipis. John A. Anderson photographed the Sioux on the Rosebud Reservation between 1885 and 1900. He showed life inside and outside the lodges. From 1902 to 1911, Richard Throssel photographed the Crow reservation and Fred Miller (from 1898 to 1912) was there as well. Both men took photo studies of the outside structure of Crow covers with some interior shots. Edward Latham took pictures of the Colvinne tipis from 1900 to 1905, and Lee Moorehouse photographed the Umatilla in 1903. Julia E. Tuell was one of the few women photographers. Tuell lived on the Northern Cheyenne Reservation from 1906 to 1912 and took photographs of the people who had defeated Custer. Then there is the 1898 to 1910 volume of work of Edward Curtis, who took hundreds of pictures from the Southwest to the Northwest coast life of Indians. However, there are hundreds of photos taken by identified and unidentified photographers in the last half of nineteenth century that will probably never be acknowledged, but their work lives on in public and private collections.

Universities and libraries, including the University of Washington Library, Denver Public Library in partnership with the Colorado Historical Society, the Denver Art Museum, and the Library of Congress, to name a few, are now putting their photographic collections on the Web.

View of Sioux Indian camp.

The Cloth Tipi of the Mid- to Late Nineteenth Century

From observations made of the earliest pictures and sketches of the historic tipis, a tipi camp of cloth tipis might have some of the following characteristics:

- The tipis could face in several directions and could be either tilted or straight up and down in a more conical form.
- Some were tall and others squat in appearance.
- Tipis might be made of the striped awning, ticking with the narrower stripes, single-filled duck, or a muslin-weight material. A few photos show material that has company marks such as "Monumental Standard." This might be a cloth company or a tipi maker of the time period.
- Even in the same tribe, there could be different ways of sewing the panels together at different angles. This was very obvious with Sioux tipis.
- Patchwork repair work would be seen around the lift areas, sides, and bottom.
- The covers would all touch the ground, with the pegs going in at an angle and not straight up and down. Around and on the covers would be pieces of wood and rocks—anything to anchor the tipi and keep out the wind. Most poles would be crooked, partially stripped, and somewhat pointed from being dragged and put into the ground.
- The majority of southern-style tipis would not be painted, while the Northern Blackfoot tipis would be highly decorated with paint.
- The tipi poles would not extend too far beyond the tie point area and in some cases would barely reach the tie point.

- The poles might be wrapped around the tie point with rope once, twice, or not at all depending on the amount of rope.
- Very few streamers would adorn the tips of the poles.
- There would not be any door poles holding open the smoke flaps. The exception to this might be the Crow, Blackfoot, and Nez Perce who used the flap where the smoke-flap pole extends beyond the corners of the pockets or holes. During the last part of the century, these tribes started using a door pole out front as well as the longer cover poles to extend the flaps.
- The flaps would fold left over right facing the front for lacing pins.
- There would be no formal bottom underturn (sod cloth) for liners, if there was any liner. Liners are rectangular panels tied only at the tops and held in place with objects at the bottom. In the Northern tribes there was more use for liners during the seasons because of the severe winters and cooler nights.
- Medicine bundles might be attached to the top, back, or front of the tipi. Some might be on tripods to the side or back depending on the tribe. Most gear would be put away for storage and travel. There would not be tripods in the front for weapons.
- In a typical tipi interior, there were no altars or skulls. They appeared to be in the society lodges or those used by holy men. More adornments appeared in tipis of the late nineteenth century and early twentieth century. This was in part due to the start of the big fairs, dances, and Wild West shows.
- Gores, or triangular additions to the smoke flaps, were only found on a few of the historic covers.

Ponca encampment, 1907, Ft. Sill, Oklahoma.

- Designs would be different within the tribe and the families. From the actual covers, photos, and drawings of tipis, it is a bit difficult to tell what is a Cheyenne, Sioux, Kiowa, Arapaho, Comanche, or Crow tipi. Though there is something of a set pattern today, the families of this time period intermarried, gifted covers, or made do with what they had in material.

The Tipi from the Late Nineteenth Century to the Mid-Twentieth Century

Ernest Thompson Seton seems to have been one of the first writers to give more information on the structure and materials for building a general type tipi. He wrote profusely about Indian crafts. Seton also helped in the formation of the Boy Scouts of America, although he had previously formed his own group, Woodcraft League of America. Seton drew some of the first layouts for making a tipi cover showing a 10- and a 14-footer, both of which are still used today. In his book *Two Little Savages* (1903, 151–54), Seton explains the construction of the tipi:

> Si had not only sewed on and hemmed the smoke-flaps, but had re-sewn the worst of the patches and hemmed the whole bottom of the teepee cover with a small rope in the hem, so that they were ready now for the pins and poles. 'Ten strong poles and two long thin ones,' said Yan, reading off. These were soon cut and brought to the campground.
>
> 'Tie them together the same height as the teepee cover—'
>
> 'Rawhide rope,' he said, but he also said, 'Make the cover of skins. I'm afraid we shall have to use common rope for the present,' and Yan looked a little ashamed of the admission.
>
> The tripod was firmly lashed with the rope and set up. Nine poles were duly leaned around in a twelve-foot circle, for a teepee twelve feet high usually has a twelve-foot base. A final lashing of the ropes held these, and the last pole was then put up opposite to the door, with the teepee cover tied to it at the point between the flaps. The ends of the two smoke-poles carried the cover round. Then the lacing-pins were needed. . . .
>
> 'You can't beat White Oak for pins.' He cut a block of White Oak, split it down the middle, then split half of it in the middle again, and so on till it was small enough to trim and finish with his knife.
>
> Ten pins were made eight inches long and a quarter of an inch thick. They were used just like dressmakers' stickpins, only the holes had to be made first, and, of course, they looked better for being regular. Thus the cover was laced. (Continued in the Appendix.)

Nearly fifty years after some of the earliest observations of tipis, these dwellings still continued to fascinate anthropologists, missionaries, and general observers. In *1885 An Average Day in Camp Among the Sioux*, Alice C. Fletcher describes the everyday life of a Sioux village, including the struggles of living in a tipi. Later in 1911, with Francis La Flesche, she writes again about the Omaha in *The Omaha Tribe*. The Omaha use the four-pole style as do the Crow, Nez Perce, Blackfoot, and Comanche as compared to the three-pole setup by the Sioux, Cheyenne, Arapaho, Kiowa, and many other southern tribes. The observations of Fletcher and La Flesche cover the construction, setting up, and transporting of the lodge. Both writers comment on the effect of weather, travel, and living in a tipi, and they describe the simplicity of moving the camp and then setting it back up. (See Appendix for excerpts from both sources.)

Studies of the Hidatsa and their culture were reported by Gilbert Wilson in 1924 in *An Anthropological Paper of the American Museum of Natural History, Vol. XV, Part II—The Horse and the Dog in Hidatsa Culture (Based on the material from 1908–1918 Hidatsa or Gros Ventre . . . called Minitari by the Mandans, are a Siouan tribe speaking a dialect akin to that of the Crow.)* Wilson's account of a tipi, most of which was related to him by Buffalo-Bird-Woman in 1913, is one of the most detailed for this time period. He gives exacting information on how the tipi is placed and constructed, on the interior fires, and on the pole setup for a Mandan or Sioux-style lodge. It appears he camped with and observed life in a village, judging from the detailed notes he wrote on life in a tipi. However, there is a problem with his explanation of the pole setup for a tipi as compared to a Sioux tipi as we know it. This discrepancy in pitching poles is pointed out later in the material. Wilson's observations include the following:

Winter Lodges and Drying Stages. Our winter camp was of earth lodges, but these were smaller and less carefully built than were our summer lodges.

Our Camp on the Sandbar. About noon, we camped on the sandbar. There were about one hundred buffalo skin tipis in the camp. When we camped in a good level place it was customary to pitch the tipis in a big circle, and if the wind was calm when we pitched camp all the tipi doors faced the center of the circle. However, if we were camped along a creek that had a narrow bank, or in any other place where a circle could not be easily formed, the tipis were set up in rows or whatever other arrangement the formation of the land compelled. If there was a stiff wind blowing a tipi was pitched with the door away from the wind.

Turning a Tipi. Camped thus in a tipi, if a windstorm arose and it became necessary to turn the tipi with the door away from the wind, my husband and I and two or three neighbors, who were invited to help us, could very easily turn it around. Sometimes seven or more people turned the tipi; the larger number could handle it better, though if there were people enough to hold the foundation poles steadily that was sufficient.

First, the pins that held the cover to the ground on the outside were pulled up. Then, we went inside the tipi, picked up the four foundation poles and the one to which the cover was tied and moved the poles and the cover at the same time. The rest of the poles were now shifted about as was necessary. If the five poles were held firmly while they were moved about there was no danger that the tipi would fall down.

A Mandan tipi could be raised and turned by four persons since its foundations was of but three poles.

Anchoring the Tipi. During a windstorm it was often necessary to anchor the tipi to prevent it from being blown over. For this purpose a rawhide lariat was passed around the poles, inside and under the tipi cover, and the ends were drawn together in a noose. The noose was pushed up by means of a forked stick to the point where the poles converged, and drawn taut. Then the loose end of the lariat was drawn downward and tied to a pin driven into the ground, four or five feet from the fireplace, toward the windward side of the tent. Very often two pins were driven into the ground and crossed. If the tipi were very large, it might be anchored with a second lariat on the outside.

In a Mandan tipi, a lariat always hung in the center in readiness for a storm. The Mandan three-pole tie was weaker than our Hidatsa four-pole tie and for that reason a lariat was passed around all the poles at the tie. In the Hidatsa tipis this was unnecessary, except in a heavy windstorm, since our poles locked at the top.

The Fire. The fireplace was surrounded by stones only when wood was scarce and buffalo chips were used for fuel, but when it was abundant the kettle was set directly on the coals and the meat roasted on wooden spits. When we camped on the prairie, however, we could obtain no wood, and made our fire of buffalo chips. In that case, we roasted our meat on stones.

In our lodges in like-a-fish-hook village, the fire was smothered at night. If it became extinguished by any accident, the woman went to a neighbor who had a fire and got some coals. We followed the same custom when in camp.

As has already been said, each of the tent poles had a hole at the smaller end through which a thong was drawn. The larger ends of the poles dragged loosely on the ground, spread fan shape. Sometimes one of these tent poles broke where it was pierced for drawing through the thong. In that case, a slight groove was cut into the pole as a substitute. This, of course, was done only in an emergency; the ordinary method was to perforate the end of the tent pole.

As the tent cover lay on the horse, it made a load on either side of the animal, twelve inches thick, twenty-six inches long, and twenty-four inches wide, while the connecting portion that passed over the saddle was about eighteen inches long.

The Mandan Tent Tie. In setting up tents, the Hidatsa used a four-pole foundation. The great advantage in employing this method was that in ordinary weather it was unnecessary to draw a lariat around the top of the poles at the place where they converged to steady them and strengthen the tie. The foundation poles of an Hidatsa tent interlocked, as the fingers of the two hands may be made to interlock. The Mandan, however, used the Dakota tent tie, which needs to be reinforced by a lariat drawn around the poles at the top. The Mandan tie (see drawings on page 19): in A, the three poles are tied together for the skeleton frame. To tie these poles, they are laid on the ground and fastened at the joint. It will be observed that pole c projects beyond the others at the top. This is for the purpose of making the front of the tent slightly longer than the rear so that the smoke hole will be directly over the fireplace. B shows the skeleton frame after the tie has been made and the framework has been set up, while in C will be seen the ground plan of the completed framework. C (a, b, and c) presents the three foundation poles as already described, a resting upon b and b upon c. The remainder of the poles for the completed framework are then set up in order as shown in the following table:

a rests upon b
b rests upon c
d rests upon a and c
e rests upon c and d
f rests upon c and e
g rests upon c (under d)
h rests upon g and c
i rests upon h and c
j rests upon a and b

The tent cover is tied to the pole, j, in the same manner as in an Hidatsa tent. Then the pole is raised between f and c and the tent cover drawn around the frame.

It will be noted B that a lariat hangs from the tie. When all the poles but j have been set up in the framework, this lariat is drawn out from beneath the poles, a and b, and carried quite around the frame in such a manner as to draw the poles snugly together at the meeting point. The arrows in the diagram C indicate the direction in which the lariat is drawn. After it has been drawn once around the poles, the pole j is raised and the lariat drawn around far enough to enclose this pole. Then it is drawn inside the framework, between j and c and anchored to a short post, or pin, driven into the ground. The owner of the tent draws the cover around and laces it in place. Finally, the two poles that hold the smoke flaps are raised.

The drawing on the opposite page shows the setup for the Mandan tipi, which Wilson drew for his notes. He states that they use the Dakota tent tie for the setup. The setup is backwards from the familiar three-pole setup of the Sioux, or else Wilson has his notes drawn wrong. I did use this style to set up my 12-foot lodge and instead of one pole in the tripod on the left facing my door, there were two tripod poles on either side of the door and only one pole towards the back. The lift pole was to the south of the F pole in Wilson's directions. This is opposite of what we know as the three-pole setup and this style gives the appearance of a four-pole setup when the cover is up. Continuing with Wilson:

> The tent poles were of pine [spruce] brought to the village by visiting Crow. In spite of the fact that they did not grow on our Reservation, we always had a great many of these poles. They lasted a long time. There were fifteen poles to our tent, including the two that upheld the smoke hole flaps. The tent door was of an old cloth blanket. On the hunt, the tent door was often made of a deerskin hung fur inside so that whenever anyone went out of the tent, the fur of the door skin fell smooth against the head and body. For this reason, the fur was hung head up.

> b, articles of food piled here for safety, also any meat brought in from the hunt, skins, etc.
> h, dishes, bowls, cups, spoons, and the like used at meals, piled here when not in use;
> i, fire place,
> j and k, firewood.

> Between each bed and fire lay a log. The space between the log and the tent wall was filled with grass and the whole covered with robes. The logs were laid in this position for two reasons: to keep the shape of the bed and to prevent sparks from the fire from setting fire to the grass. These small logs were placed near the bed when wood was plentiful, especially if we expected to camp in the locality for some time. When we camped in the hills where wood was scarce, or if for any reason we were in a great hurry or it was inconvenient to obtain logs, we did not use them.

Besides anthropologists, missionaries and visiting travelers wrote down their observations in diaries and letters. A few of these have been published over the years, giving firsthand information on reservation life. Elizabeth M. Page went west to administer the word of God and help the Indians. She kept a diary of her daily life among the Indians she worked with in her book, *In Camp and Tepee: An Indian Mission Story:*

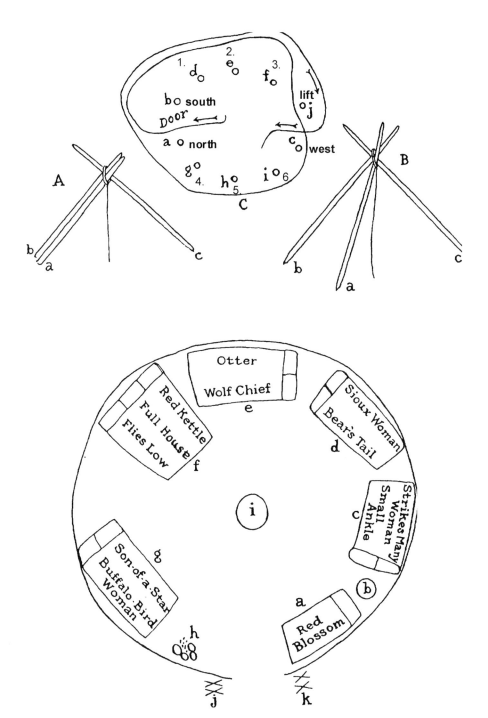

Diagrams of a Mandan tipi setup and framework. Ground plan of tent used on tribal hunt, showing position of beds, fireplace, and household utensils.

Blackfoot village in Portland, Oregon, from 1910 postcard.

Occasionally we see a woman moving about among the dingy tepees, and now and then a child ventures out from the school to visit his people. The appearance of the camp is uninviting enough. The tepees, which ordinarily look approximately white, now present their blackened cones against the white snow. A few are protected by wind-breaks made of the dried stalks of the tall weeds which grow in our river-bottoms, bound together and standing upright in a circle. One of these structures has been unable to withstand the force of the wind, and has blown over against the tepee in the centre. Beside each tepee stands the wagon of its occupant. Most of the ponies have sought protection behind the hills or in the ravines, but one team is cowering close behind the wind-break. They are but frail shelters—these hastily constructed tepees; only a frame of poles covered by an inferior quality of domestic, with an aperture at the top through which the smoke from the fire within escapes. (Continued in the Appendix.)

From 1890 to 1920, tipis started getting more formal in their look. They became taller and more decorated. Tipi poles were cut longer, especially those of the Crow, Nez Perce, and Blackfoot. The Cheyenne, Arapaho, Kiowa, and Sioux lodges were lavishly decorated with beaded medallions and tinklers or dangles on the covers. Door poles were very evident in the front of most lodges with the bottom of smoke flaps tied to them. Streamers and ribbons on the lodge poles were in abundance. Fairs and gatherings were on the increase, and it became very popular to decorate in order to show off the tipi and the interior materials. Crow Fair became the tipi capital of the world.

In *The Book of Indian Crafts and Indian Lore* (1928, 139–44), Julian Harris Salomon expanded on the Ernest T. Seton material by giving a more detailed, designed draft of the tipi cover, drawing of a liner in place, and information about pegging the liner down. This may be the first time attachments to the bottom of a liner are described. Historic photos and observed liners do not show ties on the bottom.

The poles should cross at the tie flap. There they should be tied together by the Teton method or by simply passing a rope around them three or four times and tying a square knot. Thus the tripod is made. . . .

If the tipi is to stand for some time the end of the tripod rope should be sufficiently long so that it may be wrapped around the outside of all the poles at the point where they come together. Its end is then spiraled down one of the poles. In windy weather it is fastened to stakes driven near the center of the lodge. When the lodge was to remain in one place for a long period, the poles were sunk in the ground to a depth of twelve to eighteen inches, extra allowance for this having been made when the tripod poles were measured off. . . .

To the ends of the poles the Indians often fastened streamers of cloth, buffalo or horse tails. The latter were supposed to bring fortune and many horses to the tipi's owner.

The cords on the bottom of the smoke flaps are tied to a peg placed well in front of the door. By swinging the smoke poles around according to the direction of the wind, a good draft for the fire may always be had.

A most important part of the tipi is the dew-cloth of lining. This is made of strips of cloth four to six feet wide, which are fastened to the poles on the inside of the lodge. The upper edge of each strip has tie strings on it for this purpose, and the lower is provided with rope loops one foot apart, so that it may be staked close to the ground. It is best made of drill or light canvas in six-foot sections and should be long enough to extend entirely around the lodge. Its purpose is to keep the lower part of the lodge free of smoke and the rain which runs down the poles from the beds.

Anthropologist Robert Lowie in *The Crow Indians* (1935, 88–89) gives one of the better descriptions of the four versus three-pole setup using butted poles of the Crow Indians. Lowie became familiar with the Crow Indians and their tipis through their rodeos and fairs.

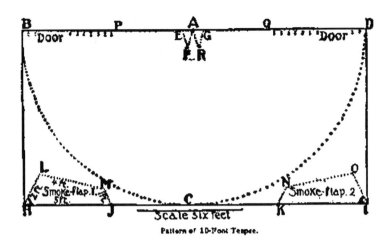

Ernest T. Seton tipi pattern, 1912.

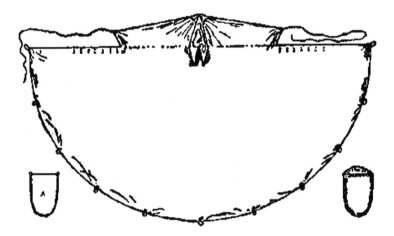

Julian Salomon–style tipi pattern, 1932.

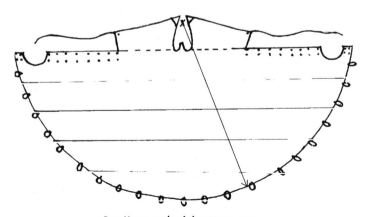

Ben Hunt–style tipi pattern, 1954.

Basic and correlated with other differences is the use of either three or four poles as a foundation for the rest. The Cheyenne, Arapaho, Teton, Assiniboin, Kiowa, Gros Ventre, Cree, Mandan, Arikara, Ponca, Oto, and Wichita use three poles, whereas the Crow, Hidatsa, Blackfoot, Sarsi, Ute, Shoshone, Omaha and Comanche use four. From observation and experience, Prof. W.S. Campbell finds that the three-pole type is the stauncher, offering greater resistance to the winds, the Cheyenne form being the most serviceable of all; the Crow variety is the most elegant in shape, though inferior in painted decoration to that of the Blackfoot, Dakota, Arapaho and Kiowa. (Continued in the Appendix.)

Royal Hassrick, an anthropologist, published *The Sioux* in 1964 based on information from 1830 to 1870. Although this book is not based on observed firsthand material, it is informative of the earlier time period. His book also has some detailed drawings of tipi covers, water bags, and backrests. Here's an excerpt: "During the spring month some of the people moved into wigwams lest the drizzling rains rot the less durable tipis. This was the time of year when tipis were repaired or renewed, from new hides collected during the fall and winter. Leggings and moccasins were made from the 'smoked tops,' and smoking of hides began in the warm weather." (Continued in the Appendix.)

Ben Hunt wrote the first of his articles on Indian crafts in 1938. They were later compiled into his book *Indian Crafts* in 1942. The drawings show a rope in the bottom hem of the cover with loops sticking out for the pegs, pocket smoke flaps, and a very circular cutout for the cover. In his popular 1954 book, *Indian Crafts and Lore,* his drawings indicate a liner but no underturn, or sod cloth, with a trapezoidal pattern smaller on the top and longer on the bottom to fit the curvature of the cover. Ties at the bottom attach the cover to the ground and there is rope at the top (101). The cover uses the Blackfoot-style pattern (96) and grommets on the bottom (98).

Reginald and Gladys Laubin in their seminal book *The Indian Tipi* (1957) show a more modern, streamlined tipi with the fitted liner that has an underturn or sod cloth. An interior rain cover (or what the Laubins called an ozan) is introduced for the first time. From this point on, almost all non-Native American tipis around the world became based on the Laubins' designs. After 1957, most books on tipi-making used the Laubins' patterns and terminology, with some embellishments to make their work appear different. Smoke-flap differences with tribal names are now identified or categorized. The tipi became oval, or egg shaped, instead of the circular pattern of the historical tipis of the nineteenth century. Based on the Laubins' drawings and the patterns for each tribe, these setups have now become the established pattern in tipi making. Reginald Laubin could be called the "Father of the Modern Tipi."

Late-Twentieth-Century Tipis to the Present

The next innovations in tipi making came with Guy (Darry) Wood of Haysville, North Carolina. In his article, "The All-American Do-It-Yourself Portable Shelter," found in an issue of *Aquarian Angel*, published in 1972, Wood further advanced tipi design. Though still based on the Laubins' book, Wood engineered the cover and the lining so that the liner fits every angle of a pole in the tipi, which makes the cover more egg shaped. He incorporated flaps on the outside cover over the door to keep water from coming in between the cover and door. He also introduced new synthetic materials like Sunbrella for the underturn, or sod cloth, on the liner, nylon chording for peg loops, polyester threads, and a synthetic blend for the cover/liner. My own tipi making is based on his designs. I am thankful for the experience of his teachings.

Very few people, if any, are making the authentic tipi of one hundred and fifty years ago. Most tipi makers today base their patterns on the Laubins'. So, what is an authentic pattern? You might have to go back to the tipis of the mid- to late nineteenth century when covers touched the ground, tipi poles were very short, and there were no formal fitted liners, rain caps, or modern materials. The exceptions to the basic look would have been the society or community tipis, the medicine lodges, and some individual family tipis showing off their battle deeds. And all of these varied from tribe to tribe and area of the country.

Timeline and Evolution of the Historic Tipi into the Modern Tipi of Today

The timeline on pages 26–28 is a summary of the development of the tipi, first made of buffalo hide, later of canvas, and now of modern materials. All early dates are approximate and vary because of inadequate information from available oral histories, vaguely written records, sketches, paintings, and undated photographic images. From the beginning of the twentieth century, the information, based on early anthropological studies, photos, diaries, articles, and books written about tipis and their construction, is more precise and detailed.

- **Before European contact, around 1500s**
  Small hide tipis on the Plains
  Hide tipis average 12 feet in size
  Reed tipis in the Northwest
  Bark tipi in the far North
  Dogs pull travois with camp gear

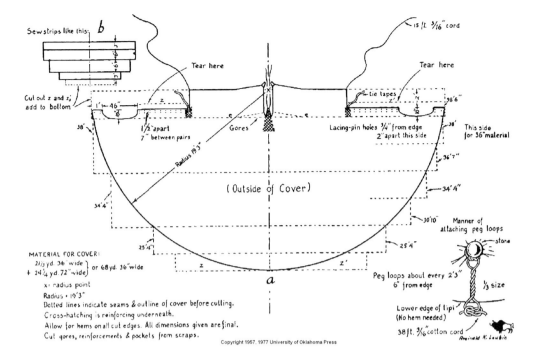

Laubins' pattern for an 18-foot Sioux-style tipi cover.

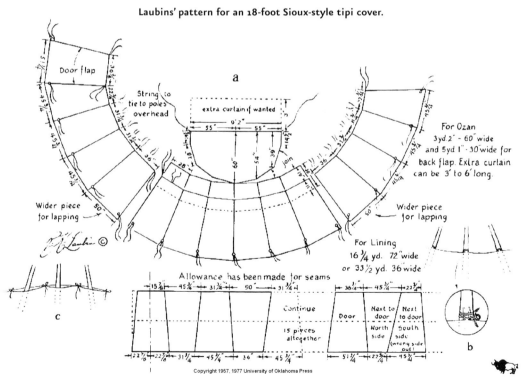

Laubins' pattern for an 18-foot-style liner/lining.

- **After the introduction of the horse, 1520s**
    Tips increase in size from 12 to 18 feet or more
    Covers do not have flap extensions or door poles
    Tipis are pegged with cover touching ground
    Slit doors—no formal door cover
    Short poles sticking out top
    Very few streamers
    One or two smoke-flap poles
    Hide linings are used

- **Fur traders and mountain men, 1800–1860s**
    Fur trade posts in northern and southern Plains
    Introduction of cloth material in tipis
    Larger hide and cloth lodges
    Slit-type doors
    Pegs are placed in ground at an angle
    Hide flaps are scalloped
    Some painted lodges and quilled decorations
    No smoke-flap ropes or door poles in front
    Some extensions on bottom of flaps
    Leather hides or robes for liners
    Some cloth for rectangular linings or blankets

- **Indian wars and frontier settlers, 1860s–1900s**
    Start of reservations
    Cloth being issued for tipis
    Decline of buffalo-hide lodges
    Many groups on the move due to hostilities
    Smoke flaps start having longer extensions
    Use of striped awning material for covers
    Some very large (approximately 25-foot) covers
    Tipis do not have door poles
    Ropes or cords attached to smoke flaps
    Cords attached to pegs holding cover
    Fur, blanket, or cloth doors
    Start of formal sewn door openings
    No rain caps
    Painted lodges
    Quilled and beaded rosettes
    Dangles or tinklers used

- **End of the Indian wars and reservation period, 1880s–1920s**
    Wild West shows and Indian fairs
    Wood platforms start to appear in Wild West show tipis
    A few door poles appear
    Decorated doors of hide and cloth
    Lodge poles get longer with some groups
    Some tipi covers are very decorated for show
    Very few buffalo-hide tipis—now made from cowhide
    Tailored oval door and variations
    Highly decorated hide and beaded rectangular cloth liners
    Crow Fair and roundups showcase family lodges
    The use of a "Gore" in smoke flaps
    Stanley Campbell (Vestal) defines the four major types of smoke flaps as
        well as characteristics of Crow and Cheyenne tipis

- **Scouts, tourists, and anthropologists discover tipis, 1890s–1940s**
    Ernest T. Seton introduces tipis to Scouting
    Introduction of the outer rain cap
    J. Salomon introduces a fitted liner
    Cloth tipis
    Tipis mostly used in the summer or family gatherings
    Great use of door pole
    Long lodge poles
    Rawhide and fancy cloth doors
    Blackfoot have highly painted lodges
    Crow, Sioux, Arapaho, Cheyenne, and Kiowa use the beaded or quilled
        rosettes and tinklers
    Pegs in at angle to hold cover to ground
    Few liners used and are made of cloth, shawls, or blankets

- **Hobbyists' tipis, 1954**
    Hunt writes the *Indian Crafts* books
    Detailed drawings on the cover and fitted-type liners
    Rain cap
    Liners are pegged down and have underturns (sod cloth)
    Cloth tipis shown at public events, like ceremonies and powwows
    Covers start to come off the ground an inch or more and the gore becomes
        standard in most patterns
    Fewer pegs for quick setup and takedown on the cover

- **First major book on history and making a tipi, 1957**
    Reginald and Gladys Laubin write *The Indian Tipi,* introducing the standards for lodges
    The fitted liner uses the trapezoidal-style pattern with underturn
    First major work on tipis gives measurements for cover and liner
    Drawings for the inside rain cover
    Introduction to the three-pole and four-pole setups
    The liner becomes a major part of the tipi
    Cover starts to lift off the ground, showing the liner bottom
    Most tipis now patterned after Laubins' book

- **Groups using tipis and innovations in tipi materials, 1950s–1970s**
    Start of the hobbyist powwows and rendezvous tipis for camping
    Hippies discover tipis; movement back to the earth and nature
    New synthetic materials in cords, ropes, and threads
    Waterproofing materials for canvas
    Fire-resistant chemicals for cloth
    Innovations in wood and concrete platforms
    Waterproof and mildew-resistant polysynthetic materials

- **Next major step in tipi making and materials, 1962–1972**
    Darry Wood writes "The All-American Do-It-Yourself Portable Shelter"
    Introduction of the formal fitted liner with the trapezoidal fitting of the angles to the poles in relation to the cover
    Use of 50/50 synthetic material in the covers
    Addition of Sunforger to the bottom of liners for extreme wet conditions
    Flaps attached to the cover going over the door to prevent water from coming in

- **Basic look of today's tipi, 1970s–present**
    (Non-Indian tipi owners)
    Follow Laubins' pattern
    Fitted liner and rain cover
    Door pole out front
    Cover off the ground by 2 to 10 inches
    Pegs driven into ground straight up
    Plain white or decorated cover
    Painted liner or plain white
    Cloth door and sewn door opening
    Fancy carved pegs and lacing pins
    Comforts of home inside, including a fire
    Try to re-create the old Indian look

(Indian tipi owners)
Family/tribal traditions or buy from a tipi maker who used Laubins' pattern
No liner in most cases or until needed
No rain cover
Door pole out front
Decorated with family or tribal patterns or plain white
Pegs driven in either at angle or straight up
Most occasions will not have a fire inside
Sometimes have a real four-poster bed, carpeting, and trunks for storage

[i] My relative Albert White Hat Sr. provided the following explanation: "The term *tipi* in Lakota means, 'They live [someplace].' In Lakota, objects are described; therefore, the word does not refer to the shape itself. The more correct term would be *tipes'tola*—"He or she lives in the sharp-pointed lodge." This explanation is taken from Albert's book *Reading and Writing the Lakota Language*, 35.

Pete Gibbs, former curator of the British Museum. Material given in conversation and e-mail.

[ii] Taken from James Creighton's correspondence, an essay on his Web site he wrote about the history of tipis, and conversations with him. Permission granted by Kathy Creighton in honor of Jim's memory.

[iii] Translations from Spanish to English of Samuel Parkman's list of trade goods.

[iv] The inventory appears in microfilm copies of *Letters Received, Adjutant General's Office*. An almost identical list, marked "A True Copy of Original Inventory," was signed by E. W. Wynkoop, U.S. Indian Agent, and appears in microfilm copies of his official correspondence.

Tipi maker Wes Housler's buffalo-hide tipi.

Styles of Tipis

In researching thousands of photographs showing various tipi groups, people standing by lodges, valley overviews of tipis, and tipis from different tribes, I have seen tipis that are tilted, straight up in back, or that have a shorter lean towards the door than the back. So, a true tipi can be tilted or not; it is up to the maker and is dependent on the materials available.

Tradition has told us that a tipi must always face east. This is also not necessarily true since a tipi should be faced with the wind at its back, which can change for various parts of the country and different weather patterns, including the day or night winds. Most of the examined photos showed tipis facing different directions even in a group. The custom of facing the tipi to the east, towards the sunrise, is a religious part of culture, though it is not known when this custom started. However, a tipi is, first of all, a dwelling that you live in and not a religious structure, unless so converted into one.

Cover Material

The first tipis were made of buffalo or elk hide, depending upon the area of the country, but most were made out of buffalo hides. The hides were taken in the spring from the cows, as the bull hides were deemed too tough. As cloth material became available in the early to mid-nineteenth century, covers started to change. The cloth material was lightweight, let in lots of light, and was easy to put together, which allowed the making of larger covers. Each tribe adapted its own buffalo-hide pattern to this new fabric material. With the rectangular shape of the cloth came changes in the smoke flaps, door openings, and the bottom pegging area.

Cloth came in widths of 36, 48, and 60 inches, with some variations in between. Widths had to be taken into account when piecing together material for the cover. Sometimes the cover was a combination of different widths. The cloth was mostly white or off-white, but the awning material came in red-and-white or blue-and-white stripes.

Each tribe did not make its tipis in a uniform pattern and this is reflected in the photographs from the time period. (See historic photos throughout this book.) Even within the same family or same tribe, patterns could be different. Included in this chapter are some of the many patterns used by the same tribe in making a cover. The drawings are taken from the hundreds of photos where seams can be seen. Although some tribes were fond of the striped awning material, the type of material used most likely depended on what supplies were available. The striped lodges were found mostly in Northern groups as opposed to the Southern Plains groups. There were, however, a few examples of Arapaho and Comanche awning cloth covers in Oklahoma.

Comanche tipi made of striped cloth.

The cloth of the Nez Perce and some Blackfoot tipis were sewn together in right angles to each other, forming an alternating stripe look. Whether this arrangement of fabric formed a strong jointed cover was up to the makers and was based on their sewing skills. A more up-to-date setup for a Blackfoot lodge is diagrammed on pages 16 to 23 of Brian Cannavaro's book *How to Set up a Blackfoot Lodge*. These new corrections are from Brian Cannavaro, who gave his permission to reprint the drawings on pages 34 and 35 of this book.

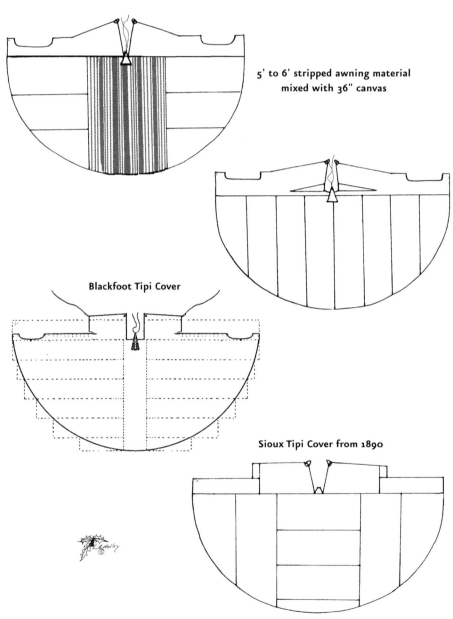

5' to 6' stripped awning material mixed with 36" canvas

Blackfoot Tipi Cover

Sioux Tipi Cover from 1890

Styles of laying canvas for a cover using 36-inch to 6-foot awning material.

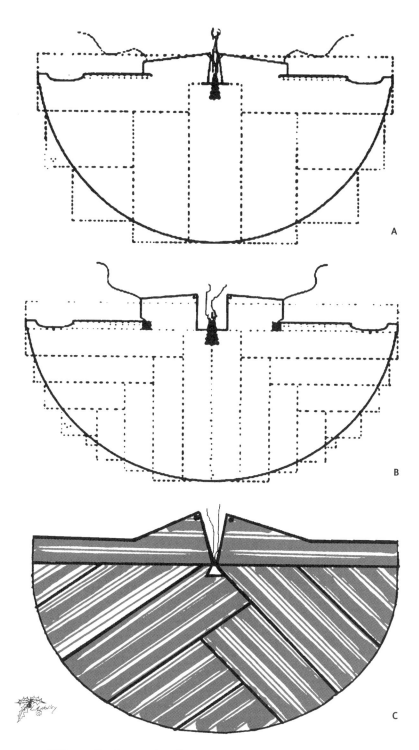

Different Nez Perce styles of cover patterns using awning material.
Material is stripped in the 4- to 6-foot size. Colors are red in most cases.

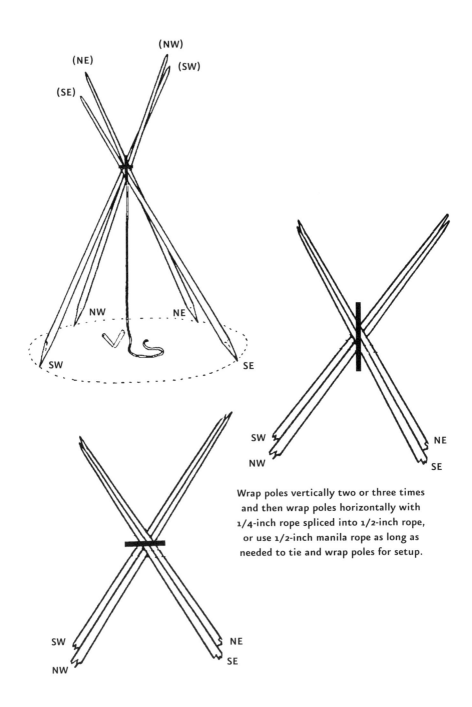

Wrap poles vertically two or three times and then wrap poles horizontally with 1/4-inch rope spliced into 1/2-inch rope, or use 1/2-inch manila rope as long as needed to tie and wrap poles for setup.

Above and opposite: Updated Blackfoot-style tipi setup.

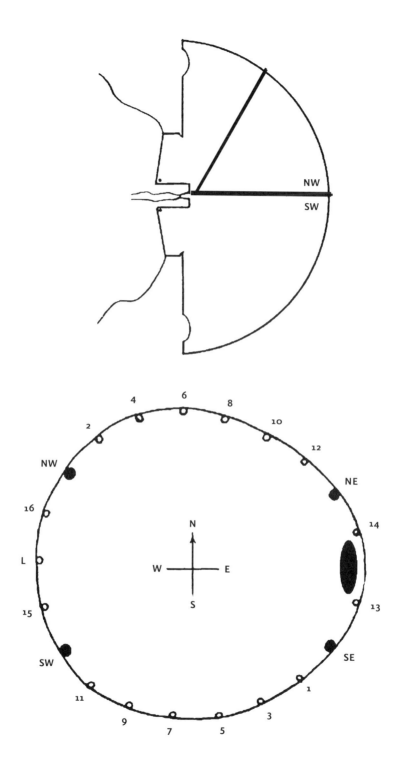

Smoke Flaps

Today, because of the Laubins and Stanley Campbell (Vestal), smoke flaps are divided into four recognized shapes: Crow (C with J-style smoke pole opening); Sioux (A and D); Cheyenne (B, C, and E); and Blackfoot (G). The Sioux and Cheyenne smoke flaps are similar in shape. The Sioux is wider with a shorter extension, if used, at the bottom. The Cheyenne tipi smoke flap is narrower with a longer extension. It is difficult to distinguish some Cheyenne smoke flaps from those of the Sioux, the Arapaho, the Kiowa, or from the many tribes using a very similar type of smoke flap by looking at photographs and sketches. There are subtle differences in the width and length and also in the way the flap is attached to the lacing-pin area.

During the mid- to late nineteenth century, many of these tribes camped together and intermarried with each other. There was also the gifting of tipis from one family to another or from one society to another of a different tribe. It is thus not unusual in this cross-cultural interchange that there was a blending of the smoke-flap patterns among the tribes.

The most distinguishable smoke-flap patterns are those of the Crow, Blackfoot, and Nez Perce (F). The Crow smoke flap is as elongated as the Cheyenne. The difference is the smoke pole going through the flap pocket or hole in the ear of the smoke flap and extending beyond. The Blackfoot smoke flap also has a hole for a pole to extend through, but the flap usually is much shorter in length but wider. The Nez Perce smoke flaps also have a hole for the pole to go through the corner area, but this triangulates back towards the lacing-pin area and does not seem to have the extensions of the Sioux/Cheyenne styles.

The drawings in this chapter are not broken down by tribal styles, but show the three main ways of attaching the smoke pole. They also show how each of the smoke flaps look in relationship to the lacing-pin area.

In the diagrams shown here, smoke flap A could be identified as Sioux and smoke flap B as Cheyenne in an older traditional style without the gores. Gores are the triangular insert in cloth flaps that Native Americans started adding around the turn of the twentieth century to help cover the smoke-hole area. The old hide tipi flaps would stretch around the poles while the cloth tipi smoke flaps stayed the same shape, not stretching to cover the smoke-hole area. With the addition of this extra piece of cloth, the gore area design covers more of the tripod opening in inclement weather. Diagrams C and D are described as Cheyenne or Sioux depending on the width of the flap. D shows an extra piece of cloth added to the front edge making it wider and more in the style of a Sioux tipi. Extensions on the bottom of the flaps can be found on both tribal styles. Flaps, if they are used, can vary in length.

Sewing a hole in the corner pocket of smoke flap C would change it into the Crow-style of flap and possible Nez Perce flap where a smoke pole went through the corner pocket area. Smoke flap F is used by Sarcee and Nez Perce. There are differences within these groups such as length, width, and use of pockets or sewn holes.

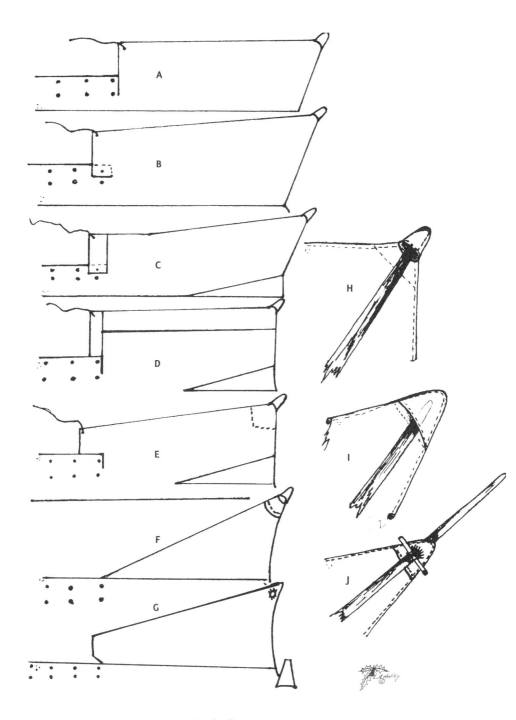

Smoke-flap styles.

The way smoke flaps attach to the lacing-pin area can also be different within each tribal group. The drawings on page 39 reflect some of the different views of the front of a lodge, which vary according to the time periods of the last part of the nineteenth into the early twentieth century.

Differentiating Sioux and Cheyenne tipis by the way they place their smoke-flap poles is not always possible by viewing the photographic evidence or sketchbook drawings. Cheyenne tipi smoke-flap poles have been described as meeting in the back while the Sioux's crossed (Laubins 1957, 46).

In the hundreds of observed images of both groups, poles were crossed or not. There was no uniformity. In many cases, smoke-flap poles are not seen in use or only one is shown, and there are no door poles out front to tie the smoke flaps to, as is commonly done today.

Four-foot-tall Southern Cheyenne tipi, 1907.

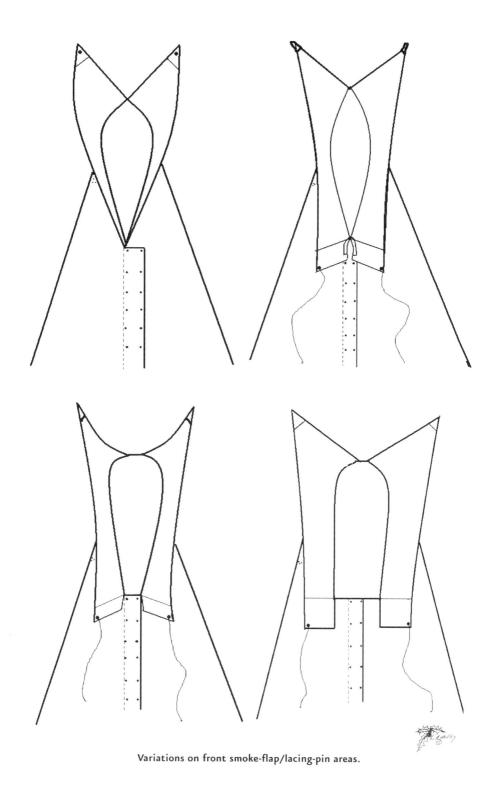

Variations on front smoke-flap/lacing-pin areas.

Materials and Steps for Making the Tipi Cover

This chapter covers the entire process of making a tipi cover, including the materials, workplace setup, patterns, layout, and the sewing process. Construction of the lining, preparation of the poles, and care of the tipi will be covered in subsequent chapters.

Materials for Making a Tipi

- canvas
- thread
- cording/tie tapes
- pencils or markers
- grommets
- rulers
- safety glasses
- steam iron
- linen waxed thread
- sewing machine
- needles (for use with sewing machine and for use by hand)
- scissors
- glue
- leather
- tables
- butcher/kraft paper or cardboard
- long roll of 4-foot-wide plastic (optional)
- marbles and/or round river pebbles

Canvas/Cloth Materials

Cotton canvas is the material I prefer for making tipis. It breathes, which minimizes condensation inside the tipi when a different temperature exists on the outside, and it has the perfect amount of stretch for a cover. It is subject to mold, mildew, and ultraviolet-ray damage; however, special treatments have been developed to combat these conditions.

Cotton and synthetic canvas can be purchased from canvas supply houses, fabric stores, and awning stores. Major canvas suppliers are in the Resources of this book. Many tipi makers will also be glad to sell you canvas. A few tipi makers sell tipi kits. Various weights and grades of canvas are available.

Almost all tent companies will describe materials, assorted canvas used in tipis, and the weight of the canvases in their brochures so it may seem a bit repetitive. But it is a good idea to read it all so you don't waste your time and money on a poorly made tipi. Depending on where you live, what you choose is up to you. The original tipi was designed for drier climates, without much humidity. We have now adapted the lodge to fit our lifestyles and weather.

Different Weights of Canvas

Canvas can be purchased at various weights. The lightest is 8-ounce duck, and the heaviest is around 26 ounces. The weight refers to the number of ounces per square yard. The lightest is naturally the cheapest. Use 10- to 12-ounce lightweight canvas if you plan to move your tipi a lot. If your tipi is going to be semipermanent or where there are a lot of storms, use a heavyweight canvas, 12 to 14 ounces. The bigger the cover, the heavier the weight of material you will want for the cover.

Sunforger Marine Finish Boat Shrunk is the premier cotton canvas fabric for tipis used in regions of high humidity, such as the Great Lakes region or the southeastern United States. This is the canvas that I prefer and recommend for tipis. It is available in 10.10 ounce and 12.65 ounce weights, both suitable for tipis. The heavier weight provides greater strength but the lighter material can be used when the goal is to hold down the overall weight of the tipi. Sunforger Fire Resistant canvas has the same treatment for water repellency and mildew resistance, but has an additional flame-retardant quality that meets the California standard (CPAI-84), which has become the industry-wide standard. Many states now require all tents and tipis to be fire resistant. That does not mean they are fireproof. I have seen five lodges burn to the ground due to negligence and my 12-footer was one of them. Fire resistance is a good quality, but it cannot compensate for carelessness. Marine-treated 10.10-ounce army duck is another excellent fabric for tipis. The fabric has a high thread count and the weave is even, consistent in strength, and will not leak when touched.

Although Sunforger and army duck are the two best cotton canvases for tipis, other canvas types can be used in some situations, notably in arid environments. Army duck is seldom, if ever, specially treated to resist mold and mildew. Nor is it preshrunk, and both it and single-fill duck will shrink drastically, so your 18-footer may end up a 17-footer if you don't allow for shrinkage. Single-fill duck is made with coarse single-ply yarns and has a tendency to leak when touched. The two single-fill (see Resources) weights for tipis are 12 ounce and 14.90 ounce. The latter has 20 percent more cotton in it and is more durable and water repellent.

Synthetic canvases are an alternative to the cotton canvas that I prefer. Fifteen-ounce Starfire is a 45 percent polyester/55 percent cotton fabric with an acrylic topcoat. Each application of acrylic is heat sealed onto the base fabric for added strength. It is water, mildew, and fire resistant, and meets CPIA-84 standards. It is soft, flexible, easily cleaned, and will last a long time, but it cannot be painted. Polaris is a 50 percent cotton/50 percent polyester blend. It is UV-resistant, mildew resistant, breathable, water repellent, and flame retardant. It remains flexible in extreme temperatures and is recommended for tipis that will be set up for extended periods of time. It can be painted with acrylic paints or exterior latex house paints. Sunbrella is an acrylic material that has the advantage of being very strong and extremely decay resistant. It cannot be painted, but it comes in an amazing array of colors, including many bold stripe patterns. This material does not breathe or meet CPAI-84 standards, but it is an excellent material to use on the bottom of a liner, the part that touches the ground.

Dean Wilson related this story about camping with the Blackfoot at one of their dances and the materials they used for their lodges:

> I have danced on the Piegan and Kainai (Blackfoot nations) reserves each year for the past five years—and almost everyone lives in tipis during the dances, including us dancers, and I have noticed that almost all of the tipis are hand sewn, use much lighter canvas than the commercial ones I own. They are not treated with anything (flame retardant or mildew treatment)—none are Sunforger canvas at all—all are very large though (they used to laugh at our little 16-foot and even our 18-foot one), but the covers are quite light. I asked several families if they used lightweight, untreated canvas specifically to keep it light to raise the large lodges. Without fail everyone responded the same way—this was all they could afford. Ah, Napi! Humour and lessons at the same time!

To sum up, in choosing your canvas material, keep in mind where you will be camping, the weather conditions in your area, how large your tipi will need to be to accommodate all the people you expect, and how much weight you can manage.

Selecting a Sewing Machine

The original hide tipis were sewn together using bone awls and sinew, and then later with steel sewing needles and cotton threads. The whip stitch, also called the overcast stitch, was used. Later in the nineteenth century, a few wealthier Indians gained access to the first hand-turned wheel or crank-driven Singer machines that were available after 1854. But these machines were expensive and very few were seen on the Great Plains. The electric sewing machines became available around 1920 before many areas of the country had electricity, but the old treadle sewing machine remained in use well after World War II.[*]

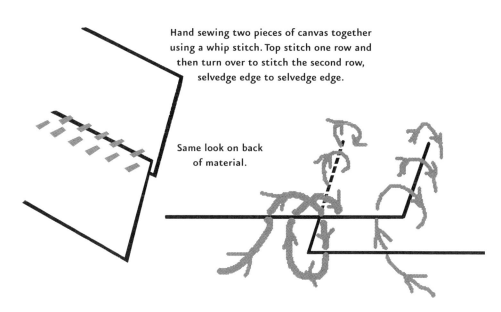

Hand sewing two pieces of canvas together using a whip stitch. Top stitch one row and then turn over to stitch the second row, selvedge edge to selvedge edge.

Same look on back of material.

Old hand-sewn method of piecing a tipi cover together without a sewing machine.

I made two tipis with ordinary household sewing machines before switching to an industrial sewing machine. My first tipi, in 1978, was made on a Singer Featherweight Sewing Machine my dad bought for me in 1964. The tipi was an 18-foot lodge made from 12.48-ounce Vivatex that had to be fitted into the machine arm on each pass. I used Singer leather-weight needles to get the heavy cotton thread through the canvas. With the two, four, and six layers of canvas, I broke or bent needles every other pass or so. I wore safety glasses on the job as broken needles shot everywhere. When the tipi was finished, all the gears of my machine had to be recalibrated. My next sewing machine was an old Singer foot

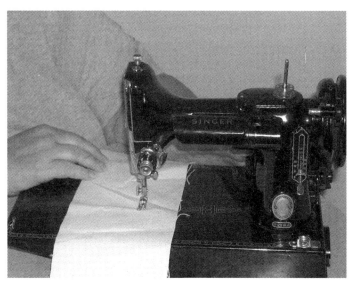

1964 Singer Baby Sewing Machine Linda Holley used to make her 18-foot lodge.

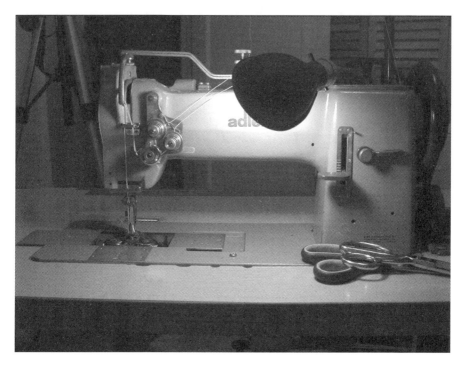
Adler Industrial Double-Needle Sewing Machine.

treadle machine. It had a much bigger arm to work with and heavier gears to work the thicknesses of canvas. The job was much easier and I broke fewer needles, but it became clear that if I were to continue making tipis I would have to have an industrial sewing machine.

I next purchased a 3/4-horsepower, double-needle Chandler Adler industrial sewing machine, with a forward and reverse stitch. The reverse stitch is great for locking your stitches, whereas without it, you have to pick up the lever and move the cloth back in order to sew forward again. The double-needle feature enables you to sew the large panels to each other with one pass rather than two. Other features of the Adler are the large opening in the arm for fitting the canvas through and the "dog feet" that grab the material and walk it past the needles. Look for these desirable features on any model of industrial sewing machine that you consider purchasing or renting. Regardless of the machine, wear safety glasses and shoo bystanders away when sewing canvas because when needles break they can shoot out six feet or more.

Choose a good sewing machine that has metal gears and a large neck opening and is strong enough to sew through six layers of canvas. Many of today's machines are made with plastic gears and internal parts that cannot withstand heavy-material sewing for long periods of time. After every tipi, the sewing machine will have to have its gears recalibrated.

If all you have is the old home sewing machine, do your best with what you have. Check with awning shops to see if they will sew the main parts for a price and you can do the remainder. And, of course, there is the old standby of hand sewing, the way the Indians did it.

Thread

The supplier of the canvas should also be able to supply thread. Any strong, rot-resistant thread will do. One such is a heavy, bonded, UV-resistant Dacron/polyester thread. Another is Filco thread, which has a polyester core wrapped in a cotton shell; the polyester core provides strength and durability, and the outer cotton shell will swell to fill the holes made by the needle when sewing.

Hand and Sewing Machine Needles

Leather needles for sewing machines are some of the largest for household machines. These are sturdy enough for use with canvas. You must take it slow and easy when going through more than four thicknesses of material. Some thicker areas may have to be hand sewn. For industrial or heavy-duty sewing machines, use sizes 110, 120, and 135 to 160, the latter being the heaviest. The heavier and stronger the needle, the bigger the hole; this can be a problem because it leaves a bigger hole where leaks may occur. A good size needle for most jobs is about 120 to 135. Always check your sewing machine manual to determine proper sizes and lengths of needles for your sewing machine and make sure the needle you are using is compatible with the machine.

Most needles used in sewing canvas are three-cornered or Glover's needles. They have very sharp edges, which cut their way into the fabric. Other needles are round ended and fairly blunt, with much less tendency to cut the fabric. The blunt needle moves the threads aside and allows them to "heal" more rapidly and form a much tighter waterproof barrier. The needle eye should be the same or a bit larger than the thread used. It is not necessary to use a larger needle than the job or the thread requires. The only things I hand sew are the buttonholes for the lacing pins, where I use a blanket stitch to reinforce the area surrounding the hole.

Cording/Tie tapes

Hardware stores sell 1/4-inch cotton or nylon cord. The choice is yours on materials for the ties used on the smoke flaps, liner, door, and cover. About 50 feet or so should do the trick. Nylon cord has the advantage of not rotting, freezing, or staying wet. Cotton will mildew and freeze to the ground, and it stays wet longer, making takedown a slower process, but it does look more historic. Tie tapes and loops can be used in place of cording for the bottom of the tipi and smoke flap. Make these by folding a 3-inch-wide strip of canvas (cut on the bias) over twice and sewing it down. You can also purchase tapes by the roll from the dealer from whom you buy the canvas. You will need 10 to 15 feet of tie tape.

Scissors

Whatever scissors you use, make sure they are sharp at all times. Straight-blade scissors are preferable. A type of scissors called "polyester," or "tiny teeth," scissors are made for fine cutting where special control is needed. They are great for bias cuts and small, rounded holes in the lacing-pin area.

Pencils or Markers

Use #2 pencils for most drawing on canvas. Remember, pencil marks do not erase on canvas. If you have to erase, use a white eraser and not the red type. The latter does not come out of the canvas and will continue to show later. Never use markers except on paper for making pattern designs. Markers do show up better on patterns than pencil. Tailor's chalk also works on canvas and does not leave marks; it just dusts off.

Glue

Use Elmer's Glue or any white glue for gluing the cover panels together. Do not use carpenter's glue because it leaves a yellow residue. White glue will dry clear and is not affected by the weather. When it does get wet, it will just fill in the seam and sewing holes.

Leather

If not making or using cloth cords, use good commercial or brain-tanned deer hide for the leather ties at the top of the liner and door. Cut a strip 21 inches by 3/8 inches. Pull both ends to stretch the strip. As it stretches, the width will narrow down. If it cracks or breaks, cut another one a bit wider, say, 1/2 inch. Cut at least thirteen or more of these ties, depending on the size of the tipi. See bottom photo on page 88.

Grommets

Brass size #4 male and female grommets are needed for the two- or three-piece liner sections where the liners join together in the bottom overlap area. Use one set for the two-piece and two sets for the three-piece liner. None are needed if you are making a one-piece liner.

Rulers

Twelve-inch to six-foot rulers or straight-edge pieces of metal or wood are needed. You'll also need a fifty-foot tape to make measurements and patterns for the canvas.

Tables

Card tables, dining room tables, or cafeteria tables are great for laying out the canvas and patterns. Getting material off the ground will help your back and help you be more accurate when cutting your cloth. You will need a large enough area to glue and iron the strips together. You will need a table at sewing-machine height to work the canvas.

As an alternative, you can do this on a long area of clear floor that can withstand the heat of an iron.

Four-by-eight sheets of plywood set up on sawhorses can be substituted for tables. A couple of coats of polyurethane or other varnish will put a smooth surface on the wood to help in the movement of the canvas.

Steam Iron

Use a Teflon-coated steam iron to iron together the long panels of the cover. I prefer Teflon because the glue will not stick to the surface, creating a gummy, sticky residue on the bottom plate that has to be constantly cleaned.

Butcher/Kraft Paper or Cardboard

Use paper or cardboard to make the patterns for the liner and the small pieces of the cover. If I'm making more than one tipi, I prefer cardboard for its thickness and ability to hold an edge for longer periods of time. For one tipi, the paper will work. Large pieces need to be 5 to 6 feet wide and 25 feet long. Paper or cardboard patterns can be pieced together with duct tape.

Waxed Linen Twines (thread)

Waxed linen twines will be used for the buttonholes and can be found in large needlecraft stores or in boating or leather craft stores. Any tough, heavy cotton or linen thread will do. Coat the thread with beeswax, thread it on a needle, and fold it double. Twist and coat it again with beeswax.

Long Roll of 4-Foot-Wide Plastic (optional)

Roofers' plastic or any plastic sheeting should be used to keep the canvas clean when it is measured out for the cover and liner. Roll out about 50 feet of it on a driveway or grassy area and peg down both ends to keep the wind from blowing it around. Walk on it with stocking feet.

Marbles, Round River Pebbles, or Bottle Caps

The bottom edge of the tipi cover can be attached to the ground in one of two ways. The first method is to sew loops onto the bottom of the cover. The pegs are then driven through the loops into the ground. The second method is to wrap marbles or round river pebbles into individual "pouches" about three inches above the bottom edge of the cover with cord ties, using clove hitches. The long ends of the cord ties are then attached to the pegs, which are pounded into the ground. Both methods are traditional and are documented on the old tipis. The advantage of the marble or pebble ties is that they can be moved along the cover where needed. The sewn-on ties cannot be moved. Two disadvantages of the pebble ties is that they should be redone after a long period of time so that the cloth doesn't thin out around the pebble or marble and they do pop out, requiring replacement.

Craft stores carry the marbles in round or half shape and in regular or large size. I use a large marble in the middle back of the tipi cover to quickly show me the middle back for my first peg, and regular marbles for the rest. I always carry extra marbles because the cord ties sometimes pop open and the marbles get lost. Do not use round, wood-type marbles as they can mildew, swell, and break apart in time. This can cause the canvas to rot as well.

Preston Miller, who owns the Four Winds Trading Company in Montana, related to me how some Crows used old beer bottle caps to tie into the cover. These might work in a pinch, but they can cut the canvas over time. A 45-caliber lead muzzle loading ball can also be used in an emergency.

Tips to Get You Started

- Get all materials and tools ready before you begin.

- Know the size of the tipi you want to make. Go for what works for you and what you can put up by yourself.

- The pattern given in this book is based on a Cheyenne-style tipi. You can change the pattern to fit your needs.

- If making this yourself, have some weights around to hold the canvas down or tight when worked. The weights act like extra hands.

- Don't let all of your friends get involved right at first. Choose one and work from there. I call them "tipi slaves," and they just love to help . . . for a while. The usual drinks, food, and the awe of making a real Indian tipi are often the best pay.

- Working at table height is better than on the floor.

- If you are on the floor, make sure it is free of clutter and wear knee pads.

- Anywhere the canvas is spread out or worked must be free of dirt, hair, or pets. All these things can get sewn or "shown" on the surface as streaks or paw prints.

- Wear clean socks or have clean feet when walking on the canvas. Keep your hands clean, too.

- If it is hot, wear a sweatband to keep moisture out of your eyes and off the cloth.

- As you unroll the canvas, look for imperfections. There can be notes written in the seams by the processor, factory slices or cuts, or little items woven into the selvedge edge like small sticks, cigarettes, and whatever else got picked up off the factory floor. You would be surprised what can show up on your "clean canvas."

- Once you cut, there is no turning back.

- Study the pattern you want to use so that you don't have to take any unnecessary steps. You save material if the pattern is laid out properly, but there is always a scrap pile.

- Remember, any mark made in pencil on the canvas is darn near impossible to erase.

- If working outside, do not pick a windy or rainy day to measure or lay out the work.

- All seam directions should point down or away from water movement—similar to a roof shingle. You do not want water to get up and under the seams and leak in.

Making Your Tipi

Patterns in this chapter give detailed measurements for the cover and liner, proper angles for the fitted liner, approximate tripod tie points, and the number of poles needed. Each pattern is complete, making it easier to buy the canvas for cutting. Buy at least 15 percent more canvas than you need for the cover and liner because you still need material to make the door (6 feet, or 2 meters). You also might need some extra fabric in case there are mistakes in cutting and measurement. Leftovers can be made into bags for the tipi or a small awning, depending on how much is left over. Measurements for the cover are given in panel numbers with #1 being the complete smoke flap, tie point or lift area, lacing-pin area, and door. Panel #2 through the largest number become progressively shorter in length.

Everyone has his or her own way of making a tipi. My way works for me and may give you some insight into how easy or confusing that process can be. For those individuals who are picture oriented, I have included several drawings and photos to help.

Czech tipi encampment.

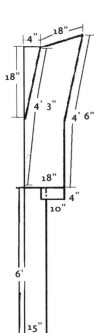

10' Tipi Dimensions
41 yards
36" wide for cover, liner, and door

Tie Points

Tie Points	
Radius	10' 6"
Lift	9' 3"
North	9' 6"
South	9' 4"
Door	10' 6"

Tipi Liner Panels for 9 poles + 2 smoke		
Panel #	To Lift	To Door
Door	86 deg.	86 deg.
1/2	81 1/2	75 1/2
3/4	87 1/2	71
5/6	92	67
7/8	94	66

Approx. 24 yards

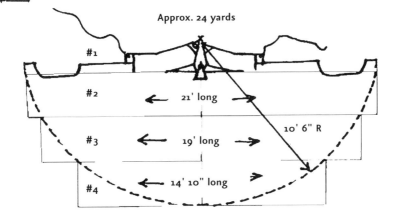

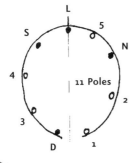

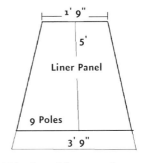

Add 12" mud flap or underturn

Ten-foot tipi dimensions.

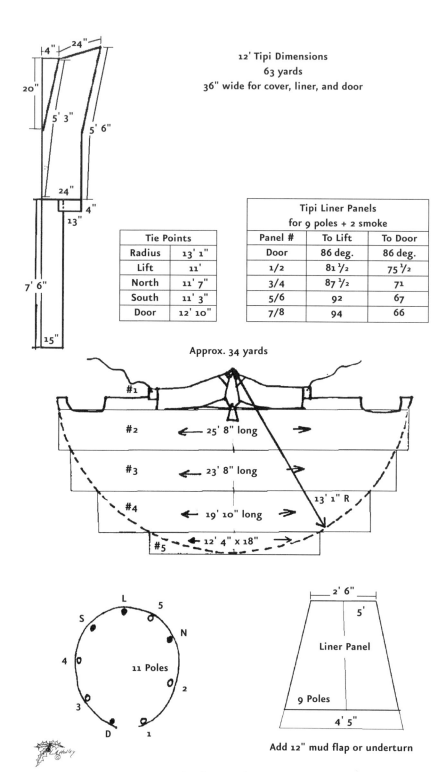

12' Tipi Dimensions
63 yards
36" wide for cover, liner, and door

Tie Points	
Radius	13' 1"
Lift	11'
North	11' 7"
South	11' 3"
Door	12' 10"

Tipi Liner Panels for 9 poles + 2 smoke		
Panel #	To Lift	To Door
Door	86 deg.	86 deg.
1/2	81 $\frac{1}{2}$	75 $\frac{1}{2}$
3/4	87 $\frac{1}{2}$	71
5/6	92	67
7/8	94	66

Approx. 34 yards

#1
#2 ← 25' 8" long →
#3 ← 23' 8" long →
#4 ← 19' 10" long →
13' 1" R
#5 ← 12' 4" x 18" →

11 Poles

Liner Panel
9 Poles
2' 6"
5'
4' 5"

Add 12" mud flap or underturn

Twelve-foot tipi dimensions.

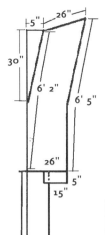

14' Tipi Dimensions
80 yards
36" wide for cover, liner, and door

for 12 poles + 2 smoke		
Panel #	To Lift	To Door
Door #1	82 ½ deg.	82 ½ deg.
2	82 ½	82 ½
3/4	85	80
5/6	87	78
7/8	88	77
9/10	89	76
11/12	90	75

Tie Points	
Radius	15' 3"
Lift	13' 4"
North	13' 3"
South	13' 3"
Door	15'

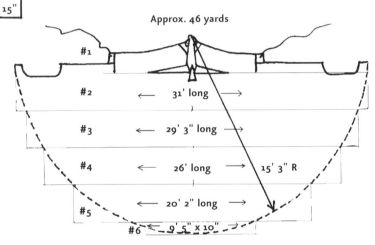

Approx. 46 yards

#1
#2   ← 31' long →
#3   ← 29' 3" long →
#4   ← 26' long →   15' 3" R
#5   ← 20' 2" long →
#6   ← 9' 5" x 10" →

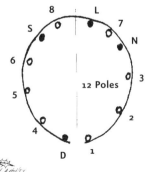

8 L 7
S
6   N
         3
   12 Poles
5
         2
4
   D   1

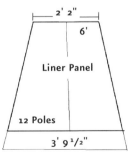

2' 2"
6'

Liner Panel

12 Poles

3' 9 ½"

Add 12" mud flap or underturn

Fourteen-foot tipi dimensions.

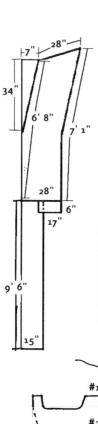

16' Tipi Dimensions
85 yards
36" wide for cover, liner, and door

Tie Points

Tie Points	
Radius	16' 4"
Lift	14' 3"
North	14' 3"
South	14' 3"
Door	16' 1"

for 12 poles + 2 smoke		
Panel #	To Lift	To Door
Door #1	82 ½ deg.	82 ½ deg.
2	82 ½	82 ½
3/4	85	80
5/6	87	78
7/8	88	77
9/10	89	76
11/12	90	75

Approx. 52 yards

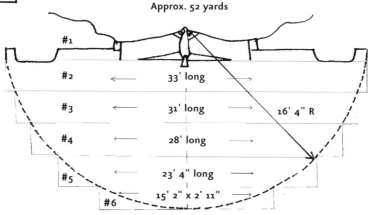

#1

#2 ← 33' long

#3 ← 31' long → 16' 4" R

#4 ← 28' long →

#5 ← 23' 4" long →

#6 15' 2" x 2' 11"

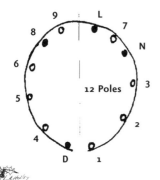

9 L 7
8   N
6
5   3
    12 Poles
4   2
  D 1

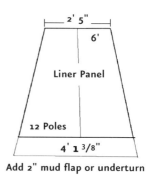

2' 5"
6'
Liner Panel
12 Poles
4' 1 3/8"

Add 2" mud flap or underturn

Sixteen-foot tipi dimensions.

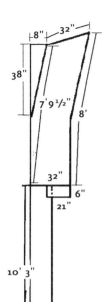

17' Tipi Dimensions
95 yards
36" wide for cover, liner, and door

8" · **32"**

38"

7' 9½"   8'

32"

6"

21"

10' 3"

15"

Tie Points	
Radius	17' 5"
Lift	15' 6"
North	15' 5"
South	15' 5"
Door	17' 2"

Tipi Liner Panels		
for 12 poles + 2 smoke		
Panel #	To Lift	To Door
Door #1	82 ½ deg.	82 ½ deg.
2	82 ½	82 ½
3/4	85	80
5/6	87	78
7/8	88	77
9/10	89	76
11/12	90	75

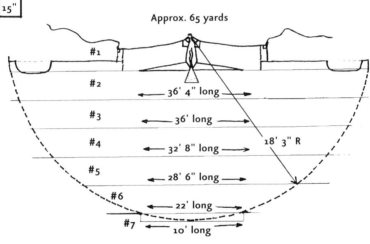

Approx. 65 yards

#1

#2 — 36' 4" long

#3 — 36' long

#4 — 32' 8" long — 18' 3" R

#5 — 28' 6" long

#6 — 22' long

#7 — 10' long

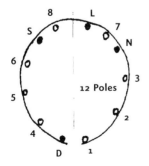

8   L   7
S   N
6
12 Poles   3
5
4   2
D   1

12 Poles

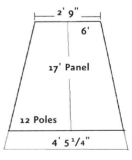

2' 9"

6'

17' Panel

12 Poles

4' 5¼"

Add 12" mud flap or underturn

Seventeen-foot tipi dimensions.

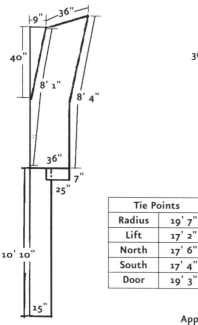

18' Tipi Dimensions
125 yards
36" wide for cover, liner, and door

Tipi Liner Panels		
for 15 poles + 2 smoke		
Panel #	To Lift	To Door
Door #1	86 deg.	86 deg.
1/2	84 1/2	83
3/4	86	82 1/2
5/6	87	81
7/8	88 1/2	79 1/2
9/10	89	78 1/4
11/12	89 1/2	78
13/14	90 1/2	77 1/2

Tie Points	
Radius	19' 7"
Lift	17' 2"
North	17' 6"
South	17' 4"
Door	19' 3"

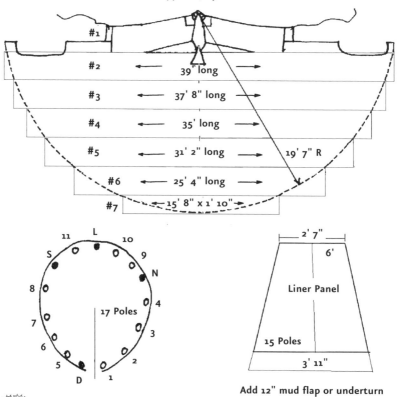

Approx. 76 yards

#1

#2 ← 39' long →

#3 ← 37' 8" long →

#4 ← 35' long →

#5 ← 31' 2" long → 19' 7" R

#6 ← 25' 4" long →

#7 ← 15' 8" x 1' 10" →

11 L 10
S 9
8 N
7 4
17 Poles
6 3
5 2
D 1

2' 7"
6'
Liner Panel
15 Poles
3' 11"

Add 12" mud flap or underturn

Eighteen-foot tipi dimensions.

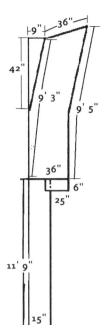

20' Tipi Dimensions
135 yards
36" wide for cover, liner, and door

9" 36"

42"

9' 3"

9' 5"

36"

6"

25"

11' 9"

15"

Tie Points	
Radius	21' 5"
Lift	19' 9"
North	19' 6"
South	20'
Door	22'

Tipi Liner Panels for 17 poles + 2 smoke		
Panel #	To Lift	To Door
Door #1	88 deg.	88 deg.
2/3	84	85 1/2
4/5	86	82
6/7	88 1/2	80
8/9	89	83
10/11	90	79 1/2
12/13	90	79
14/15	86 1/2	76
16/17	89	80

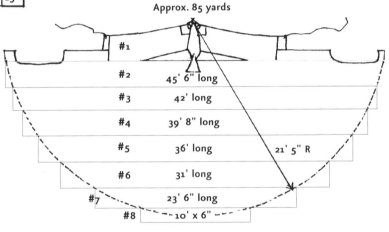

Approx. 85 yards

#1

#2 · 45' 6" long

#3 · 42' long

#4 · 39' 8" long

#5 · 36' long · 21' 5" R

#6 · 31' long

#7 · 23' 6" long

#8 · 10' x 6"

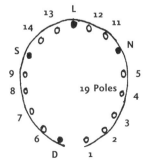

13 · L · 12 · 11

14 · N

S

9 · 5

8 · 19 Poles · 4

7 · 3

6 · 2

D · 1

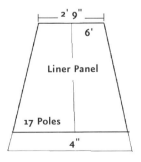

2' 9"

6'

Liner Panel

17 Poles

4"

4"

Add 12" mud flap or underturn

Twenty-foot tipi dimensions.

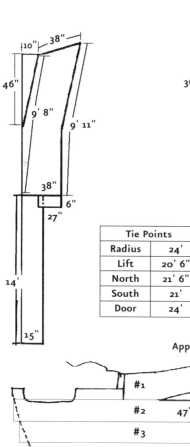

22' Tipi Dimensions
140 yards
36" wide for cover, liner, and door

Tie Points	
Radius	24'
Lift	20' 6"
North	21' 6"
South	21'
Door	24'

Tipi Liner Panels		
for 19 poles + 2 smoke		
Panel #	To Lift	To Door
Door #1	88 deg.	88 deg.
2/3	86	83 $\frac{1}{2}$
4/5	87 $\frac{1}{2}$	82 $\frac{1}{2}$
6/7	88 $\frac{1}{2}$	81 $\frac{1}{2}$
8/9	89 $\frac{1}{2}$	80 $\frac{1}{2}$
10/11	91 $\frac{1}{2}$	79
12/13	92 $\frac{1}{2}$	78
14/15	93	77 $\frac{1}{2}$
16/17	94	76 $\frac{1}{2}$
18/19	94	76 $\frac{1}{2}$

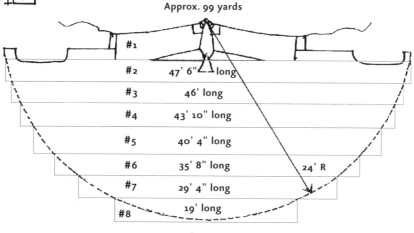

Approx. 99 yards

#1
#2 47' 6" long
#3 46' long
#4 43' 10" long
#5 40' 4" long
#6 35' 8" long
#7 29' 4" long
#8 19' long

24' R

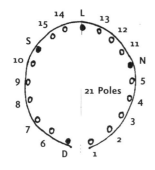

21 Poles

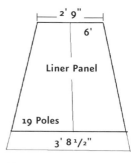

2' 9"

6'

Liner Panel

19 Poles

3' 8 $\frac{1}{2}$"

Add 12" mud flap or underturn

Twenty-two-foot tipi dimensions.

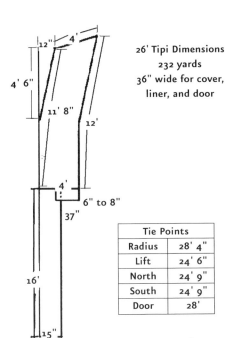

26' Tipi Dimensions
232 yards
36" wide for cover,
liner, and door

12" 4'
4' 6"
11' 8"
12'
12"
4'
6" to 8"
37"
16'
15"

for 25 poles + 2 smoke		
Panel #	To Lift	To Door
Door #1	88 deg.	88 deg.
2/3	87 ½	84 ½
4/5	88	85
6/7	88 ½	84
8/9	89 ½	83 ½
10/11	90 ½	82 ½
12/13	91	81 ½
14/15	91 ½	81
16/17	92	80 ½
18/19	92 ½	80 ½
20/21	93	80
22/23	93 ½	79 ¾
24/25	93 ½	80

Tie Points	
Radius	28' 4"
Lift	24' 6"
North	24' 9"
South	24' 9"
Door	28'

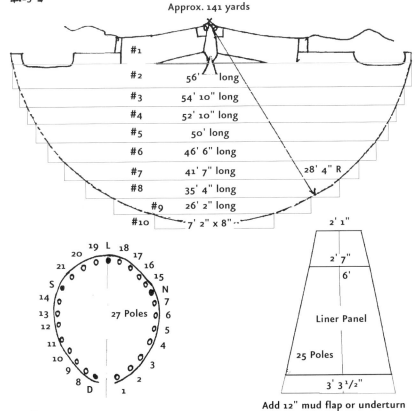

Approx. 141 yards

#1
#2   56'   long
#3   54' 10" long
#4   52' 10" long
#5   50' long
#6   46' 6" long
#7   41' 7" long
#8   35' 4" long
#9   26' 2" long
#10   7' 2" x 8"

28' 4" R

19 L 18
20   17
21   16
S   15
14   N
13   7
12   27 Poles 6
11   5
10   4
9   3
8   2
D   1

2' 1"
2' 7"
6'

Liner Panel

25 Poles

3' 3 ½"

Add 12" mud flap or underturn

Twenty-six-foot tipi dimensions.

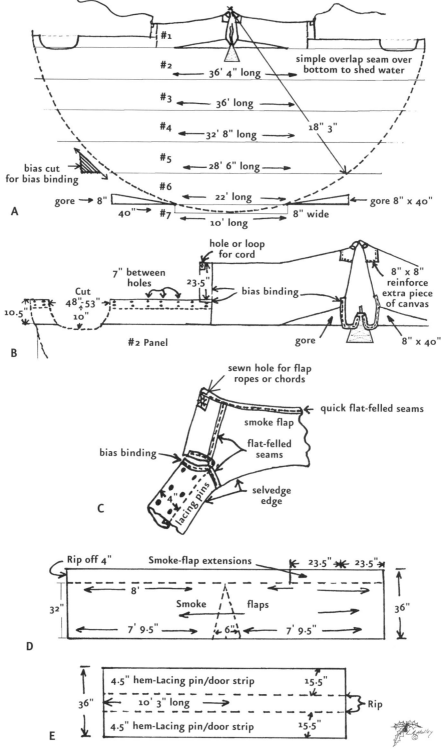

A

#1

simple overlap seam over bottom to shed water

#2 ←— 36' 4" long —→

#3 ←— 36' long —→

#4 ←—32' 8" long—→

18" 3"

#5 ←— 28' 6" long —→

bias cut for bias binding

#6

gore → 8"   ←— 22' long —→   gore 8" x 40"

40"→ #7 ←—10' long—→ 8" wide

B

hole or loop for cord

7" between holes

23.5"

bias binding

8" x 8" reinforce extra piece of canvas

Cut 48"-53"

10.5" 10"

#2 Panel

gore

8" x 40"

C

sewn hole for flap ropes or chords

quick flat-felled seams

smoke flap

flat-felled seams

bias binding

selvedge edge

4"

lacing pins

D

Rip off 4"   Smoke-flap extensions   23.5" 23.5"

8'

32"   Smoke / flaps   36"

7' 9.5"   6"   7' 9.5"

E

4.5" hem-Lacing pin/door strip   15.5"

36"   ←— 10' 3" long —→   Rip

4.5" hem-Lacing pin/door strip   15.5"

Seventeen-foot tipi cover, approximately 65 yards/36-inch material.

Making the Cover

Preparing the Panels

The first step in making the tipi cover is to prepare all the paper patterns and have them ready to trace onto the canvas. Then, you will measure out the different panels that comprise the cover and cut them to length. To do this, spread plastic sheeting on your driveway and roll out your canvas there, or use your hallway or living room. Have two people help, if possible. If no help is available, one person can do it, using a large weight on one end of the canvas to hold it down tight. Measure the length with at least a 40-foot tape measure. Run it out and lay it alongside the canvas. Before cutting, always measure twice. Measure the longest panels first and work down to the shortest panels. After measuring the first panel, cut the canvas off at the bolt end and bring the two raw ends together, folding the entire length in the exact middle. Pull the canvas tight with one person or a

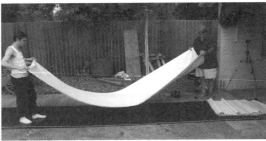

To find the middle of the panel, bring the raw edges together, pull tight, and mark the middle at the selvedge edges. Open back up to fold sections into neat piles.

weight holding the two raw ends together and the other person holding the middle fold. Make a little mark on both selvedge edges on the inside and outside to establish the center of each panel for future reference. Repeat this procedure for all the panels cut. On the raw edges, in the corner, mark the panel number. Unfold and stretch the canvas back out.

To get the canvas to fit into the arm of the sewing machine, you need to narrow the canvas. Fold the canvas lengthwise, with one selvedge edge folded two-thirds of the way over toward the other selvedge. Then fold the folded material one more time lengthwise, so that two-thirds of the width of the canvas has been folded twice, and one-third remains one thickness, with no folds over it. Fold this narrow width of canvas accordion style to make working the long lengths of canvas easier. Handling the canvas panel by panel, with careful marking and neat folding, is the key to easy sewing and avoiding confusion.

A. Fold the panel strip for a tight crease two-thirds of the way to selvedge.
B. Fold down, still keeping a tight hold on the canvas. C. Flip again for a double fold and then accordion fold toward one end, forming a pile.

If marking more than one tipi at a time, mark each panel with the panel number and the size of the tipi. For example, panel #2 for an 18-foot tipi would be "2/18." Once I was making five tipis at a time, and I cut all the panels at the same time with insufficient marking. It was very embarrassing to set up the poles for an 18-foot tipi and discover the cover was for a 14-footer. It certainly looked strange all squished up there on those big poles.

Once you have all your panels cut, marked, and folded neatly, put them away, except for panel #1.

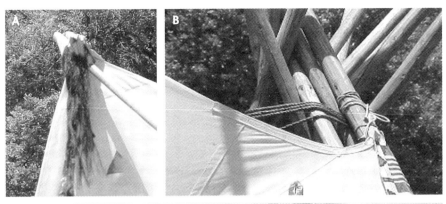

A. Smoke-flap pockets and reinforcement area. B. Gore, tie point, and lift reinforcement. C. Additional flaps over the door area to prevent rain from going between door and cover. Door fits under the flaps.

Panel #1

It is here that the real work of building the tipi begins, as most of the work in making the tipi is in panel #1. Panel #1 consists of the smoke flaps with gores, the lift area or tie flap, the lacing pin/door strip, and the door.

Smoke flaps consist of the pockets in which the poles will set to hold the flaps erect, reinforcement pieces, the gores, extensions to the bottom of the smoke flaps, and the biased seam tape. Smoke-flap pockets are made from the four pieces of canvas as shown in the drawing. For each pocket, sew two pieces together

Tie Flap for Lift Pole

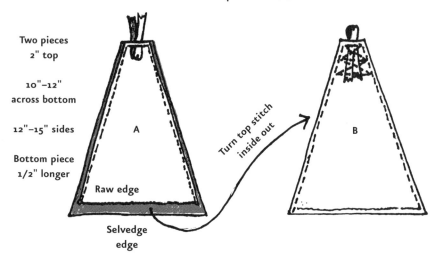

Two pieces
2" top

10"–12"
across bottom

12"–15" sides

Bottom piece
1/2" longer

A

Raw edge

Selvedge
edge

Turn top stitch
inside out

B

Smoke-Flap Pockets—
Cut 4 pieces, 2 for each smoke flap.

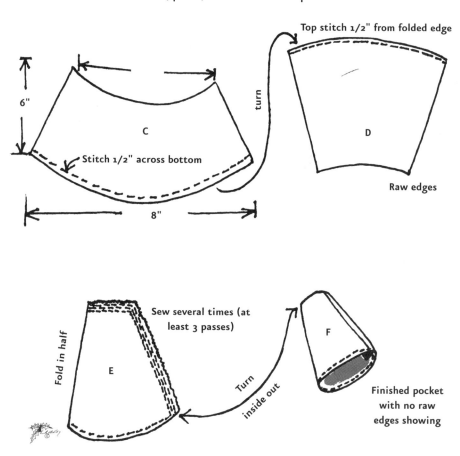

6"

C

Stitch 1/2" across bottom

8"

turn

Top stitch 1/2" from folded edge

D

Raw edges

Fold in half

Sew several times (at
least 3 passes)

E

Turn
inside out

F

Finished pocket
with no raw
edges showing

across the longest width and then turn inside out and top stitch on the folded seam. Fold lengthwise again, making a cup or pocket, and sew from the smaller end to the larger. Sew several lines of stitching to reinforce the seam. Next, turn it inside out to give a smooth exterior appearance. Inside this pocket is where the tip of the smoke-flap pole will rest, so it must be strong enough for the pole not to punch through. Set aside the smoke-flap pockets; they will be sewn to the smoke flaps later.

After making the smoke-flap pockets, sew the reinforcement on the inside corner of the main smoke-flap panel. This piece of cloth can be cut from scrap material. Try to cut the longest edge on the selvedge so you save a step by not having to turn under a raw edge. Cut the tip off so it can be folded later without bunching up too much material.

The tie flap for the lift pole is the piece that attaches the whole cover to the tipi. While lifting the tipi up, the entire weight of the tipi will be on this tie flap, so it needs to have sufficient size and strength to stand up to a lot of weight and wear. This area will be reinforced with rope, heavy 1-inch nylon tape, or pieces of canvas that are cut on the bias, folded lengthwise, and sewn several times to form a tape. Whichever you use, these pieces should be cut about 8 inches long. This is the tape that will have a rope or cord attached to it and tied to the lifting pole. Cut two pieces of canvas in a trapezoidal pattern (A and B), one a bit larger than the other. Sew up one side. Before sewing across the top, fold a piece of the strong tape, making a 1- to 1-1/2-inch loop through which the tie rope will later be inserted. Place this to the inside of the trapezoid, the closed end of the loop facing toward the bottom end of the trapezoid. Stitch it down as you sew across the top. Now sew down the other side of the trapezoid, leaving the bottom end open. Reach up inside the trapezoid and pull the tie tape down hard, turning the trapezoid inside out. If there are raw edges at the bottom, turn the bottom raw hem toward the inside of the trapezoid that will face the tipi cover. Smooth out all the edges and top stitch them. Then sew back and forth across the trapezoid in a zigzag pattern to further strengthen the area.

The gores should be cut so that one long side is selvedge. Each gore is sewn on the inside of the smoke flap, putting the raw edge of the gore to the selvedge edge of the flap. Move it in about 1/2 inch from the edge and sew a single line from the top of the flap to the bottom tip of the gore. Now fold the gore over and sew along the selvedge edge of the smoke flap from the bottom tip of the gore to the top of the gore. This is called a single-turn hem and it hides the raw edge of the gore. The selvedge edge of the gore is now facing out to form a new edge for the smoke flap. It will be sewn to panel #2 when panel #1 is sewn to panel #2.

The next step is to cut and sew the two extensions to the bottom of the smoke flaps. This extension is used mainly on the Cheyenne- and Sioux-style lodges and among other tribes that use the same pattern. It can be left off entirely if you wish. If you are changing the width of the smoke flaps from the size shown here in order to reflect a certain tribal tradition, remember to change the measurements of the extensions to fit your altered width. In cutting the flap extensions,

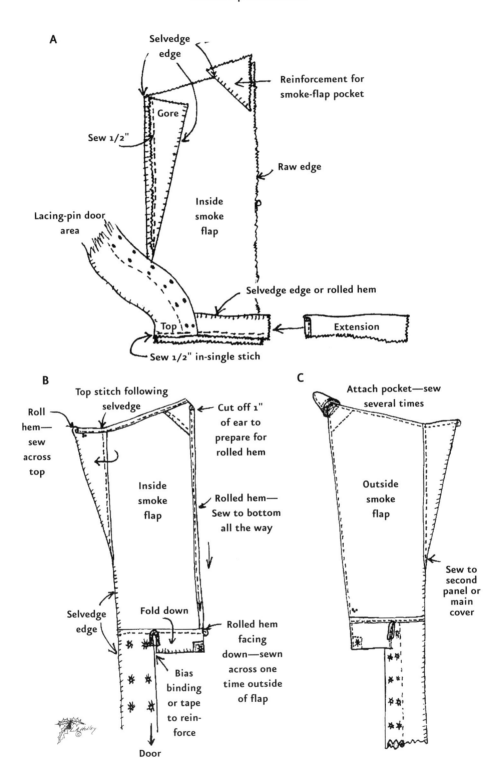

A

Selvedge edge

Reinforcement for smoke-flap pocket

Gore

Sew 1/2"

Raw edge

Inside smoke flap

Lacing-pin door area

Selvedge edge or rolled hem

Top

Extension

Sew 1/2" in-single stich

B

Top stitch following selvedge

Roll hem— sew across top

Cut off 1" of ear to prepare for rolled hem

Inside smoke flap

Rolled hem— Sew to bottom all the way

Selvedge edge

Fold down

Rolled hem facing down—sewn across one time outside of flap

Bias binding or tape to rein-force

Door

C

Attach pocket—sew several times

Outside smoke flap

Sew to second panel or main cover

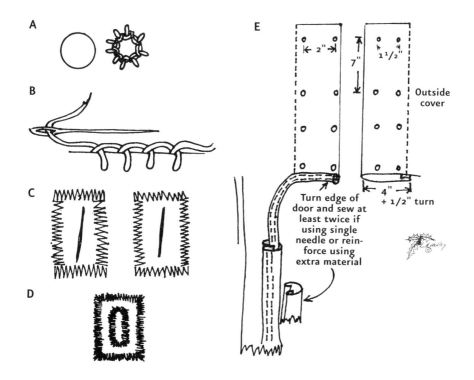

Lacing-pin hole constructions. A. Size of cut hole 5/16 inch. B. Button hole stitch. C. Machine button hole. D. Machine-sewn outline and cut hole. E. Left over right.

you can eliminate the need to hem the bottom if you place the extension pattern on the selvedge edge. If you don't use the selvedge edge, hem the bottom edge of the extension with a double-turn hem. The edge of the extension, which will be sewn to the flap, will be left raw at this point, but will shortly be sewn to the bottom of the smoke flap. For the moment, set the extensions aside and proceed with the tie flap.

The lacing pin/door strip piece runs from the bottom of the smoke flap to the bottom of the tipi on the finished tipi. There are two such strips and the lacing pins that hold the tipi together down the front are inserted into holes made through these strips. To make a lacing pin/door strip, turn the raw edge under 1/2 inch and iron the crease all the way down the strip. Turn it under again for a 4-inch hem and iron it down. Sew this 4-inch hem down near the edge formed by the 1/2-inch underturn. Repeat the process for the other strip.

Buttonholes are about 7 inches apart vertically, on the left panel are 2 inches apart horizontally, and on the right panel 1½ inches apart horizontally.

After measuring and marking your buttonholes carefully (see drawing B on page 60 and drawing E above), cut each hole with very sharp scissors or a hole-punch cutter to about 5/16 inch. Then take some heavy waxed linen or cotton thread, and using a buttonhole stitch, hand sew each hole.

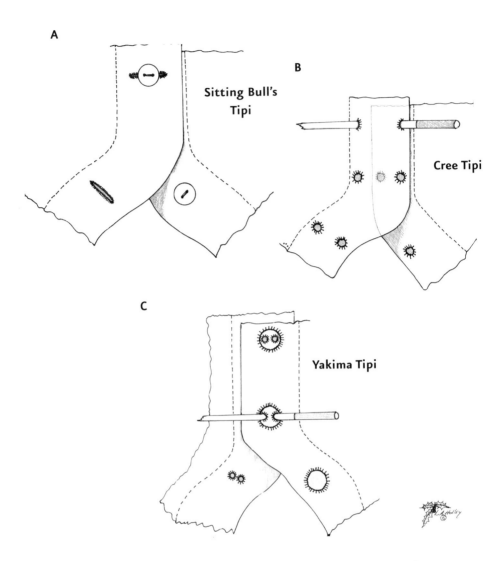

A

Sitting Bull's
Tipi

B

Cree Tipi

C

Yakima Tipi

Lacing-pin exceptions. A. Sitting Bull's tipi, Sioux 1890. B. Cree. C. Yakima.

Some people use a sewing machine to make the buttonhole and either single or double stitch the hole. A heavy-duty machine can do this. Others insert an extra piece of canvas inside the 4-inch hem and then cut the hole and leave it raw, unstitched, because they feel the thickness of four pieces of canvas won't rip. My preference is to hand sew the holes for a finished look and to make a kind of seal around the lacing pin. This gives an authentic appearance to the lodge as compared to machine-stitched holes. There are exceptions to multiple lacing pins. An old photograph, taken around 1890 by David F. Barry, shows Sitting Bull's tipi (A) with actual buttonholes and buttons holding the front together, rather than lacing pins. The buttons appear to be about 1 inch in diameter and spaced about 8 inches from each other down the front to the top of the door opening. Another picture shows a Cree tipi (B) with two lacing-pin holes in the front and one in the back panel. The last picture is a Yakima tipi (C) that shows one big lacing-pin hole in the front and two smaller ones in the under strip or left side panel.

Since the lacing pins are made of wood, they will swell when they get wet. You can avoid excessive swelling by putting a wax or varnish finish on them.

With the lacing pin/door strip essentially complete, it is time to assemble the different parts of panel #1. Begin by matching up the smoke-flap extensions and the lacing pin/door strip to the base of the smoke flaps. Line these two pieces up with the bottom inside of the smoke flap. Aligning these pieces correctly will give a streamlined shingle effect on the outside of the cover. Sew the lacing pin/door strip section to the smoke flap, stopping 1 1/2 inches from the outer fold of the lacing-pin hem. This is slightly overlapped by the extension, the hem of which does not quite meet the other seam. Fold down the lacing pin/door strip and the extension toward the bottom of the lodge cover. Then sew a rolled-hem (double-hem) facing, turning under the raw edges left from joining the sections. This hem will face downward in a shingle effect.

The door opening is an integral part of the lacing pin/door strip, and it is necessary to consider the type of door you want before finishing panel #1. There is a wide range of choices in door openings for your tipi. The old buffalo-hide tipis usually had no formal opening. The bottom corners were just folded back, leaving a triangular door, or the bottom one or two lacing pins were left open and people squeezed in and out until the hide stretched and formed a sort of saggy door

CHIEF OF COMMANCHE INDIANS AND SQUAW,
OKLAHOMA

opening. When canvas tipis were introduced, these methods continued to be used, but with some additional, more formal, door treatments. Quanah Parker, the famous Comanche leader, had a tipi with a triangular door, pointed at the top and squared off at the bottom just above the lacing pins. Others began cutting oval doors, some low to the ground and others high. The latter are associated particularly with the northern tribes, probably because of the snow buildup in front of the door. One thing to remember, however, is that the higher your door threshold, the higher up you will have to step to get in and out of your lodge. This can be a problem for visitors and children and even yourself if you don't lift your feet high enough to clear the threshold. It has been the source of a lot of broken bones. It is a better idea to just pull out the pins on the bottom and leave it unpinned until you need it pinned at night to keep the weather out or when you go away for a while. The threshold below the door opening takes a lot of stress and abuse, so it needs to be reinforced.

The door opening can be made as tall as you need for your purposes. But remember, when severe weather sets in, a smaller door opening keeps more weather out.

Door covers in early times were just pieces of leather, old furs, or old blankets suspended over the door to keep out the wind, rain, sleet, and snow. Later, the rawhide or parfleche door covers, with their colorful geometric designs and the U-shaped, Cheyenne door covers, often with lanes of beadwork, came into use, as did the circular door covers. Some were simply decorated rectangles of fabric. Today there are some highly tailored doors and door covers, which keep out the worst of rains. Many have special flaps on the cover to prevent water from running down between the door and the door cover. Nowadays almost all door covers are made out of the same material as the cover.

Three ways to make a door opening for your tipi:

For an authentic-looking door that is both simple and practical, just leave the lacing pin/door strip straight, all the way to the end. When the tipi is set up, fold

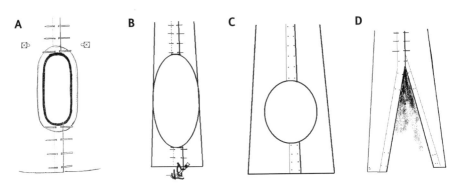

Four types of door openings. A. Reinforced, oval, high-off-ground door attachments.
B. Oval-cut door. Peg in front. C. Round-cut door high off ground.
D. Slit door, not tailored, just straight. Lacing pins optional at bottom.

the bottom corners back to give a triangular opening all the way to the ground, with no canvas door threshold.

For another authentic look, do not make a formal door opening; just leave the lacing pin/door strip straight all the way to the end. When the tipi is set up, the lacing pins are put in place both above and below the entry area. You enter by stretching your arms forward through the slit and pushing the fabric aside. In time the fabric will stretch to some degree and form a somewhat saggy door opening that looks very much like that of old-time tipis.

For a more formal, cut-out door, make a template from paper or cardboard—or use a nice rounded platter or plate—to establish the curves at the top and the bottom of the door opening. Decide how far from the bottom of the finished tipi you want the door hole to begin, and how high you want the top of the door to be. Then, draw in these curves at the top and bottom. Since the second panel of the cover has not yet been sewn to the first panel, only the curve for the top and bottom of the door can be drawn at this point. The side of the door will be rather straight, following the line where the first panel is sewn to the second panel.

Set the completed first panel aside while you sew the other panels together. Later you will sew panel #1 to the rest of the tipi.

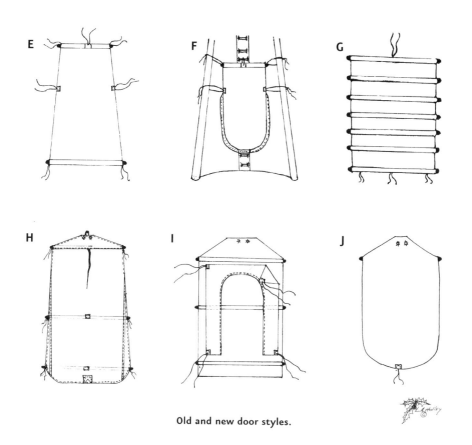

Old and new door styles.

Main Body of the Cover

You are now ready to put the **strips for the main part of the cover** together. Start with the bottom (or smallest) panel and work your way up to the #1 panel. Now the little mid-marks of each panel become important. It works best if you have a large area in your backyard, house, or driveway to lay out a full cover. Then you can start from one end and work to the other. It is the way I made over three hundred tipis.

Lay the shortest panel out on the surface where you are going to work and find the mid-mark. Then line up the next shortest panel parallel to the shortest panel with the two mid-marks matching up. It is not necessary to unfold them completely as you will start from the midpoint and work to each end. The larger panel will be longer on each end than the shorter panel, and it will start forming a shingle effect.

Accordion-folded panels ready to glue and sew.

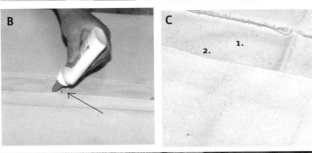

Mid-marks for centering canvas panels. Top always goes over the bottom to give shingle effect.

Ironing the two panels together.

Get an iron (set it on the highest setting) and a bottle of glue ready. With the two panels right next to each other at the mid-mark, run a thin bead of glue down the shorter panel to the end. Carefully lay the longer strip panel over the shorter strip panel by covering one selvedge edge over the other by about 1/2 inch. This will cover the glue. Take the iron and move it slowly along the selvedges until you get to the end of the glued area. Do not leave the iron in one spot too long as it will leave scorch marks. This is not a permanent way to hold a tipi together, but it's

Top thread

Canvas

Bottom thread

Simple overlap seam: The free edges are selvedged; material is overlapped 1 inch. Spacing between double stitching is 5/8".

Quick flat-felled seam: The raw edges are turned 1/2"; material is overlapped 1 inch. Spacing between double stitching is 5/8".

Double-turn hem: Material is folded 1/2" twice and stitched to enclose raw edge.

French seam: First material is aligned and stitched 1/2" from raw edges. Material is subsequently reversed and stitched so as to flatten and enclose raw edge.

Single-turn hem: Material is folded 1/2" once and stitched to another surface, thereby enclosing raw edge.

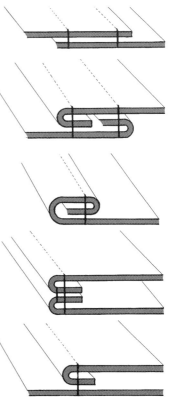

Diagrams of sewing stitches, seams, and hand-sewing seams.

better than clothespins or needles. If it comes apart, reapply the glue and iron the material again until it sticks. The heat sets the glue, which keeps the two pieces of canvas together until you sew them. If two people are working together, one person can do the overlapping while the other irons. Repeat this process on the other side of the mid-mark for the same two panels. After you finish gluing and ironing, carefully accordion fold the two panels. Take them to the sewing machine and sew. If you have a one-needle machine, make two passes. This type of seam, called a simple overlap, is just as strong as the flat-felled seam. When done properly, it will last the life of the cover. The old-style tipis were made with an overlapping seam.

Repeat this process for the remainder of the panels, continuing to sew the next larger panel to the rest of the cover.

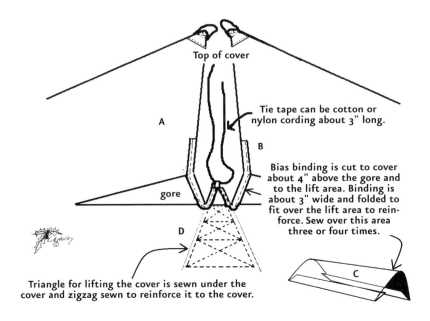

Top of cover

Tie tape can be cotton or
nylon cording about 3" long.

A

B

Bias binding is cut to cover
about 4" above the gore and
to the lift area. Binding is
about 3" wide and folded to
fit over the lift area to reinforce. Sew over this area
three or four times.

gore

D

C

Triangle for lifting the cover is sewn under the
cover and zigzag sewn to reinforce it to the cover.

Attaching smoke flaps, gore, and lifting tab on section 1 panel.

Lay out the smoke flaps and triangle for the tie point on panel #1. They should match from the mid-mark of #1 to the bottom where the bottom of the lacing-pin section meets. Glue the lifting tie to the cover at the midpoint. I usually put this under the panel instead of on top to act as a buffer where it lies on the lift pole. Starting 3 1/2 inches on either side of the center, overlap the gores, smoke flap, and lacing-pin section on top of panel #1. Carefully fold when finished and start on the other side of the tie flap and do the same thing. Fold toward the rest of the pile and sew straight down one end to the other.

To cut the door, sew the lifting triangle in place and attach the reinforcing bias binding to flaps and gore, as shown in the diagrams. If you have an industrial sewing machine, run the reinforcements more than once. The threads will strengthen the area.

When you unfold this completed panel, stretch it out as tight as possible to get as much of the curves out as possible. Then refold the smoke-flap area and #1 panel back on itself to make a nice tight bundle. Next find the mid-mark on the bottom of panel #1 so it can be matched to the mid-mark of panel #2.

Take the completed panels out and unfold and then refold again so that the selvedge edge of the largest strip is under the next largest panel at the mid-marks. Always work from the middle out on both sides and accordion fold when finished. After all the main panels are sewn together, it is time to attach panel #1 to the main body. You should have two rather large, neatly folded piles (you hope). The #1 strip will go through the arm of the sewing machine. Carefully glue and join the sections by using your fingers and hands, stretching the canvas to fight the curves. Fold to create a small compact pile in that area. Match the mid-marks for #1 to #2

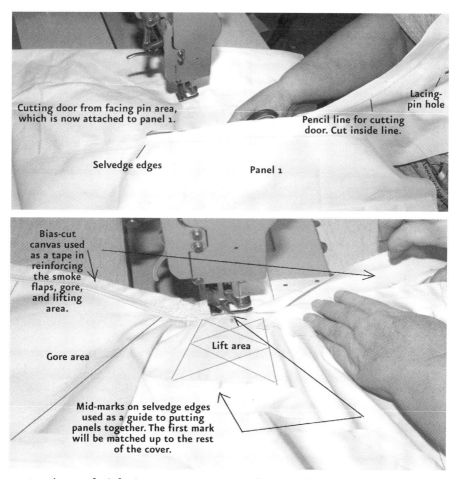

Cutting door from facing pin area, which is now attached to panel 1.

Lacing-pin hole

Pencil line for cutting door. Cut inside line.

Selvedge edges

Panel 1

Bias-cut canvas used as a tape in reinforcing the smoke flaps, gore, and lifting area.

Gore area

Lift area

Mid-marks on selvedge edges used as a guide to putting panels together. The first mark will be matched up to the rest of the cover.

Attachment of reinforcing canvas tape to smoke flaps and lift area. Cut door opening.

and start the process of joining the two major areas. This is not going to be easy, as there is a natural curve to some panels. When all is done, sew.

Now that the #1 panel is sewn to the main body of the cover, it can be taken out for the final trim and to attach the bottom cords. Spread the cover in a clean grass area or put it on a big plastic tarp in a parking lot. An abandoned lot is always good; no cars will roll over the cover. Using a big nail or a tipi peg, use a cord attached to the lift tie and peg the cover to the ground. Stretch the cover down the middle back and pin the small panel at midpoint. Next pull the first seam from either side to lay as straight as possible and stick nails in the lacing-pin holes at the bottom of the door area. Smooth out the entire cover until it is nice and stretched. Peg big nails or heavy rocks/bricks on the other corners of the panels to keep the cover taut and straight.

To cut the outside curve/bottom of the cover, the radius point is drawn. Check several times before cutting. To find this point, place a big nail or peg between the smoke-flap pockets and measure out to the edge of the cover. The closer the peg is to the tie point, the more you will have a shape of a cone. The farther out to the

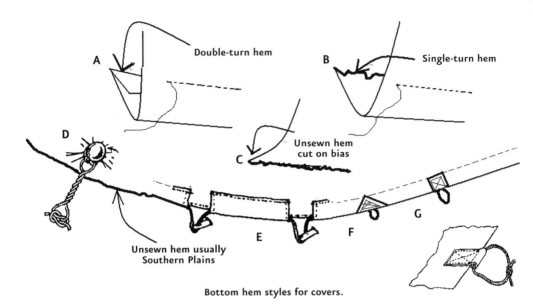

Double-turn hem

Single-turn hem

Unsewn hem
cut on bias

Unsewn hem usually
Southern Plains

Bottom hem styles for covers.

smoke-flap pockets the radius is moved, the shorter the back or tilt of your tipi. All measurements can be adjusted to the size and shape needed. Use a non-stretchable tape measure and start marking your pivot, or circumference, with a pencil or tailor's chalk. Trim along the mark, staying to the outside. Once cut, the edge can be left unfinished for a Southern-style look, which has very little raveling, or the edge can be turned and sewn for the more Northern-style of tipi bottom.

Diagrams of different styles of tailored bottoms and ties have been included in this chapter. The choice is up to you; this will be determined by your use and the area of country in which you live.

For the unfinished bottom, cut as many peg loops as needed. These are spaced anywhere from 18 to 25 inches around the bottom. Since the pegs hold down the cover, I prefer more loops and I just do not use all of them unless needed. Peg loops are cotton cord or 1/8-inch nylon about 25 to 9 inches long depending on if you want the cover touching the ground or not. If you use the nylon chord, which does not freeze in cold weather, melt the ends before attaching them to prevent unraveling and slippage. Put a square knot in the ends of the cords and then attach a marble or some round, smooth object using a clove hitch. With smoke flap and tie point cords added, you can fold the cover and store until use.

This is only one way of making a tipi. There are many other ways depending on styles, tribes, and number of family members in a tribe. Another popular way is to cut the smoke flaps and lacing-pin area out of the same strip and not as separate pieces. The gore would be the only other separate piece added. It would be reinforced with a heavy-duty twill tape, as would the tie point, which would be heavily sewn on the cover. Other stress areas would be over sewn with more canvas and tapes to strengthen them.

* Lee Bryant., "Ask the Expert," *Doll Craft Magazine*, July 2002, 86–87.

Old-style buffalo-hide liner.

The Liner or Lining

A bit of confusion has arisen over the official name for the liner or lining of the tipi. Many Sioux Native Americans residing on the reservation and Sioux dictionary translations indicate the name used for the liner is the *ozan*. However, the Laubins used the word *ozan* to refer to the rain cover (Laubins 1957, 53). In this book, the ozan is called the liner. In the next chapter, the covering above the head that protects from rain is referred to as the rain cover. The liner has also been known as the *o'zan*, and *óza* with a nasal "n," *ozanpi, woza* (n) (Warcloud 1989, 43), *oh-WON-eh-OH-zon* or *Wo-zon*.[i]

A dew-curtain, called an óza (pronounced with a nasal "n"), was hung all around and was long enough to be tucked under the carpet. This was

77

made in matched pieces, with strings attached for tying them together and to the tipi poles. Many an oza, (ozan), was elaborately decorated at about two to four feet intervals with vertical bands of fancy work in patterns of bright colors—or so painted. This dew-curtain, which was tied to the poles at a height of perhaps four feet, and the sloping tipi wall, together formed a little circular alley-way, like a lean-to in shape. And there all surplus foods and robes were stored, as well as extra personal belongings of the family, all packed in proper containers. This storage area was insulation as well, and the inside of the tipi was always noticeably warmer because of it. The dew-curtain was usually of either doe or calf skin. This summer curtain was purely for decoration and was hung only across the back of the ticatku (place of honor). If anything, this was more elaborate than the winter-curtain whose primary purpose was to protect against extreme cold.[ii]

The liner's purpose is twofold. It helps insulate the tipi's interior, and it also serves to block the draft. Historically the liner was made of tanned hides. Two hides were sewn together head to head, tail to tail, or side to side. Later cloth was hung

Cheyenne tipi cloth panel or liner.

from the tipi poles by a rope of rawhide or braided buffalo hair. Often liners consisted of several sections that overlapped when in use. These liner pieces could be decorated with paintings or horizontal lanes of quillwork or beadwork. Some have dangles. Tipi liners are typically about 3 to 5 feet high. There have been references to a liner going around the whole interior of the lodge. A single liner made of hide or cloth would be too heavy and bulky to encircle the lodge, so it probably means

there were two or more rectangular liners, which appear as one complete liner. The later cloth liners carried over this rectangular shape and style (Cheyenne-Arapaho beaded liners and most painted muslin liners). When the liner is adorned in historic style, it can be a striking addition to the overall historic appearance of the lodge's interior.

Original cloth liners were rectangular shaped. Since these panels were not fitted, they basically hung straight down from the tie point. Then parfleches, beds, or whatever else was on hand were piled on the liner to push it back as far as it would go. Dried food, extra storage material, saddles, or whatever was not needed at the moment could be stored between the cover and the liner. This created a lodge with a very small living space, but with lots of storage area behind the liner.

Liners could also be made of blankets, Russian shawls, calico-printed cotton, and any other cloth that could be found. The old,

Above: Southern Cheyenne summer tipi, 1913.
Below: Interior of Crow lodge.

decorated shawls seemed to be popular in the Northern Plains for Crow tipis. Stripped awning material and printed cloth were also popular.

The lodges of the nineteenth century did not use a liner in the warmer times of the year. Photos of the Plains tipis rarely show liners. However, liners are pictured on the Northern Plains tipis, used where temperatures can get very cold even in summer. In some photos the liners are not just in front of the poles, but in many cases between the cover and the poles. This seems to help with some insulation because many tipis are made from lighter materials, such as muslin. Also the cover and these interior liners go all the way to the ground, blocking out all drafts. An interesting point to remember is that Native Americans could adapt more easily to warm and cold temperatures than we can today, as they spent all their life outdoors.

There are no pictures of liners pegged to the ground by the poles. All the liners that I've seen had no ties or attachments at the bottom. The only ties were at the top of the lining, which could be tied to a rope or pole on the inside of the lodge. Many tipis had liners that overlapped each other, or there was just one in the back going over a bed area.

Today's linings or liners can come in all types, sizes, and materials. These materials can be canvas, natural muslin, calico-patterned cloth, brain-tan, or commercial hides. As tipis got larger and more elaborate, liners became more tailored to fit the angles and number of poles. Today we have two types of linings: the pole liner and the rope liner. The pole liner is attached directly to the pole at the top and bottom. The rope liner is attached to a rope, which is wrapped around the poles about 5 to 6 feet above the floor space. The bottom on the same liner is attached to pegs or another rope wrapped around the butts of the same tipi pole or tied to the bottom of the tipi pole. There seem to be several ways and combinations to putting up a lining. However you choose to put up your lining, it adds to the beauty and mystery of the lodge. Privacy was not a main concern as women and men dressed in front of each other until the coming of the missionaries. So "privacy" curtains are a new concept.

Ernest Thompson Seton describes a liner in his articles on tipis for Scouting. Pictured are pieces of rectangular cloth that hang from the tipi poles. The articles do not mention how it is attached at the bottom. In later books, Ben Hunt draws pictures of liners without an underturn but shows a cut curve with small ties attached at the bottom for pegs.

In *The Indian Tipi* by the Laubins, we start seeing the tailored, fitted bottom underturn liner of cloth. The trapezoidal sections for the liner are drawn out with good instructions and measurements for an 18-foot lodge. Their book was the basis for all the other books based on this style of tipi.

Should a liner have a "sod cloth" or should it underturn at the bottom? A sod cloth does help seal out the cold winds when other articles are put on top. Being cloth, however, it will mildew or rot over time. If the underturn is made out of the synthetic cloth, it will be rot resistant. My opinion is that if you have a liner, you should fold it under. But if the climate is good and you want to travel light, you should leave the liner at home.

To tie my liner down, I have long loops or ties at the ends of the seams. These line up with my poles and are simply hooked under or tied to the bottom butt of the poles. This saves me from having to use more pegs. Because of the length of the loops, the liner doesn't stick out beyond the cover and catch water.

So, do you need a liner in your lodge? No! Today we have pitched the tipi cover so high off the ground that the liner becomes just an unnecessary extra cover to keep out the weather. Does a liner keep you cooler in summer by forcing the air to flow upward, creating a better draft? Not from my experience of camping in the 100-degree temperatures of the South and West. The tipi is actually cooler without the liner during the summer. In cooler weather, with or without a liner inside, a fire burns easily. The smoke flaps and door opening control the airflow more than any liner. Today the liner has become simply a big privacy curtain in the daylight hours and a "shadow catcher" at night.

Materials for the Fitted Liner

All the equipment, materials, and cloth listed in the previous chapter, "Materials and Steps for Making the Tipi Cover," are needed here. If you have already made the panels, which go together and form the top and bottom of the lining, then put the glue and iron away. If you are going for the 9-foot-tall liner, then another strip can be added to the 6-foot liner. This does add more weight and angles at the top following the natural curve of the tipi. In a 24-foot or larger tipi, a very tall liner can be used for winter living. These liners also require extra ties vertically to a rope or pole to support the sagging middle sections.

This is also the time to decide on a one-, two-, or three-piece liner. For a small tipi, a one-piece is OK. But, because of weight and maneuverability, when you get into the big tipis, like the 18-footers, three pieces may be a better choice. The fitted liner dictates the shape of the cover and how it looks from the outside.

The lining can be made from either a 10-ounce material or a calico/muslin cloth, which is lighter still. It does not have to be from the heavier canvas. It is all up to you. If you do go for the lightweight material, a regular sewing machine will suffice to sew the liner. The underturn, or sod cloth, can be a longer extension already built into the panels or it can be added cloth sewn to the bottom. The pattern in this chapter is a tailored style and requires a protractor (which can be made of cardboard or wood), a ruler, and a long straight edge of 6 to 7 feet.

Ties on the liner are placed at the top and bottom, which attach to the tipi poles. This eliminates the need for an extra rope at the bottom or pegs to anchor the lining. Some people still use a rope wrapped around the poles to attach the top of the lining instead of just the pole. The most time-consuming aspect of pitching a tipi is hanging the lining, especially if you're using the fitted styles. Compared to a tailored liner, hanging the liner in the old way is fast but not neat, nor does it give a wrinkle-free look.

To get the geometric arrangement that fits the poles, you will need to use a large protractor. Sometimes you can find a large one in a teaching supply store. Or you can make one by using the biggest one you can find and enlarging it onto a piece of cardboard or wood. The size I made, and worked with for twenty-five years, was 2 feet across and high. Find the center and then 60 degrees to 90 degrees on both sides. The long 7-foot stick or straight edge is for continuing the lines at the top and bottom. Kraft, butcher, or any paper large enough to draw a full-scale pattern works when making designs. A heavy board or Masonite paneling works great if you want a more durable pattern. The patterns only have to be drawn and cut once but can be used hundreds of times. Remember, there are half as many panels as there are poles, plus the door area. That means if you have a twelve-pole lodge, you have to have at least five panel patterns (which will make two exact panels) and one for the door, which makes six. The door area is drawn only one time. Total cloth panels will be twelve plus the door for thirteen liner pieces to make the one-piece liner.

The diagrams below show how to find angles for the fitted liner. If you want to make a new size or add more poles, they show the measurements for angles. You do not have to be a real math wizard to figure this out or know how to use a CAD program for mechanical engineers. The fitted angles also help in the regular rectangular-panel liner.

All panel patterns should be cut true to their angles or the liner will be thrown off. There will be some imperfections in the cloth, curves, and in your drawing ability. Be as exact as possible with very little deviation. If your measurements deviate from the given patterns by as much as half a degree or an inch, go back and recheck. A tiny bit off will not hurt too much.

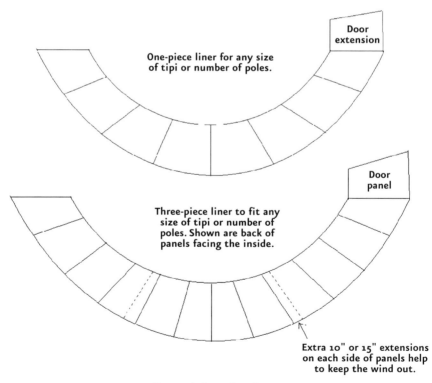

Door
extension

One-piece liner for any size
of tipi or number of poles.

Door
panel

Three-piece liner to fit any
size of tipi or number of
poles. Shown are back of
panels facing the inside.

Extra 10" or 15" extensions
on each side of panels help
to keep the wind out.

One- and three-piece liners.

A

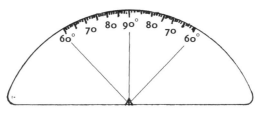

Make a large cardboard protractor with a radius of 25".

B Pattern can be used with any 12-pole frame. Goes with the 14', 16', 17' in this book.

Cut 3/4" twill tape or leather strips for top laces. They should be about 24" long. Need to go around poles twice and tie in bow. Cut one end to an angle's point ≻ and thread through awl hole in each seam about 1/2" from top, or sew in.

Cut bottom edge even before adding mud flap.

75°

12
D
4
90°
76° 10
89° 8
77°
88° 6
78°
87° 4
80°
85° 82.5°
82.5°

5
6
S
8
L
N
7
2
3
9
76°
75°
90°
82.5°
82.5°
11
1
1

Door flap

8" ties for overlap

85° 80° 87° 78°
89°
77°
88°

5/16" reinforced hole or heavy brass grommet for peg hole

Peg ties

Hem edges unless using selvedge edge

Mud flap 12" to 15" wide and as long as the liner panel is added on using a flap fled seam. Material is canvas or synthetic material to help reduce mildew or rot.

D

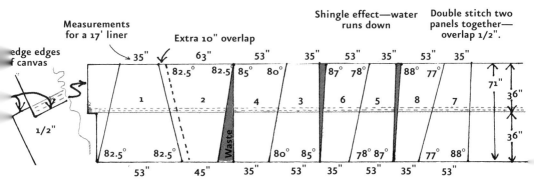

Measurements for a 17' liner

Extra 10" overlap

Shingle effect—water runs down

Double stitch two panels together— overlap 1/2".

edge edges f canvas

1/2"

Pattern for 17-foot tipi liner.

Two strips of the cloth should be sewn together to make a long panel of about 50 to 75 feet. This all depends on how big of a tipi you have chosen. Most liners measure a little less in canvas yardage than the cover. If more sections are needed, you can add them later.

The pattern can be adjusted to a shorter vertical version by measuring down 12 inches from the top. I bend the pattern at this point, and let this be the new top line all the way across. This will leave you an extra 12 inches or so at the bottom and will form the underturn, or sod cloth, on its own.

Construction

Cut the pattern drawings with number one as the door covering. Number one and number two panels are the same angles. Number three and number four panels are the same angles and so on until you are finished. The acute angle (an angle getting less than 90 degrees) faces the door, and the obtuse angle (an angle getting closer to 90 degrees) is at the lift pole or lift area. Make sure panels are stacked in the way they will be sewn and reverse each panel in the opposite direction of the other to have the correct angles to the door or lift pole. See drawing B on page 83 and the drawing on page 85. When sewing these sections together, it will create the shingle effect of the seam facing downward on every section. If not, water can collect in the seam and drip in. Always double check to make sure angles are facing in the right directions before sewing. Ripping out is no fun and takes time.

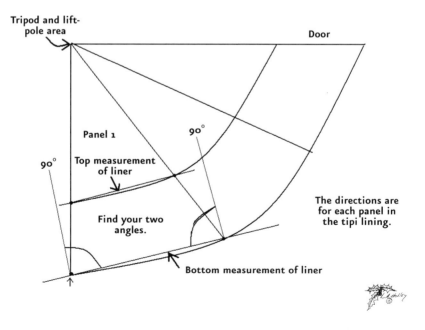

Finding the angles of a fitted liner with any number of poles.

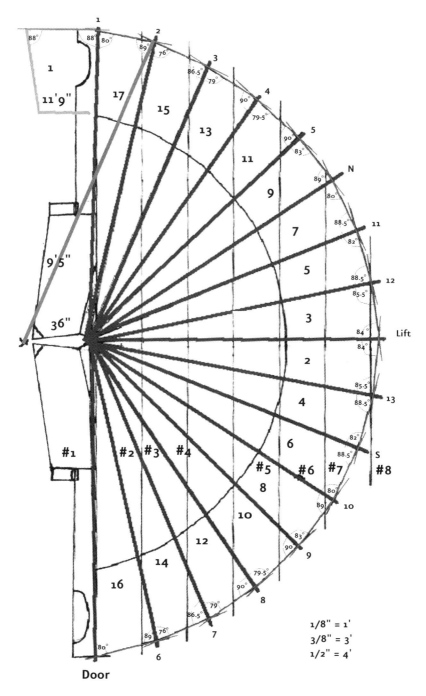

1/8" = 1'
3/8" = 3'
1/2" = 4'

Door

Twenty-foot tipi showing working drawings for position of poles and 6-foot liner.

Drawing the liner panel. Protractor and long straight edge are used to draw the first pattern for a liner panel. Draw the back edge, bottom, and front side of the pattern following straight line. Bottom edge is drawn in if sod cloth is added to pattern. Makes a shorter 5-foot liner plus underturn. Or slide pattern down to opposite seam for a full 6-foot-size liner panel and add 10 to 12 inches for a sod cloth.

Try to work with only one section of the panel in the arm of the sewing machine. You do not want piles of canvas in the way.

After the pieces are sewn with either a flat-felled, overlap, or just two-edges-put-together seam, then add on the 8- to 12-inch sod cloth or underturn. This can also be done with any of the stitches pictured. For neatness and smooth folding, the flat-felled seam is the best. But if your machine cannot handle the thickness, do whatever works for you.

Next put on the leather ties (cotton tape) at the top and 1/4-inch nylon cords at the bottom of each panel seam. The ties at the top are 22-inch-long strips or what will reach around the thickness of your poles. On the top, use the awl to punch the holes for the leather and hand or machine sew the cotton ties. The bottom of the joined seam has a marble inserted with an 18-inch nylon cord to tie it to the bottom of the tipi pole. These are placed on the opposite seam from the top tie. Where the two major panels come together, sew in a 2-inch reinforcing piece of

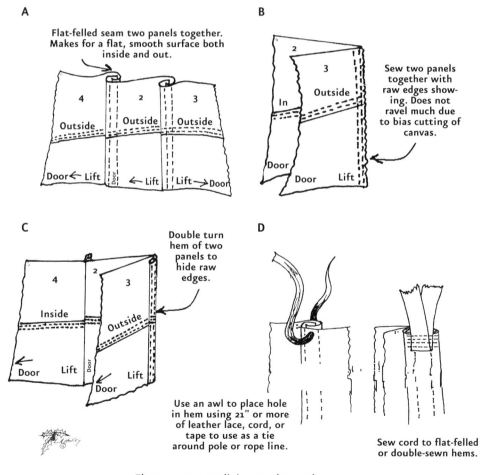

A

Flat-felled seam two panels together. Makes for a flat, smooth surface both inside and out.

B

Sew two panels together with raw edges showing. Does not ravel much due to bias cutting of canvas.

C

Double turn hem of two panels to hide raw edges.

D

Use an awl to place hole in hem using 21" or more of leather lace, cord, or tape to use as a tie around pole or rope line.

Sew cord to flat-felled or double-sewn hems.

Three ways to sew lining panels together.

cloth and install a size 4 or 5 grommet. One panel fits into the other at the 10-inch overlap. This keeps the draft out on the side and from going up the panel. It is also possible to hand sew this hole, and then reinforce it several times with waxed linen thread. However, under stress, this has a tendency to stretch out and can tear. This is the only area that I use a metal grommet because of the strength. After the tipi is pitched, the grommet does not show.

Stitches per inch on
overlap seam.

Awl for piercing canvas.

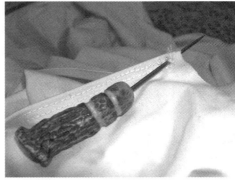

Leather with cut tip
used for liner ties.

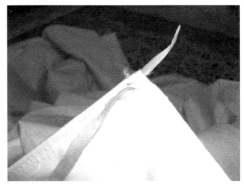

[i] From e-mail correspondence with Benson Lanford based on conversations with the late Milford Chandler and Buechel. Full quotes can be found in the Appendix.

[ii] E-mail correspondence with Peter Gibbs quoting Ella Delorias's papers on the usage of *oza*. Full quotes can be found in the Appendix.

1938 Czechoslovakia Woodcraft encampment showing rain caps.

Rain Covers
and Rain Caps

When standing inside a tipi and looking up at the gaping smoke hole, the new-comer to tipis invariably asks, "How do you keep the rain out?" This is a good question indeed and the subject of this chapter. The simple, brief answer is you use rain caps and rain covers. But it is actually more complicated than that.

In all the known daguerreotypes (tin types), glass negatives, photographs, sketchbooks, journals, or writings, there is no illustration or mention of a cover on top of a tipi to protect it from rain. The first time that it appears is when Ernest Thompson Seton illustrated it in his book *Two Little Savages*, first published in 1901. Seton may have adopted the idea from the Missouri River Indians who

French tipi made by Guy Vaudois, showing a rain cap, with tie downs at three corners.

covered the smoke holes of their earth lodges with their buffalo-hide bull boats. It is unlikely that Seton ever observed this practice applied to tipis either among Indians of his day or in historical documents. Because of the heavy weight of the boat, the uneven length, and the thin tips of the poles, it is unrealistic to assume that a tipi could support a boat. Moreover, throughout much of the Plains region such boats were rarely used.

The next time a drawing of a tipi with a rain cover appears in tipi literature is in Ben Hunt's book *Indian and Camp Handcraft,* which was largely a compilation of articles that he had published in the magazine *Industrial Arts and Vocational Education* in 1938. His tipi illustrations, apparently based on Seton's drawings, show a bowl-shaped cover and rain pouring down. In later drawings, Hunt depicts ropes holding the storm cap in place. The use of rain caps today is more prevalent in Europe, particularly in England, France, and Germany, than America.

Interior Rain Covers

Could some kind of rain covering have been used inside the early lodges? There is a possibility with the Wild West shows and other entertainment at the turn of the century where tipis were on display. Some type of interior cover could have been used inside to protect the occupants from the many storms that happen in the East. However, from all the photographs and descriptions of the time, no picture or information can be found of either an outside rain cover or inside rain cover. If one was used, it was probably a piece of cloth that was tied up inside on the poles to keep the water from the occupants and then taken down when not needed. Spare hides, blankets, robes, and cloth were the only practical, known materials for this time period.

Makeshift awning material stretched for rain cover over liner
for Linda Holley's 12-foot tipi.

Drawstring rain cover.

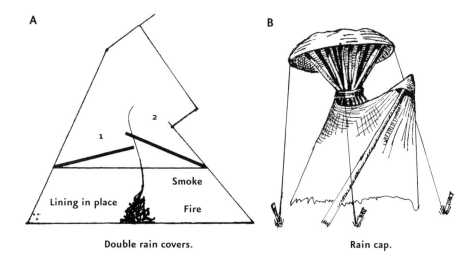

A

1

2

Smoke

Lining in place

Fire

Double rain covers.

B

Rain cap.

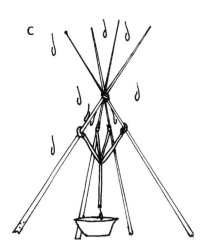

C

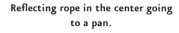

Reflecting rope in the center going
to a pan.

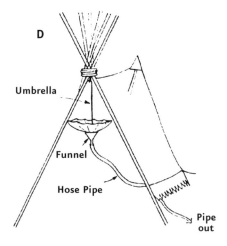

D

Umbrella

Funnel

Hose Pipe

Pipe
out

New Zealand Jaia Tipis' way of keeping
water off your head.

In America the preference seems to be for the interior rain canopy, which the Laubins called the "ozan." In Lakota, the word *ozan* really refers to the lining, not the overhead rain canopy, so the words *rain cover* or *rain canopy* will be employed here. Rain canopies appear to be a rare exception rather than the norm until the Laubins published *The Indian Tipi* in 1957. They brought us the fitted or tailored interior rain cover. Historically, the portable tipi was designed for the Great Plains, where there is little rain but a constant wind. Typically the storms and rains that hit the Great Plains move through fast, driven by the wind. Any objects that got wet would dry out rather quickly due to the low level of humidity. The success of the Laubins in introducing the tipi to people living outside the arid Plains region, in wet and humid climates such as those found in Oregon, Florida, and the southern Appalachians, has resulted in far greater use of the interior rain cover today than in earlier times. Refer back to bottom drawing on page 25.

Today the interior rain canopy is a large piece of cloth, preferably a water-repellent, fire-retardant, lightweight canvas that fits overhead, from one side of the tipi to the other. It angles down to the sides and back, just above the lining, so that water will run off the canopy behind the liner. Properly set up, the rain cover will prevent water from dripping onto the beds. After a rain is over, if there are any items that got wet, perhaps from water coming under the tipi, they can be placed on top of the rain cover to dry out, assuming they are not too heavy. The rain cover is also effective in retaining and reflecting heat.

Tipi makers can sell you a fitted rain cover or you can easily make your own with a large piece of painter's cloth, treated material, or any water-resistant cloth that will fit the interior of your lodge. A fire-retardant material is a good idea. It is easy to take a piece of cloth, marbles, and string or leather ties and attach the rain cover to each tipi pole above your head level using the same marble-tie system employed to make stake loops. Stretch it across from side to side and then angle it down and back, attaching it to each pole as it angles down to the back sleeping area. If there is extra material overlapping the liner, cut it so that it fits behind the lining, forming a flap. All this can be done for just a few dollars.

In my own tipi, I use two of these rain covers to keep out the heaviest of storms and to keep in the warmth of a small fire. One goes from the back to the middle and the other goes from the front to the middle. They meet above the fire area, with one overlapping the other by a space of about 12 or more inches so the smoke can escape. Each cover slants back to the lining so that any moisture can drain out behind the liner.

Alternative Methods of Interior and Exterior Rain Covers

Another possibility for a rain cover is to use a fitted drawstring cover that attaches to the lining and gathers in the middle with a hole for smoke to pass through.

Here is a tip to consider from Jaia Tipis in New Zealand:

I know [one tipi owner] who will pass a 1/8-inch cord over his pole cluster and hang an umbrella upside down in the tipi. He pulls the upside down umbrella all the way up to where it will touch as many poles as possible and ties the cord off. He has also poked a small hole near the tip of the umbrella and runs a cotton string out the hole and down to a stake on

Specialized plastic interior rain cover diverts the water back to the outside.

the ground so [that] as the umbrella fills up, [the water] goes out the hole near the tip of the umbrella, down the string and ends up in the grass where his stake is. It works for him.

Another elaborate system for deflecting interior water is to put little flags on the inside of the tipi poles about 3 feet from the lift area so that water drips into the rain cover before it gets to the liner. Or simply tie a piece of cloth to the poles with ropes or strings to poles and have it drain into a pan in the middle of the tipi. The most innovative method of this type of rain cover, which uses clear plastic for the light advantage, is from Rainbow Tipis.

On the outside several ideas have been developed lately of what would be called rain caps. These are attached to the outside poles, covering all the exterior poles and the smoke-hole area, preventing the rain from getting in. The Europeans seem to prefer this outside rain cap or cover and were probably influenced by the early works of Seton and Ben Hunt. In using these, you may have to cut your poles much shorter in order to get the cap to cover the whole area to be protected. Then the cap should be tied down with at least four pegs in the ground to prevent it from flying off and damaging the top poles or cover. Some caps are attached to the tipi poles themselves and stay up for the season. For the beauty of the lodge and poles, I prefer to use an interior rain cover.

In the last fifty years, the interior and exterior rain covers have evolved greatly. Each person seems to be coming up with his own idea of how to keep the rain out. The important thing to remember is that whatever works for you works.

Poles, Pole Care, and Pole Maintenance

Whether you get your poles from a commercial source or you go out and cut your own, the next step is to get them ready for your tipi. If you have access to trees in your area, check them out. But also check to see what the laws are on cutting them down. The easiest way is to cut down poles on private property, but you can also check with your local National Forest office about obtaining a cutting permit. Buying poles can cost from $100 to $450 for a set, plus transportation. Some poles can cost from $15 to $25 or so each, depending on whether they are stripped of bark or not.

Any tree that is straight, light enough to handle, and does not have a heavy sap can be used for tipi poles. But also make sure trees are hefty enough to support your cover, liner, and interior rain cover. It your poles are too thin, add more poles to your setup until you can get better, thicker ones. Some of the best trees to use are lodgepole pine (Indians preferred these), some cedar, tamarack (also known as larch), southern cypress, Douglas fir, Wisconsin balsam, and longleaf pine. Bamboo has also been used, but I would not recommend it because of the rings that will drip water. The choices are different all over the country or the world. Trees selected should come from a heavily wooded area so that the stands grow as straight as possible. Make sure you can walk or float the tree out. Whatever you choose, be sure to get the following:

- permission to go on property to cut poles
- a friend or two to help
- bug, snake, bear, and alligator repellent
- good handsaws or chainsaws
- a first aid kit and someone skilled in responding to accidents
- a truck with racks or trailer to get the trees home

Always yell "timber" when cutting. Nothing like a tree falling on you from out of the blue, even in a swamp.

Fresh poles can weigh four or five times their weight when newly cut. Our cypress poles lose 50 to 75 percent of their water weight in twenty-four hours after being stripped. Then they are easier to pick up and work in the other stages when they are light and dry.

In getting your own trees make sure you choose a time of the year when the sap is rising. Here in the South, where we use cypress trees, the preferred time is in the early spring. If you can start stripping the bark in the first forty-eight hours, in most cases, you can use a knife to peel it from bottom to top like a banana. After several days you will have to use a drawknife to start debarking the tree because it is not as easy once the water or sap has evaporated. Some people put their trees in small ponds, streams, or some area of water containment to soak the bark.

If you have ordered your poles from some other part of the country, they will probably arrive in a very dry state bundled together. It is a very good idea to order the poles pre-stripped to reduce the cost of shipping. This will add to the cost of your poles, but in the long run it will save you a great deal of time and trouble. Some dealers do such a good job of stripping the poles that very little work is needed in final preparation.

Poles should be kept off the ground because of the risk of rot, mildew, and bugs. When working with my poles I prefer to get them off the ground away from the dirt and to make it easier to pick each pole up. If your poles need to be stripped

Drawknife stripping through bark. Bevel
should be facing down.

of their bark, they will have to be set up off the ground so that you can use a drawknife or other way of debarking them. You will need either sawhorses, two large tripods set about 10 or 15 feet apart, or any other platform on which you can set a pole to be stripped down. It is also nice if you have a friend who can help hold the pole and turn it while you do the stripping.

A drawknife with about a 12-inch blade is good enough to strip your poles, but any knife with a sharp blade will do. To get a good, clean cut, make sure that the bevel is facing down. A bevel that is facing up has a tendency to gouge out the wood. You want to glide between the bark and the inner wood. Work with the blade coming toward you with long clean cuts. Short, jagged cuts cause cutting marks in the surface of the wood, which will create more work for you later.

Today there are other tools that can be used for stripping poles. Electric 3- and 4-inch planers are wonderful for shortcutting the process. These work great on smooth-bark trees, more so than on pine trees and other trees with jagged bark. After stripping the poles with a drawknife, I like to use a 4-inch planer to smooth down and get rid of any jagged edges that may have been left by the blade. I also use a rasping tool, like a Stanley Sureform, to smooth down small limbs or indentations that may have been left.

The next process involves sanding down the pole. Wait a week or so after stripping the bark until the wood has dried out. Hand sanding is a great way to get around all the curves that you are going to find. Do this in an up-and-down or top-to-bottom motion when the pole is completely dry. You can start with a heavy grit and then work your way to a finer sandpaper. It is not a good idea to use a circular orbiting sander as it leaves swirling marks on your pole, which will allow water to follow the grooves and drip into your lodge. It is possible to use a belt sander.

A final step is cutting your poles to the length that you would use in setting up the tipi. The butt of the pole should be pointed for ease in setting up and keeping your tipi in place on the ground. This is accomplished by standing the pole up on a wood block and then taking an ax to chop off sections of the butt at an angle, forming a point. It can be four- to six-sided or whatever works for you. Take your drawknife or electric planer to finish off the cuts for a smooth look. Do not make your angle too long if you are using the butt to tie the liner to as the liner will slip up the pole.

A flat butt skips across the ground when setting up the pole. The pointed butt will dig into the ground, making it easier to maneuver the poles into position by walking them up and into the crouch area. The rounded-off tips help prevent the pole from splitting and make the poles look better.

Treating Poles

Poles will weather and eventually fall apart from dry or wet rot. To protect your investment in time and money, you should follow these steps.

- Before using your poles, paint or spray one of the following solutions on the poles:
  - Thompson's Water Seal or Behr water seal
  - a solution of 1/2 linseed oil to 1/2 turpentine or shingle oil made by Chevron, which is cheaper than linseed oil
- Pour deck sealer into a large, tall bucket and soak both ends of the poles in the sealer for a day or two until the ends have entirely soaked in the liquid. This waterproofs the tips. Waterproofing on the bottom of the pole need not go up more than 6 to 8 inches. The top end should be coated, if possible, as much as it is exposed above and beyond the top of the tipi (the UV protector in the sealer helps the upper parts, too). Try to do this every two to three years or when the wood seems to be a bit thirsty. This is also good for wood stakes.

Pole racks store tipi-pole sets. The green waterproof cover protects the poles.

- Do not be concerned when a dry pole soaks up a tremendous quantity of liquid. Let the poles dry well before using them so they don't stain the cover.
- If your poles have already started to weather, treat mildew with the same bleach solution. Living in the humid parts of the country, this is a must before applying any other treatments. Scrub the pole with a brush and a solution of 1/4 cup bleach in a 2-gallon bucket of warm water. Let the pole area dry completely. This will kill the mildew and stop it from spreading. Then follow up with any of the above sealers.
- Though some people do this, I would not store poles by leaning them in a crotch of a large tree or leaving the poles up in the frame and leaning the smoke-flap poles and lifting pole with the bundle. In wet climates the poles will rot at the bottom or be eaten by termites or other bugs. There are "bore bees," which look like bumblebees, that will eat holes in the poles to lay their eggs. Those holes can run 12 inches in the interior pith of the pole, thus weakening them. If this has already happened to your poles, fill the holes with a polymer plastic resin to harden the tubes.
- Store poles off the ground and covered. They will last longer out of the sun and weather. Ideally, storing poles indoors (horizontally and well supported to prevent warping) would be the best for when they're not in use, but not all of us have a 23-foot garage or barn wall to put them on. You could build a rack system that puts the poles a few feet off the ground. The racks can look like an H with one or more tiers to support two or three sets. At least four of these the length of the poles will help support the weight. Make sure you cover all the poles to protect them from rain, sun, and insects.

Fixing Broken Poles

Tripod poles that are broken cannot be restored to their original strength. But they can be used as one of the fill-in poles, not as a tripod pole. Gorilla Glue with some duct tape can stick most poles back together. Rawhide, like they used in the old days, that has been wetted, sewn on tight, and then left to dry will form a very strong sleeve. This could be used along with the glue. Remember that rawhide tends to stay moist in humid climates. If you are at home, make a special sleeve for the broken area and pour in clear cast or some other plastic-like material to make a hardened sleeve. This can also be accomplished with fiberglass mending kits.

Whether or not to split the poles for storage or transportation is a question that is asked many times. It can be done but the results are poles that are not as strong as full-length poles. To join them together, some people use a sleeve material made from metal or plastic. This means you must carve away portions of the pole to fit into the top and bottom of the sleeve. It does work, but water going down the pole will leak as it hits the sleeve casing. However, in very wet weather, you can tie a piece of leather just above the cut and the water will run down the pole until it reaches the leather and drips onto the rain cover or behind a liner. There is also the problem of constant shrinkage of the wood as it ages. On the upside, it does make transporting poles much easier.

Pegs, Lacing Pins, and Rain Sticks

Pegs for the outside cover hold down the tipi in all types of weather. Depending on the area of setup, wood pegs should be about 18 inches long and 1 inch thick. The size of the tipi will depend on the number of pegs you need. In my case, I carry four sets with me: a short wood set of 15 inches, a longer wood set of 24 inches, and a steel set. The 24-inch circus long pegs are for very sandy soil, while

Two full sets of wood pegs.

the steel set is for rock-hard ground that breaks wood pegs. It is nice to know what the ground is like where you are going to camp, but that is not always possible. I have left wood pegs in the ground where I could not get them back out after finally pounding them in. This is extra material to cart around, but the pegs hold the tipi cover down in windy weather and it is important that it is securely tied to the ground. I also carry a pointed steel pick about 15 inches long (to first dig a hole in the ground before pounding in the wood pegs). That makes it much easier to drive wood pegs into a hard surface.

Pegs and hammers.

Bring a steel hammer for this job in addition to a good wooden mallet for the pegs.

For pegging the cover to the ground, you will need twenty to twenty-five wooden pegs. Always cut extras as they break with age or split. Any hardwood you can find will be good enough. If you know trees, you can look for hickory, maple, ash, oak, or chokecherry. My sets are locust from North Carolina, ironwood from Texas, and chokecherry from Florida. In a pinch, use 1-inch round dowels cut down to size.

Sharpen the pegs to a point at one end and leave about 6 inches of bark at the other to catch the rope you will be tying to it. Another way to catch the rope is to carve a ring around the top of the peg.

Lacing pins insert into the pairs of holes down the front to button up and close the cover around the poles. Make them out of the same wood as the wooden pegs. These sticks should be round pointed, 12 inches long, and about 3/8-inch thick. Lumberyards have dowels you can buy and cut to size. If you wish, leave about 4 inches of bark on the pin for carving rings in a decorative manner. Strip off the bark on the rest of the stick. Put floor wax or a polyurethane finish on the lacing pins to protect them from the weather and make them go into the holes easier. Canvas swells when it gets wet, and it becomes very difficult to get the pins out or in. Make as many lacing pins as needed for the pairs for holes down the front of the lodge. My 12 foot lodge only takes about eight whereas my 17-foot lodge takes fifteen.

Rain Pegs: Get together about thirty 5-inch sticks 1/4 to 1/2 inches thick. These will be used after your lining is up. They are inserted between the rope or leather ties that tie the lining to the poles and the poles themselves; they keep water running down the poles by forming an uninterrupted channel.

Rain pegs are used anywhere you want the water to continue to run down the pole wherever there is an interruption on the tipi poles by ropes or other materials, such as decorative ropes for hanging items.

Tying cover to lift pole. Lacing pins inserted into cover.

Rain sticks.

Darry Wood rain stick used to channel water and hang items.

Tipi storage box for setup materials.

Pitching or Setting Up a Tipi

Materials

Get a good storage box to store materials in for setting up your tipi. This box can be made from wood, rawhide, or canvas. It will take a great deal of punishment so choose a material that holds up to constant use. My own box shows some of the items I carry:

- A good book on tipis for reference on setting up a lodge
- Ropes for tying the tripod together and wrapping the poles, along with some extra rope for hanging items in the interior
- Ribbons or cloth for the tips of poles (streamers)
- Lacing pins in their pouch
- Buffalo hooves made into a door knocker for outside
- Rawhide cylinder container that holds the rain pegs
- Small broom for dusting off items inside and outside the lodge
- Rawhide box to hold these items

You will develop your own storage system for the items you will need to set up your tipi.

Rope: You will need about 25 to 45 feet of $1/2$-inch manila or hemp rope to tie the poles together at the top. Hardware and large discount stores should have manila rope. Hemp rope is OK, but wet down and stretch out your rope until dry before setting up the tipi. Some ropes have threads that stick out and can get under the skin. Wear gloves if this poses a problem. I have two sets of rope that are used for miscellaneous purposes. The set I use depends on the occasion of the camp I am attending. Use a $1/2$-inch by 25-foot braided horsehair rope spliced into 12 feet of good $1/4$-inch manila rope for the old-time look. The $1/4$ inch x 12 foot of rope ties the tripod and then wraps around the other poles placed in the crotch while the horsehair part hangs down into the middle of the lodge. This style of rope is still strong enough to hold down my 17-foot lodge in a big storm. The rope on the right is my basic rope for everyday use. It is $1/2$ inch x 25-foot hemp spliced into 12 feet of $1/4$-inch hemp rope that is tied around the tripod. Do not use a nylon rope as it will slip and does not grip into the poles.

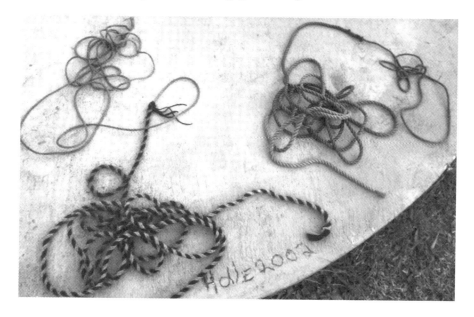

I have found it necessary to carry different sets of pegs, hammers, and steel stakes. This is a lot of material to carry around, but I have never regretted bringing the extra items. If you ever have to abandon or cut a set of pegs off level in the ground so no one will trip on them after you are gone, you will bring an extra set, too. Following is a set of materials you might want to consider for your special box to be used in setting up your tipi.

Camping Tools and Pegs

- Pegs. (See page 100, #5–9.)
- Lacing pins.
- Rain sticks. (See page 101, bottom two photos.)
- Large, carved oak mallet. I use this to place the anchor peg(s) and to pound in my wood tipi pegs so the heads don't splinter. (See page 100, #1.)
- Plastic dead-blow hammer for those with weak hands who might need a little help. (See page 100, #2.)
- 3-pound steel hammer or an ax with a flat metal end for driving in the steel or iron pegs. (See page 100, #3.)
- 22-inch pointed steel bar to loosen up for dry, hard, or frozen ground for the wood pegs. (See page 100, #4.)
- 28-inch, or longer, thick pegs for sandy or loose soil. Florida has some very sandy areas and covers can lift straight up if not firmly pegged down. I call these the "circus" pegs, and for a good reason. (See page 100, #5.)
- Locus wood pegs approximately 20 inches long with no bark. (See page 100, #6.)
- Chokecherry wood pegs carved and painted for show. (See page 100, #7.)
- Center peg for tying down the tie rope inside the lodge. This peg has a crook in the top to wrap and tie down the rope securely. Two pegs can also be used for this purpose. (See page 100, #8.)
- Steel set of pegs for rock-hard ground. (See page 100, #9.)

After getting your material and poles together, choose a good level area, clear of brush, rocks, and debris for the setup. The area needs to slope so that water drains away from the lodge, should not have overhanging branches, and should have enough space for you to be able to maneuver your smoke-flap poles. If setting up on a platform, concrete pad, or a smooth flooring surface, have someone else there to help you hold the poles in position while setting the poles. If possible, try to put your tipi in a protected area that has the least exposure to the wind. It is important to face the front of the tipi away from the prevailing winds. This allows the smoke to be drawn upwards and out of the tipi properly. Although a tipi can be comfortable in the broiling sun, an ideal place would be to pitch yours northeast of a tree (or trees) in the summer for late morning to evening shade. But make sure that it is not a tree like an oak that will leach tannin stain onto your cover or a pine that can drip sap onto the cover.

Setting Up the Tripod

The setup described in this chapter is for a three-pole tipi. Know beforehand the size of your tipi and how many poles it takes for the inside. Drawings of seven different pole setups are given for a comparison, with an extra one to design on your own. As with most three-pole sets, the Laubins' tripod pattern is used. Streamers should be put on before poles are placed into position.

It does not matter which style of wrapping is chosen for the tripod. What does matter is that it works for you in getting the poles up without slipping. Most people use the Laubins' method (A), a clove hitch tied off with a couple of half hitches. Others find that the Seton woven wrap (B) or the Ben Hunt wrap (C) work for them. See page 106 for the three styles.

Choose the four heaviest poles in your group. Three of these will be for the tripod and the fourth is for the lift pole. Mark your poles in some way that will let you know which are the north, south, east, and lift poles. Make sure all poles have a pointed butt. Flat bottom poles will skid when setting up. The lift pole should be the longest pole sticking out over the crown of the grouping. Some people like to make a fancy "war bonnet" effect with all the poles the same height to create a flared look from a distance. Originally, poles were positioned for strength in weather and not

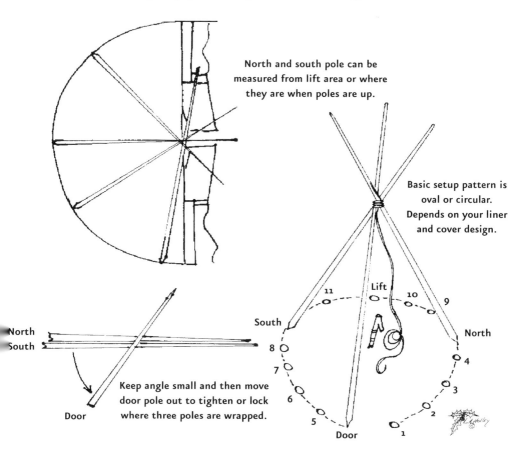

North and south pole can be measured from lift area or where they are when poles are up.

Basic setup pattern is oval or circular. Depends on your liner and cover design.

Keep angle small and then move door pole out to tighten or lock where three poles are wrapped.

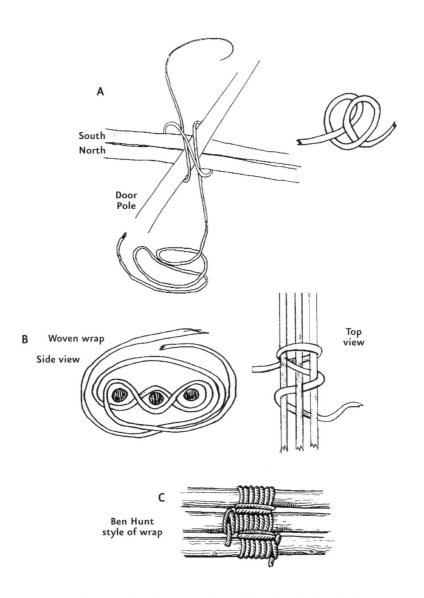

A

South
North

Door
Pole

B Woven wrap

Side view

Top
view

C

Ben Hunt
style of wrap

Different styles of wrapping the tripod. A. Clove hitch method.
B. Woven wrap side view. C. Ben Hunt style of wrap.

for looks as we do today. Rain, snow, canvas shrinkage, or strong wind are all going to bend in the frame somewhat. If the poles are relatively stout, they will mostly spring back and return to near their original straightness when the cover is dry. Weak poles do not tend to recover and only get worse as time passes. When this happens, the poles may warp and need to be turned or twisted back out.

Trying to get an hourglass look with the poles or using overly long pole extensions out the top of the cover adds to the tie-point thickness and increases the opening for water leaks. Four to six feet makes them easier to handle and is a good look without overdoing the length. The north and south poles are laid next to each other with the door pole crossing over. No measurements are given here because everyone will have different numbers. Use your 35-foot rope and tie a clove hitch to pull the three poles tightly together, leaving about 5 or more feet of rope to later wrap around about three more times and finish with a square knot. A little trick to help keep the tripod from slipping: place the door pole closer toward the north and south pole, and after tying them off, kick the door pole back out to position. This locks or tightens the knot by putting pressure on the rope.

Lift the poles into place by standing at the north and south pole butts and using your foot to brace and pull on the tie rope to start the process of bringing the poles up. Two people can do this quickly if one person stands on the butts and the other person walks the poles up with the rope. I am 5 foot, 1 inch and can put up 28-foot poles by myself. It does take leverage and practice. Another way is to peg the tipi pole butts down so they do not move and then pull on the tie rope while walking the poles up until they are vertical. Still holding on to the rope, spread the north and south poles. Hang on to the south pole and push the north pole out and away from you. If it all feels somewhat balanced, walk to the north pole and bring it into place. Then set the whole tripod into position. Looking from the outside, the door pole is always to the left and the #1 pole is to the right. Place the rest of the poles into position, following the pattern starting with the right door pole (#1), placing it even with your tripod door pole. Leave enough room so that your shoulders do not touch the poles when walking between them. This allows you to enter the tipi with ease.

Depending on the style of tipi, poles should be slightly in from their final position, with the exception of the door pole. When working the cover and liner, it is easier to bring poles out than in. Take the lift pole rope out of the south pole area. Then move in a clockwise direction around the set of poles. Wrap your tripod at least two to four times. Come in the north pole area and set the rope in the center by pulling tightly. Then tie it to the anchor peg. This will steady the poles during the cover and liner setup.

The Cover Setup

There are three basic ways of attaching the cover to the lift pole. You want to make sure it does not slip when lifting and this can be done with a good leather tie or cotton ties (1). Place a small peg into the wood (2), and (from an old photo of a Cheyenne tipi being set up*) carve a small curve (3) indention around the tie area and tightly tie the cover. Do not put a V-shape groove as this will weaken the pole, which may cause it to snap later. Then move the lift pole and cover into place. Again, if you are the only person around, place two pegs into the ground to brace the butt of the lift pole and then walk into place. This is a bit more work, but better than the butt sliding out of position or skidding away.

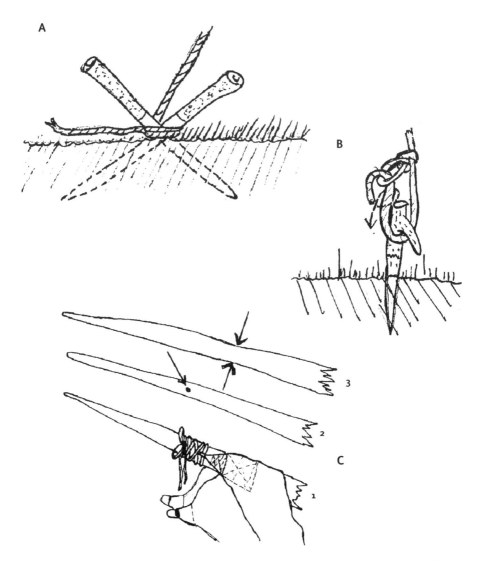

A. Placement of anchor pegs. **B.** Single anchor peg with truckee knot. **C.** Tying cover to lift pole.

Bring the cover around and put in the lacing pins, left over right, as you face your tipi. Left over right is the standard way, but in some of the old pictures the reverse can be seen. Just make sure that the lacing-pin holes for the top part of the cover (the left) are a bit farther apart than the two holes underneath, which are closer together. This helps divert water from leaking directly inside. Also bring a small ladder if the lacing-pin holes are much higher than your reach. It can be very dangerous standing on makeshift items. Leave the bottom lacing pins out until the liner and cover are just about set. This makes going in and out much easier and the danger of broken limbs caused by tripping on the closed door opening is lessened. In the final stages of setting up, put the pins in and set the cover by moving the poles in or out as needed. See photos on page 101 for placement of pins.

Setting up the tripod.

Hanging a Rope Liner

If you used a pattern in this book to make your fitted lining, then you are going to have an oval-shaped tipi. The Laubins said "that the floor plan of a properly pitched tipi is oval or egg shaped, rather than round. The tipi cone is also tilted and steeper up the back than the front" (Laubins 1957, 27). Some tipis do come in round and oval footprint shapes. The structure can tilt more toward the front than back, as well as the true shape of a cone. So, what is your tipi? Again, if made from the pattern in this book, it will have a slight tilt to the back and have a liner that will form an oval shape with the poles.

In making the lining using the old way with rectangular panels, it will most likely be a rope liner and can be set up using any of the positions shown. All these methods are shown in pictures of Northern and Southern tribal tipis using a rope. 1 and 2 were mainly used in the Northern tipis with 3 being used with the most rope liners. Panels are tied at the top, hang down, and then items are pushed against them to the sides. The more formal rope liners, connected to ropes or pegs at the bottom, are a modern addition in the last sixty years.

Hanging the Fitted liner

Inside the tipi, locate the lift pole and tie the bottom base cord of the liner to the butt of the pole. Make the tie tight with a square knot. Then working from the lift pole toward the door, secure all the other bottom ties on each side of the lift. Once this is complete, the bottom ties do not have to be untied. They can be left tied for the next setup. This will leave a loop to slip over the butts. If your liner is in more than one section, place the ties of the end panel into the grommet hole and tie to the pole tightly. Try not to have the ties ride up the butt of the pole. Ropes are difficult to tie on poles that are not butted, but have a straight-across cut. They can slip up the pole, making the bottom of the liner loose. To prevent slippage, place a small nail or wood peg (B) at the base of the pole.

With the bottom of the liner attached to the butts of the poles, stretch the liner and shift poles as you work from the lift pole to the door. Next lift the top of the liner up to the pole and tie it into place using the leather/cotton ties. The leather ties grip better than cotton. If the cotton ties do slip, slightly wet the strips to give them some grip to the material. Wrap them around at least once and then tie a bow in the front of the pole. Start pulling poles in and out as needed to get the wrinkles out of the liner. The last panel to the north of the door wraps around the pole. This extra panel is used at night or during inclement weather to seal the tipi by bringing it across the opening to the door pole and tucking it behind or tying in front. If the liner is not smooth, you may have to go back around, moving poles in and out to the door to get the fitted look (A). Two people can do this with one person inside directing the person on the outside to move poles in or out or to the door. You need to learn to read the wrinkles in the canvas so you know whether to pull out or in. This is an easy liner to set up once you know how. My own way of setting up is to put the entire lining up first and then the cover. Since the measurements on the poles are already fixed and marked from experience, the cover can go up when I need it. I like to put all my materials inside while there is a breeze and good weather, and then put the cover on. However, this method does drive people crazy! When not using the fitted liner, the cover can be set up to the ground and poles set in a more circular final shape. Using a rope or tying directly

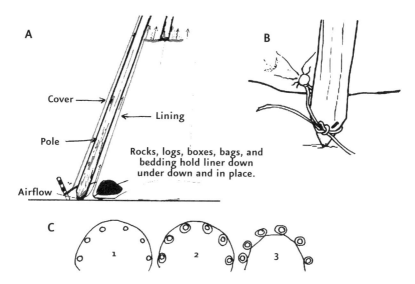

A. Airflow and liner placement. B. Attaching liner to butt of pole. Single or double cord attaching liner to butt of pole. If poles are not butted, tap in a small nail to help keep the line from sliding up. C. Three top lining setups—last one is used the most.

to the poles, I will use old shawls and blankets as a liner only where my sleeping area lies. The bed holds the bottom of the liner in place.

Linings do not have to be placed in front of the poles. Some are placed between the poles and cover, forming a double thickness of the cover, which then goes to the ground. A few others weave under, over, and between poles, with no ropes or ties.

Pegging Down the Cover

Start with the lift pole and peg this area down first, and then pull on the cover to get out wrinkles. This sets up the cover for the rest of the pegs. Next, go to the front and peg down the loops on either side of the door. Again, pull the cover and shake it before pegging in the two pegs. This will insure that your door will not be pulled out of place. If the cover is to go all the way to the ground, drive in the pegs at an angle to the cover. If the cover will be several inches off the ground, drive pegs in straight up and down, with the loops doubled over and twisted on the peg. This will lock the loop in place and make it possible to slide the loop down if it comes up without hammering the peg still farther into the ground.

The last item is to set the interior anchor peg and attach the tripod rope with a tight truckers knot, sheepshank knot, or whatever knot works for you. To prevent movement inward of the poles or traveling in strong winds, the anchor peg helps the poles "bite" into the ground. If not corrected, traveling poles can cause the tipi to fall over or move a few feet.

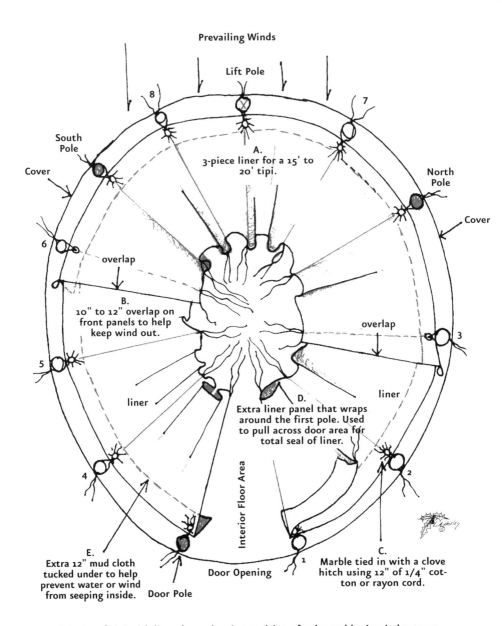

Prevailing Winds

Lift Pole

8

7

South Pole

Cover

North Pole

Cover

A.
3-piece liner for a 15' to 20' tipi.

6

overlap

B.
10" to 12" overlap on front panels to help keep wind out.

overlap

3

5

liner

D.
Extra liner panel that wraps around the first pole. Used to pull across door area for total seal of liner.

liner

4

2

E.
Extra 12" mud cloth tucked under to help prevent water or wind from seeping inside.

1

C.
Marble tied in with a clove hitch using 12" of 1/4" cotton or rayon cord.

Interior Floor Area

Door Opening

Door Pole

Interior of tipi with liner down showing position of poles and basic wind pattern.

Smoke-Flap Poles

Next the smoke-flap poles are placed in the pockets of the flaps. These poles need to be sturdy and not bent around the cover. Too many people choose thin, long poles for this and they snap or wrap around the tipi under pressure. Since they have to take the wind without breaking, choose a stout pole that fits from ground to pocket in an open position from the back side of the tipi to front. Lastly, put the door on over the door opening, securing it in place.

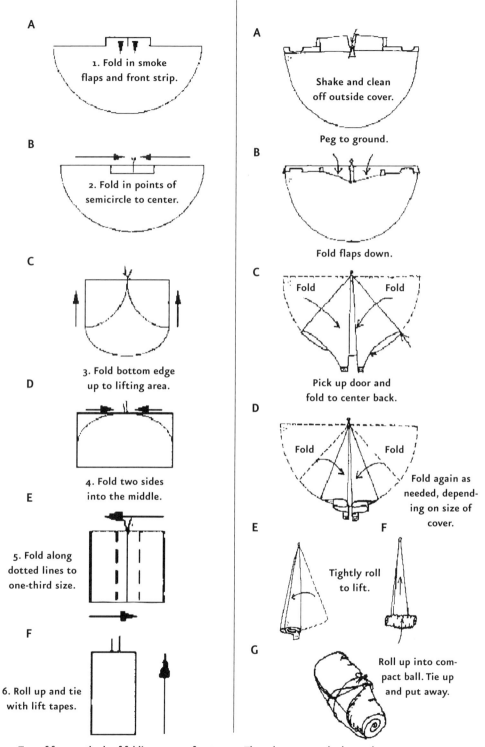

A

1. Fold in smoke flaps and front strip.

B

2. Fold in points of semicircle to center.

C

3. Fold bottom edge up to lifting area.

D

4. Fold two sides into the middle.

E

5. Fold along dotted lines to one-third size.

F

6. Roll up and tie with lift tapes.

A

Shake and clean off outside cover.

Peg to ground.

B

Fold flaps down.

C

Fold   Fold

Pick up door and fold to center back.

D

Fold   Fold

Fold again as needed, depending on size of cover.

E   **F**

Tightly roll to lift.

G

Roll up into compact ball. Tie up and put away.

Two of four methods of folding a cover for storage. The other two methods are shown on page 114.

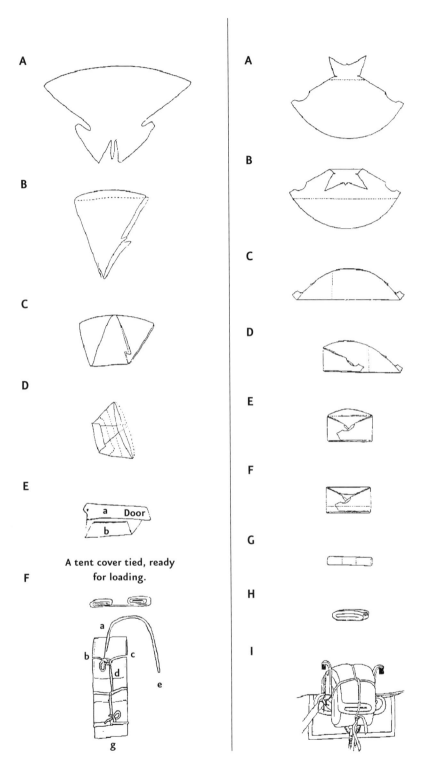

A tent cover tied, ready
for loading.

Folding the Cover or Takedown

There are four possible ways to fold a tipi. A, C and D are examples of the old ways to fold for loading on a pack horse, travois, or for storage. Example B is an easy way to fold right on and off the lift pole. While the cover is still on the poles, undo the lacing pins and vigorously shake both sides of the cover, one side at a time. Also take a broom and hit the inside, knocking out the dust. Grab the lacing-pin area and walk it to the lift pole, forming a pie wedge. Go back to the fold and repeat about three times, depending on the size of the cover. Start on the other side and fold again, following the same procedure. The back of the tipi now looks like a giant thin triangular wedge shape from little top to larger bottom. At this point, take a rope and tie it around the cover and lift pole at about eye level. This keeps the cover from slipping off the pole. Then gently ease the lift pole down. Two people can reverse the steps they used in setting up; one person reverses his or her setup steps.

While the cover is still on the lift pole, take the pole out and sweep or brush off the cover as it is tightly rolled into a ball from base to top. Tie the cords on the tie point around the cover, if they reach, and you should have a tight little ball of canvas. This is particularly helpful in keeping your tipi dry if the surrounding ground is wet.

Problems with Canvas in the Cover or Liner

- Wrinkles are most likely caused (assuming the tipi was cut correctly) by the tripod tie being too low and/or the poles being too spread out at the base to fit the lining. The lower tie point prohibits the cover from sliding down the pole structure and forming a nice snug fit.
- Some wrinkles are caused by not pulling on the cover and then pegging it down to work out wrinkles as you peg from back to front.
- If you have a sagging liner or the rope or ties have slipped, retie the rope or bring the pole in or out.
- Rains coming in from the top can be caused by smoke flaps not being wrapped around tight enough, or the tie point might be too high, making a bigger opening than can be covered.
- A rough bark spot or splinter on the pole creates drips. Use your finger or a long stick to guide the water down the pole. Redirect the water on the surface by touching the dripping area until it flows down.
- When water is coming in through the canvas or splattering inside, the cover needs to be re-waterproofed.

* Phillips Collection of Cheyenne tipi setup. Oklahoma Photo #1755, "Cheyenne Tipi Setup," date 1927. My observations of the photos.

A cane windbreak helps keep the hot western winds and dust from getting into the tipi.

Living in a Tipi

Smoke Flaps

Long ribbons fluttering from pole tips aren't simply decorative; they're the wind sock that helps to determine which direction prevailing winds are blowing. This allows you to set your tipi's smoke flaps accordingly. The diagrams on page 117 show eight ways to adjust or use the flaps to adapt to the weather. Figures A through C show the placement of flaps when wind and rain are coming from the sides; E shows the placement when winds are from the back. Figures G and H have the flaps wide open and the sides of the tipis are rolled up or spread out to act as a sun shade. Rolling up a side of your tipi cover and dropping portions of the liner will provide your camp with both shade and breeze on those hot, sticky July/August afternoons. On the shady side of the lodge, roll the side of tipi cover up to a height of 4 feet or so. Prop the rolled-up cover on a couple of forked sticks. On the opposite side, drop the liner and side that best takes advantage of any cross breeze. Figure D comes from a picture labeled as "circling winds." Both flaps are shown rolled up on the poles. I only saw this once on a Cheyenne lodge.* Most interesting is Figure F that shows the use of reed walls made of cattails or sunflower stalks built around the tipi to keep the high winds and dust out. In Oklahoma photos, many Cheyenne and Kiowa tipis were seen with this

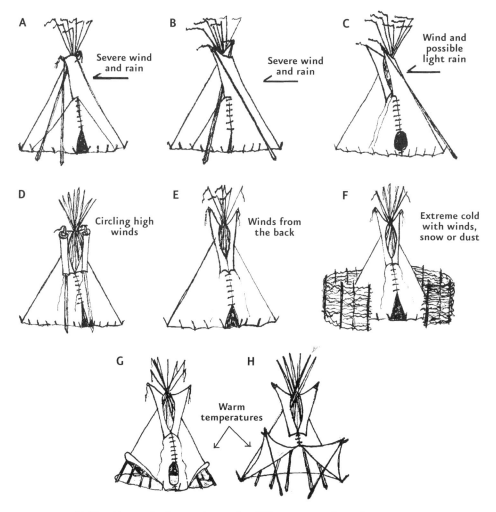

Setting the smoke flaps and camp for different types of weather.

surrounding wall. Outside were arbors of willow and reeds. This gave shade for cooking and just sitting around. Depending on the part of the country you live, there are different solutions to rain and wind problems.

Extreme Winds

Though the shape of the tipi makes for a very wind-resistant structure, a strong gust can shift a lodge. You should frequently check poles for movement and kick or move them out regularly to keep the canvas taut. Crow tipis use ropes attached to the lift poles that go out to the back or sides for a distance and are then pegged down. This keeps lodges from walking or moving out of position. Sioux and Kiowa tipis use similar ropes that surround structures about midway and are then

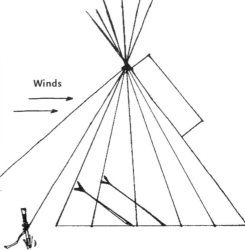

Forked sticks to help brace poles. Rope attached to lifting pole that is pegged down in the back. This method is used by the Crow/Blackfoot and others but can be used by any tipi owner to support the tipi in very high winds.

Winds

Gary and Luella Johnson Crow family pattern tipi. Note ropes at back.

pegged down to the sides. Sticks can also be placed on the inside to brace weak poles in extreme winds. I have used these methods in winds clocked at over ninety miles per hour, and they do work. But it is always best to start with good poles, and by good poles I mean ones that are hefty, strong wood. Weak poles will cave in from the pressure of the wind against the sides of the cover.

One way to keep the poles from moving is to bury the bottom of the poles. This trick also works when the door pole is too long and you do not want to start over. Cheyenne women used this trick when door poles were too long. The Crow talked about making holes in the ground with an ax to keep poles from moving.

The following is a system that Arrow Tipi Co. uses: they drill a 1/2-inch hole through the pole 4 inches from the bottom, slanting the drill toward the bottom of the pole so that the drill exits the pole 2 inches from the ground. Rebar pegs may be used, but the pegs should be 3/8 inch or #10 rebar and up to 30 inches long. A hook should be formed on one end. The peg must be a snug fit in the drilled hole. The peg is driven into the ground through the pole at a slant until flush with the top hole opening. The hook on the peg should be turned to the side to allow for removal.

Cold-Weather Camping

Fires should be small and their size and location depends on the size and shape of your lodge. Many people cut a hole for a fire about 2 1/2 feet toward the door from center. Stand directly under the smoke-flap opening, and then take a step or two toward the door and cut your fire hole. Make sure it is not in the way when you step into your lodge. Also consider how close the fire is to the sleeping areas.

Stuffing grass between the liner and the cover is the old-time way of adding some insulation; however, you might not want to do this because mice and other little animals use it for food and nesting. Pete Roller, of *Whispering Wind Magazine*, experimented with fiberglass insulation by using plastic sheeting on both sides instead of grass stuffed between the two liners and the cover (Wilson 1924, 242). He also used a rain cover with a double liner and found it to be very warm with his small stove. This setup is a great idea for a permanent camp, but not for weekend setups.

Liner or Lining Use

A liner does more for insulation than for circulation. Take the liner down when it is hot and put it up when it's cold. Roll the sides up on hot days. On hot humid days, the liner does not help the airflow.

Floors and Platforms

Traditionally there are no floors in tipis. It was common to put down animal robes and trade blankets for a floor covering. Today we use all types of materials to keep the dust, dirt, water, and critters out of lodges or protect the valuable robes from damage from wet ground. Some floors are canvas, old rugs, clear plastic, painter's cloth, and heavy-duty Weblon synthetic plastic, which you often see used on trucks for cover tarps. However, if you are in an area where the ground is mostly dirt, rock, or sand, you might want to consider having a solid floor. You can get a solid floor in different colors, depending on the material.

I live in a wet area of the country where biting ants and spiders are a real problem, so a floor has become a necessity. My need is to keep the moisture out and to protect my buffalo hides. I have a floor going from side to side and front to back and going up a foot and over the sod cloth. All this is hidden by the multiple robes and blankets on my "green" floor covering. My floor of choice is a Weblon material that can be purchased from most canvas and awning shops. It is more expensive than most flooring material, but it is worth the price if you have ever had heavy rains flood your tipi and all your gear ended up soaking wet from groundwater. If buying this material, do not let the supplier sew the edges or the center seams. The seams should be heat welded together without any sewing holes. Once you get it home, cut the material to size or just fold it over for protection from water going

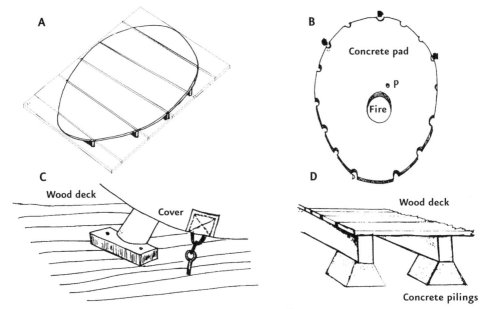

A

B

Concrete pad

P

Fire

C

Wood deck

Cover

D

Wood deck

Concrete pilings

Platforms to support a tipi off the ground.

over the edges in a very heavy rain. It may feel like you are walking on a rubber raft with the water underneath, but it definitely saves your gear. But do not cut a fire hole as the water will come up and over the fire-hole opening. Since I use a propane wood log fire that does not give off heat toward the bottom, I can have solid floor construction. A drawback to "plastic" floors is that if water drips in from above or the door opening leaks, the water stays on the surface until it dries up. It can be like living in a small wading pool after a heavy rainfall. Leak proof your lodge as much as possible to prevent this.

Most water comes from the ground underneath the tipi. If you are going to live in your tipi, build it on some sort of foundation to get it off the ground. These foundations can be wood platforms, gravel, very sandy mounds, or concrete pads. If your area is flat, make your platform at least 3 to 4 inches high so your lodge will be above the standing water. A lot depends on the soil's drainage. You can trench your tipi all around the outside, draining water away from the camp. Be aware, however, that many campgrounds or facilities will not let you trench because this can cause damage to the ground.

Concrete pads can be poured in your backyard or chosen camping area. I had a 16-foot circle pad poured in my backyard for my 17-foot oval lodge. I didn't go with an oval shape for the pad because I wanted the water to drain from the front and the poles to just touch or be close to the pad. You can either build a fire hole right into the concrete or you can set the fire on top of the concrete. Putting a hole in the pad is easier for cleaning up ashes and it helps keep the fire from getting out of control. You can still put rock around the fire whether it is in the ground or on top of the pad. A few concrete pads have indentions for each pole or special metal brackets to hold a lodge pole in place. These keep the poles off the ground to prevent rot and bug infestation.

Wood decks can be built anywhere and can be built in any shape or of any height. Most people build these in off-location places where there are animals that might be of concern or for that great view of the surrounding landscape. If you decide on a wooden floor, give careful thought to the choice of wood and a suitable sealant. Treated or untreated wood is generally available everywhere. Leave suitable gaps between each board for the water to drain off and away from the tipi. There are also synthetic decks or porch boards that do not rot, decay, or absorb water. They last forever and never need to be treated. Remember, if your deck is elevated, air is an excellent thermal insulator. It conducts very little heat, but it will lose heat through convection. Insulation will be considerably better if your floor is constructed to minimize air movement.

Several tipi companies now offer portable wooden platforms and permanent decking for tipis. If you are not a skilled craftsman, this is a way to go for comfort and protection of equipment. Look at companies' brochures and Web sites to get ideas for your permanent camping.

Beds

Any bed you can get in the lodge will work. Remember that the lodge sides slant in so that a bed frame cannot come off the ground very high without giving up room. The more real-sized furniture placed inside a tipi, the less room there is for living, unless you have a very large lodge. Traditionally beds are situated on the ground with fur robes and some padding underneath (Wilson 1924, 242). In some cases, beds are constructed off the ground using supports from the backrests and small logs to guide the size. Backrests form the head and foot of the bed (B). The bed structure in the photo below comes with more permanent campsites that allow for the luxury of an interior bed with bags, beaded liner, and other gear.

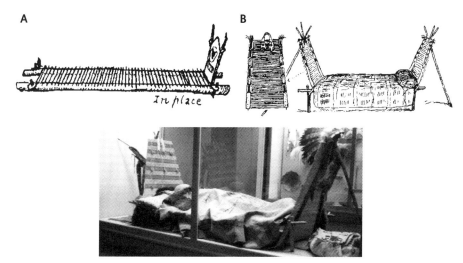

Backrest beds.

Bathroom and Washup

If you are going to an event such as a powwow or rendezvous, you will find porta-potties and other facilities. In some cases, there are real bathrooms with sinks and water. But for those of you who take your lodges out to the deep woods for longer periods of time, you have to take your own water and bathroom with you. There are many self-contained potties that can be used in your lodge or the old 5-gallon paint bucket with a toilet lid on top does it for me. You can buy chemicals to help biodegrade the waste at camping stores and other retail outlets that sell camping goods. And then you can dig your own outhouse away from the tipi for privacy and sanitation.

For a good shower, there are solar setups using 5-gallon black bags, or you can heat the water over an open fire and sponge on and rinse off. Do this away from the lodge so that water does not splash on your cover or run into the tipi. My pref-erence is a small, covered area away from the camp where I can wash, brush my teeth, and clean my hair without messing up my camp. If you are into a more modern shower, there are the battery-operated types that will suck up the water from a warm or hot pot and then spray it on you like a real shower. No picking up heavy bags or containers of water for a gravity-fed rinse of the solar types.

Heating Your Lodge

The basic materials for a fire in your lodge are as follows:

- Good lighter for starting the flame
- Small firewood, either cut or broken to size
- Cleared area in the center or towards the front of the tipi
- Rocks or fire brick to circle the flames
- Small shovel or rake to clear the area of all grass and roots
- Metal plate of some type to keep the fire off the ground
- Rocks, metal ring, or fire brick to set the metal plate or galvanized garbage lid
- Fire extinguisher or at least 5 gallons of water for safety

Once you have your lodge set up almost everybody wants to have a fire. Do you have to have a fire inside? No! Most cooking was done outside. After all, do you cook in your living room or bedroom? But when the weather does turn cold and there is a need to conserve firewood, cooking in the tipi keeps you warm and can be used to cook your food. The kind of fire you have in your dwelling depends upon the size of the tipi, whether or not it is a cooking fire, the weather, and how many people are inside. If you do have some kind of flooring in your lodge, do not put straw or any combustible material underneath it. Make sure the flooring itself will not catch fire. Several fires have started when people got their insulat-ing material too close to the fire and the tipi burned to the ground. The fire traveled underneath the floor and caught the lining on fire as well as other combustible items.

A small fire is better because it is easier to control than a big fire. Too big of a fire can send sparks into the smoke flaps of your tipi and outside, which can set the grass on fire. A small fire also uses less fuel in maintaining the camp. The type of wood used is determined by where you camp in the country. Many people bring one or two night's worth of firewood with them. I like to bring in a day or so worth of good split oak wood and pine. Pine is a fast-burning wood while the oak is a slow-burning wood that makes coals. Some people bring enough wood for the week because they are not too happy with the firewood they get at the campground. It can supplement the type of wood found in the area.

Keeping the fire burning in a lodge is very different from keeping it burning in your house. You need to keep it burning fast. That way it produces less smoke and draws the smoke outside faster. Using smaller pieces of dry, split hardwood will keep your fire burning longer and keep the amount of smoke down, making it more comfortable in your lodge.

Whether you build a round or rectangular fire pit is not really determined by the tipi tribal style. What does matter is if your fire is on the ground or if you dig a pit. By putting the fire directly on the ground or on some material such as dirt or sand, the heat will spread out around you. Clear a 3-foot area of all grass and burnable material. If you are digging a pit and digging the grass plug out, dig the hole deep to get out all of the grass and roots. Put the plug at least a foot away from the fire or outside the lodge. Heat kills the grass on the sides of a fire pit. Depending on how long you are camping, you can keep the grass plug watered and replace it when you leave, after making sure that there is no heat coming from the fire pit. I put water in the hole and replace the grass plugs and water them again. The grass grows back in a week or so.

Putting rocks around your fire is good for keeping heat and the fire in their area. Some parts of the country do not have rocks so you might need to bring your own. Being from Florida, I bring rocks almost everywhere I go, and this included a trip to Wyoming. I did not consider that Wyoming has lots of rocks. That's why they call it the Rockies. Fire brick, which can be obtained from fireplace shops, ceramic stores, some home improvement centers, and kiln builders, can also be used. It is lightweight, retains heat, and helps protect from some sparks.

Dianne Best (Jin-o-ta-ka), a woman I corresponded with, told me that when she was down on the Cheyenne River Reserve, she was talking to the old people about winter life in the tipi and asked about ventilation (since she had been told they often stuffed dry grass down in the space between the covering and the ghost sheet liner). She was told that it was common to dig a shallow trench extending from the outside of the lodge cover to the fire in the center. The trench was then covered with branches (so you didn't trip on it). This allowed cold air to reach the fire without making the draft on everyone inside.

With today's problems of forest fires, it is a good idea to bring extra fire-safety items like rocks and a fire extinguisher. Some areas will not let you have a ground fire unless you have protection to keep it from spreading. Bring some cheap garden dirt, such as vermiculite, from a garden center. It does not absorb heat. Then on top of this foundation, place a metal rim, galvanized garbage lid, a few fire bricks, or a wok to hold the fire. A wire screen can also be used to stop sparks from flying. These are some alternative ideas if camping rules do not allow you to dig a hole. At historical sites, certain private areas, national parks, Disney World Wilderness Campground sites, and "rocky areas" where campfires are still not permitted on the ground but in contained pits off the ground, these suggestions may prove helpful to you. It is always a good idea to find out before you get to the site if a ground or pit fire is allowed.

Your lodge should always have the wind at its back, but it doesn't matter whether your tipi is facing east, west, north, or south. Winds can come at you from all directions. They can change from day to night, season to season, and with cold to warm fronts. On the Great Plains, most of the wind is from the west going east, but at night it can change to the opposite direction. In the Southeast, the winds swirl in from out of the southwest and then change to the east because of the ocean temperatures, which cause land and sea breezes. Use that local information to decide in which direction to face your tipi.

If you build a fire outside the tipi to cook on, like I do, be on the watch for sparks and changes in the wind direction. I saw a lodge go up in flames because of someone's fire that spread to other tipis and tents. Even if the weather appears calm, never leave a fire unattended. Losing your own tipi is bad enough, but to be the cause of such a loss to others is unbearable.

The best wood to use for fires is hardwood oak or hickory. Take the bark off to help keep the smoke down on the larger pieces of wood. Small logs of about 1 to 3 inches in diameter are great to use. Wood should always be dry and well seasoned. I have my own favorite species, but if you're in a different part of the world, what's available that burns cleanly is probably sufficient.

Split the logs into small pieces—no more than 4 inches in diameter. Don't throw on 8- and 12-inch-diameter logs that will just sit and smolder for hours. You'll find you have to spend a lot of time splitting wood and feeding the fire. It's not a log burner that you can stoke up and forget about for hours. In feeding a fire, Ken Weidner, an experienced primitive tipi camper, explains that a "feeder" piece is sometimes a piece of wood you can use that is larger than 6 inches in diameter. It is fed into the fire from the side nearest the door. You just keep pushing it in as it burns down. But do not leave it unattended before you go to bed. He continues:

The feeder does a couple of things:

1. It protects the fire from the draft from the door.

2. It acts like a kind of thermal flywheel—when the fire is burning well, it stores up heat, which it then puts back into the fire as it starts to die.

Building your fire on stones helps, too, for much the same reason as stated in #2 above. But be careful, as some stones will split or explode, partly because of trapped moisture if they are river rocks. You'll often find the first fire you make is the worst, particularly if you build it straight on the ground. As the ground dries out, subsequent fires will burn better.

Also, get yourself a length of 15 millimeters of copper water pipe, a heavy-gauge nail and a big hammer. Position the nail carefully resting in one end of the pipe and then flatten that end of the pipe around the nail by hitting the pipe with the hammer. Pull the nail out so that you now have only a small, nail-sized opening in one end of the pipe. You now have one of the most useful tools you'll ever want in a tipi—a blow pipe. If the fire is awkward, point the flattened end at a strategic spot and blow through the other end. This provides oxygen to the fire, vital for a fire to burn well. It works wonders!

I try to burn smaller wood (up to 2-inch diameter). But I've seen some guys burning large logs (4- to 6-inch diameter), but they always have a good bed of coals going before they put on the bigger wood. I still try to burn smaller stuff; it gives instant heat and burns cleaner. Also fire tending is a necessary evil in a tipi, and the amount of vigilance required increases with the size of the wood used.

As far as lifting the tipi cover up higher for better draft, I usually peg mine right on the ground and usually have no problem with draft at all. There is still plenty of air that gets in, regardless of how tightly pegged it is, unless it snows or something else keeps air from entering. The old photos seem to show the lodges pegged down closely.

If you want that "dark smoked look" top on your tipi, burn a very smoky fire and close the flaps. That way you will get it quickly. In my new tipis, I like to start a small fire with a little fat lighter (which is very sappy pinewood), sold in some grocery stores or fireplace equipment outlets. One stick is splintered apart and then I use smaller pieces of oak or other wood to make up a tipi fire or square fire. After the fire gets going and grows larger, branches and sticks can be added to the fire. When burning oak wood, you will get a nice yellowish brown tint on the inside of your lodge and on the smoke flaps. This is a nicer color than the black smoke flaps that are caused when the fire is too smoky and sometimes too big. Do not use paper as a fire starter, as it has a tendency to fly up in the smoke flaps and can set the flaps on fire or even the outside area if the conditions are right. Paper also flies around the inside and make a mess. Do not use lighter fluid or other flammable materials because they can lead to a taller, smokier fire than you expected.

Other types of fuel are the "wax logs" you get in stores. They do work, but they will leave a black, sooty coating in the top of the tipi. I saw one lodge with way too large of a fire made of these logs almost burn to the ground. Sparks got caught up in the smoke flaps and caused a small fire. Luckily for the owner a fire extinguisher was nearby. A better idea is to break or cut up these logs and use them for starting the fire and/or to supplement the flame if needed later. It is possible to use charcoal, but that can pose a big danger. If you close up all the air openings, it creates carbon monoxide buildup, which is a serious health hazard. Smoke can also be a problem if you do not change the direction of the smoke flaps when the wind or weather changes.

Crazy Cyot's description, as related to me in conversation of what can happen in a lodge when flaps are not changed or other climate changes occur, is described below. It provides a firsthand experience of living in a tipi and what can happen with winter conditions.

But I have had to lay low a few times when the smoke got thick, due to a wind change. Before I got up to change the smoke flaps, the first winter I lived in my tipis I dug a trench to the outside as before mentioned but I (forgive the lack of period correctness) laid a pipe in the ground with a ninety on it so it had about 3 feet of pipe standing above the ground so the snow would not cover it. This worked very well; it helped keep a good draft for the fire and helped to keep the inside of the lodge warmer because the fire was not pulling cold air in from the edges of the lodge. I also found that a tall liner helps to keep it warmer. I never tried the grass stuffed in the liner; I just figured that when the grass got wet and started to mold, it would help to rot the canvas faster. I found building a wind-break fence around the tipis helped, too; it also gave me a place to store firewood. I spent two winters in a tipi on the bend of the Bear River by Soda Springs, Idaho. I also found out why the Indians did not winter there: it's got to be one of the coldest places in the state.

Kerosene heaters are another way of heating a tipi. Heaters come in rectangular to round styles. A good 10,000 BTU heater will warm an 18-foot lodge as long as the lodge has a good liner and rain cover inside. I prefer the rounded heaters inside the lodge as they seem to distribute warmth in a circular motion in comparison to the flat-sided styles. Another advantage of the rounded heater is that you can put a pot of water on the top for tea or coffee in the morning. But it is not good for roasting marshmallows nor does it have the ambiance of a roaring fire. One gallon of fuel will take off the chill for the night. The drawback to kerosene heaters is the smell of the fumes and carbon monoxide. You want to make sure that there is adequate ventilation. Leaving the smoke flaps slightly open at the top will help. In all the years I have used my heater in the tipi, there has been only one small problem—the slight smell of the fumes. If your tipi is closed up too tight, there is a possibility of getting headaches from the fumes.

Another type of heater is the propane fireplace. Some of these can put out between 5,000 to 15,000 BTU. They have a circular pan of between 20 to 30 inches and have logs that look real. The logs give off heat that you can cook on. The pan is insulated on the bottom with a layer of vermiculite that protects the floor from burning or getting too hot. There are 2 to 3 inches of air space under the pan, permitting cool air to circulate. Some pans have built-in legs while others rest on fire bricks. A 12-foot hose is connected to a 20-pound propane bottle. The tank can be hidden inside the lodge or outside. Use extreme caution when handling propane, and place the propane container as far from the fire as possible.

The disadvantage to the propane fireplace is again the carbon monoxide, but I have never had trouble with the unit because of the airflow in my lodge. Another disadvantage is not being able to throw another log on the fire, which we are all prone to do. They are, however, fairly easy to unclog if some trash does end up in the vent holes. The vermiculite also helps protect the mechanics of the unit from trash or other items put in the fire. To make the fire more realistic, put rocks around the pan for effect. They look great and no one can tell the difference between gas and wood except that there are no sparks and you do not keep putting wood on the fire. Depending on how long you keep the fire going, a 20-pound cylinder of gas can last

Louis Beergeron tipi with stove and rain cover.

two to three days. I base this on personal experience of two nights in 17-degree weather. I did not heat during the day unless cooking. It is also so nice to just roll over and turn up the fire in the morning for a little hot chocolate or tea.

I have used buffalo chips with little sticks of wood in my tipi fire. I found that they did not smoke and the chips were like charcoal when they burned. Chips also gave off a warm glow with little or no smell. They should be totally dried out before using. If they are not totally dry, they can explode because the moisture inside is quickly boiled in the fire. It is well known that the Plains Indians used buffalo chips and wrapped knots of prairie grass for their fires.

Tipis are being used around the world and everyone is coming up with their own ideas of having a fire or heating the inside. In Japan, there are lodges with hibachis or wood-type, double-glass-door fire holders. In the Southwest, chimeneas of varying sizes are set up. In Europe, one gentleman came up with an elaborate underground air-piping system. The three pipes lead from the inside fire outside using the airways. This system was designed for heavy snow where the tipi is covered halfway to the top for days or weeks. Each of the three airways lead to a vertical pipe that is 3 to 5 feet above the ground and is above the snow line to provide oxygen.

For permanent or longtime living in a tipi, the ultimate heater is the cast-iron stove. The woodstove enables you to cook and heat water regardless of the weather. Stove jacks can be installed in tipis that stabilize the stovepipe to the poles. Some people have the usual fire on the floor (hearth) and the stove.

Louis Beergeron, a tipi dweller, lives in New England, where there are all kinds of wet weather. Her lodge has held up great in severe weather conditions. She put an 8-foot canvas umbrella with a wooden frame on top of her tipi poles. It works for her and she has been dry ever since. She did have to cut down the poles to get the umbrella to sit right. According to Louis, it has had over a foot of snow and ice on it and has held up wonderfully. Four straps are tied to the umbrella and poles to hold the rain cover down to the ground. The winds have howled and pulled at the umbrella, but it has withstood them. A woodstove is inside for winter camping, and it is toasty warm inside. There is no open fire, which she misses, "but you can't have everything."

To prevent a fire when using a woodstove inside the tipi, the stovepipe should be insulated where it goes through the smoke flaps or a hole in the cover. This can be done by double piping the stovepipe and by using fireproof materials around the pipe opening. Check with your local fireplace equipment supplier or tent camping store that sells portable fireplaces and see what they have in non-heat-absorbing material.

Other heating possibilities include gas generators, underground electrical lines, and solar panels for generating electricity. While living in a tipi with all the new survivalist material, camping journals, and microengineering, your life does not have to be primitive. There is an electric line laid underground that goes under my tipi cover to run my TV, computer, and a small light. I have all the comforts of home. When I want to be primitive, I put it away and pull out the buffalo robes.

* Oklahoma State Archive Phillips Collection #1760, "Cheyenne Tipi Setup."

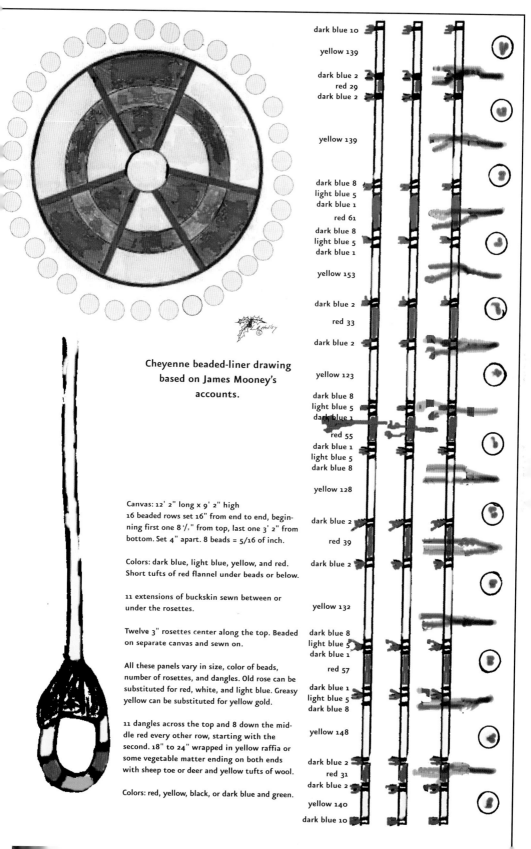

Cheyenne beaded-liner drawing based on James Mooney's accounts.

dark blue 10
yellow 139
dark blue 2
red 29
dark blue 2

yellow 139

dark blue 8
light blue 5
dark blue 1
red 61
dark blue 8
light blue 5
dark blue 1

yellow 153

dark blue 2
red 33
dark blue 2

yellow 123

dark blue 8
light blue 5
dark blue 1
red 55
dark blue 1
light blue 5
dark blue 8

yellow 128

dark blue 2
red 39
dark blue 2

yellow 132

dark blue 8
light blue 5
dark blue 1
red 57
dark blue 1
light blue 5
dark blue 8

yellow 148

dark blue 2
red 31
dark blue 2

yellow 140
dark blue 10

Canvas: 12' 2" long x 9' 2" high
16 beaded rows set 16" from end to end, beginning first one 8 '/." from top, last one 3' 2" from
bottom. Set 4" apart. 8 beads = 5/16 of inch.

Colors: dark blue, light blue, yellow, and red.
Short tufts of red flannel under beads or below.

11 extensions of buckskin sewn between or
under the rosettes.

Twelve 3" rosettes center along the top. Beaded
on separate canvas and sewn on.

All these panels vary in size, color of beads,
number of rosettes, and dangles. Old rose can be
substituted for red, white, and light blue. Greasy
yellow can be substituted for yellow gold.

11 dangles across the top and 8 down the middle red every other row, starting with the
second. 18" to 24" wrapped in yellow raffia or
some vegetable matter ending on both ends
with sheep toe or deer and yellow tufts of wool.

Colors: red, yellow, black, or dark blue and green.

Above: Buffalo-hide tipi at sunset.   Below: Tipi liner panel from Denver Art Museum.

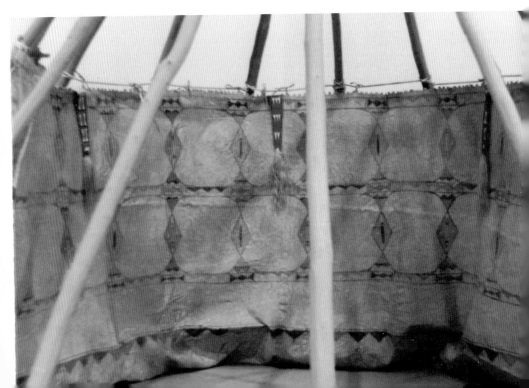

Above: Back of Linda Holley's 17-foot lodge.

Below: Sioux and Cheyenne tipi decorations for the cover.

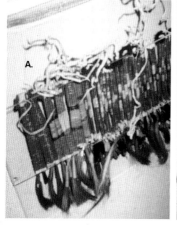

A.

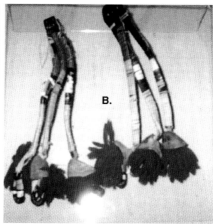

B.

David Ansonia's Swiss tipi that he painted himself.

Parleche-designed and painted 18-foot lodge.

Above: Hungarian winter tipi encampment.

Right: Czech Indian hobbyist dancers and camp.

Above: Tipi in Mount Carmel mountain range in Israel.
Below: Buffalo Days style of tipi interior.
Opposite: Modern re-creation of an old-style painted tipi by the Brewers.

Above: Interior of John Neidenthal's tipi.

Below: MNLRA Western Rendezvous.

NMLRA Western National Rendezvous in Wyoming, 1987.

Decorations on the Cover and Liner

Applying Design and Paint to the Cover

WARNING: Do not copy any designs found in this book or any other book show-ing cover designs. Many of these images are still owned by families today and they can and do get upset when they see them on other tipis. I know of a family that took their tipi to a dance in Montana only to be greeted by an angry Native American family who demanded they take their tipi down because the designs belonged to them. The other family complied and later sold the painted cover and replaced it with a plain white one.

"The painted tipis, or 'medicine,' tipis were owned by only a few distinguished families. . . . Medicine designs usually originated in dreams . . . and were handed down generation to generation. Such designs could be purchased in proper ceremonies and the 'medicine' and rituals 'passed' from one owner to another" (Laubins 1957, 243).

Kathy Brewer of Indian Images describes the use of cloth and the tribes who painted their lodges:

> Canvas, linen or cloth covers for tipis started becoming popular among the Native Americans around 1851. According to Kurz's 1851 journal, more of the wealthy men were already getting canvas for their lodges. Treaty annuity payments in the late 1850s and 1860s also were accompanied by lots of canvas bed ticking and other fabrics. As the 19th century wore on, the covers got bigger. . . . Bolder surface designs were applied with the new industrial paints and dyes that did not wash off or fade. Old photos of Blackfoot tipis, drawings of the Kiowa, Cheyenne, and Sioux depict spectacular cover paintings in their sketchbooks.

As for copyright of tipi designs, Blackfoot tipi designs (especially the stylized, elongated animals painted between the bottom surrounding base design and the surrounding top design) are family owned. Permission is needed from the tribe or the family before you use a particular design. You must also gain permission to use patterns from Kiowa, Cheyenne, and some Sioux families. Getting "the rights" from a tribe or family historically involved a feast, music, and a ritual that had to be learned with certain rites to be performed. "A painted tipi was an announcement that a sacred bundle rested within [and that] the tipi owner possessed the rites and rituals of that bundle" (Maurer 1978, 22).

You can decorate your tipi any way you see fit, with designs that are relevant to you and your family. If you want to make a more traditional-looking tipi, look at some ledger art drawings to get acquainted with the pictographic style of drawing and painting. Then do your own patterns in that style. The advantage to pictographic-style paintings is that you can decorate your tipi liner/cover with figures that do not cover it completely with paint.

Historically, the men were in charge of painting pictographic representational images (even though they were highly stylized), and the women painted geometric-type designs, as on parfleches and robes. Many nonfamily tipi designs were based on the individual's own exploits or dreams. These are the possession of just that one individual or society.

If you do not want to stick with traditional Native American designs, your creativity and imagination are your only limits. I have seen cross-stitched designs, rainbows, Scottish heraldic images, and every type of animal and geometric symbol that can be envisioned. Then there are the tie-dye tipis of the Netherlands and

Above left: Anadarko, Oklahoma, 24-foot tipi.

Above right: Karl Miller tipi, National Powwow, Crescent City, Illinois, 1990.

Left: Modern Sioux lodge, 1999.

Right: Nomadic tipi makers.

Above left and right: Rick Patterson tipi, Union Grove, North Carolina, AICA Dance. Tipi by Darry Wood.

Left: Beaded flower cover. Tipi by Darry Wood; owned and beaded by Bob Acorn.

Below left: NMLRA Western National Rendezvous.

Below right: Painted tipi by the Brewers of Indian Images.

England. Tipis have a huge canvas that can painted. Or you can always leave it white and just enjoy the tipi.

Painting the Entire Cover

If you are painting the whole cover, remember heavy paints can cause the tipi to shrink 3 to 6 inches. Make sure your canvas is of a tight weave like army duck. If it is pretreated with waterproofing solution or fire retardant, you will have to use your brushes to push the color into the weave. This will take the waterproofing and fire retardant out of the canvas. After it dries, you will need to re-waterproof and repaint the fire retardant.

Some of the old-time colors are red iron oxide (sometimes called light red or Indian red), yellow ochre, Prussian blue, chromium green oxide, and Van Dyke brown. Of course, you are free to use whatever colors you wish if you aren't aiming for an old-time look. Try painting on scrap pieces of canvas first.

For large areas, you should paint on premoistened canvas. Use sponges or wet towels. It is more difficult when the tipi is dry. The paint needs to be applied in thin coats and several coats are needed. This is better than one heavy coat! I use flat latex exterior house paint, which comes in several colors or can be custom mixed.

Give your cover time to dry before folding it up. If you have painted the whole cover, you will find that ten or more pounds have been added to the material. Any added decorations, such as appliqués, beadwork, and dangles, will also put weight on the tipi cover.

Innovative tipi owner Gary Winders (Short Bull) wanted his lodge to look like an old-time buffalo-brain-tanned hide, which is white at first and then turns a light yellow color with time. He took a piece of "smoked brain tan" to a paint store and matched it with their computer color duplicator. He mixed the latex exterior house paint with water (5 parts water to 1 part paint) in a 5-gallon bucket. He then laid his 18-foot tipi out on the ground. Using a big sponge, he went over it starting at the top and working his way down to the bottom. That way he could make it splotchy and uneven. Then he went back and applied more to the top, to the bottom, and around the door to make it look more used. Later he painted his liner with the same color by going over the pictographs that were already on the surface. This helps keep the sun out, he says, thus keeping the lodge cooler in the summer.

The Brewer family restores and makes reproduction Native American materials for museums and private individuals. Through their years of work, they have come up with some very innovative and creative ways to make materials look old. For a more aged look on a tipi, they developed this idea:

Bill sprayed [the tipi] with a very weak, muddy-colored acrylic solution, akin to tea water or coffee water, using one of those tank-style spray painters. He did it outdoors, and threw some dirt on it while still damp, and then brushed off the excess when dry. We had some black soot that had been shoveled out of an old blacksmith shop, and he used that to darken the top and flaps of the tipi to look like it had been discolored by smoke.

You can paint your canvas tipi cover with large hide-shaped areas, rather than adding additional material cut in hide shapes. This was how it was done in the movie *Dances with Wolves*, and it looked remarkably good from a distance. It may take some artistic talent, but I am sure with practice (try a miniature tipi cover or even a plain piece of canvas to start with) you could come up with a pretty good facsimile. Just look at old photos (preferably color ones, if you can find some) and try to replicate the "design" of the hides sewn together. There should be shading and some color differential in the different areas representing separate skins, but that is what trompe l'oeil is all about. This 'fool the eye' painting is really popular in the United States right now; all sorts of programs on the Home and Garden channel have ways to paint your house up in this way.

Bob Ellis's 16-foot tipi, 1975.

Painting the Designs

Before painting your cover, you might want to make a small toy paper cover, with all the designs painted or drawn to scale. It is better to make your little mistakes on paper before you paint on the big cover. I have done this before painting any of my covers. This definitely shows design flaws. It also gives you a chance to make any changes in color choices.

Use a heavy paper or kraft butcher paper for patterns or stencils. This will save on extra pencil marks that are almost impossible to erase on canvas. Use tacky light spray glues that can be applied to the back of the pattern to hold it in place. Make sure to wear socks or have clean feet when walking on the cover.

Disney World Lodge Owners, 2000. Linda Holley's 17-foot lodge.

Materials for Painting

- Water-based acrylics such as Liquitex, Golden Fluid Acrylics, and Colorplace paint
- Flat latex exterior house paints
- Paper for patterns
- #2 pencils
- White erasers (not red because these leave marks on the canvas)
- Blue or red tailor's chalk (unlike pencil, this will brush out)
- Large area to lay the cover out (peg or staple the cover to grass or weigh it down to the floor)
- Good brushes for use with acrylic paints in sizes from 1/8 inch to 2 inches

For the various designs, about any water-based color medium will do. Try several colors on similar scrap material and compare before you choose.

The pigments should be colorfast and designed to withstand exposure to UV radiation (sunlight). Dilute the fluid acrylics with water as much as 15 to 1 for a watercolor effect and 10 to 1 for most colors. You can also purchase pre-diluted airbrush colors that are pretty close to the correct consistency. A 6-ounce tube of pigment or large artist tubes can be used to paint an entire top of a tipi if diluted to a stain or slightly opaque consistency. You can mix pigments in thinned "hide glue" or "craft fabric paints." Paints that are applied too thick crack and peel even at a 50/50 mixture. Paints applied too thick will also create a very heavy cover that will result in leaks where the canvas bends. This is called crackling. The paint exposes spiderweb lines of canvas that break the paint.

For highlighting, use permanent paint pens to outline your images for sharper, cleaner edges. You might find a black or white outline accents your design. However, if you re-waterproof after using the paint pens, a halo or bleeding effect around the dark lines may happen. Try it on an extra piece of canvas to see how the paint performs.

For designs that you want to have a definite edge, the paint needs to be thicker, but not so thick that it cracks when you fold it. The only way you can find the right consistency is practice.

Put the tipi paint in plastic containers with covers so the paint won't dry out between uses. It will, however, dry out eventually. This is why you shouldn't mix the whole tube at once. Use a good-quality acrylic brush if you want to do detailed work (like pictographs), a wider brush for large areas, and a smaller one for detail areas.

Just a few notes on painting: Painting the cover makes the cover heavier and less likely to cause deteriorating trouble as the tipi wears out. Painted areas have to be re-waterproofed as the paint and scrubbing action of the paintbrush take the water-resistant chemical out of the canvas. Whatever is painted on the surface is going to cut down on the amount of light that gets through the cover.

Painting the Top and Bottom of the Cover

Paint the top part of the cover first so that you don't track over your work. One of the hardest things to do along the bottom of the tipi is to keep your lines even as you make your design. To make circular designs that follow the entire bottom of the tipi to form a border or line designs, first peg a tape measurer to the radius point of the lodge between the two smoke flaps. This will give you a good swing line to form your pattern lines. Check and recheck before marking any line. Because tipis can have a different radius point, you may have to move the tape measure a few times before getting the right measurement. Once you have the distance, either tape or hold the pencil tightly on the tape measure and start making the "swing" line.

Above: Jim Creighton's hand-stitched and painted lodge, Arizona.

Below: Interior of Jim Creighton's tipi looking up to back.

Blackfeet tipi liner, ca 1915, which belonged to Cecile Horn of Browning, Montana. Hand-stitched cotton cloth colored with crayon, Indian ink, and pencil. 24 1/2 x 5 feet, 10 inches wide.

Timber Line Tipis of England has a different formula for marking the bottom lines setting the tipi up on poles:

> A tip that people might have worked out before, but that makes marking out a tipi a lot easier, is to run bands around the tipi that you want parallel to the ground. Erect the poles and put the cover on them, but inside out. No need for the smoke-flap poles. Then to mark the bands, stand on a stepladder inside the tipi. It's a lot easier and safer than trying to mark the outside when you find yourself overreaching and in risk of falling off. Also, you don't need to move the stepladder about as much.

Blackfoot painted hide liner, Denver Art Museum.

The next step is to get your colors together and start painting. The cover can be painted on the ground or put on tables. For large areas, sponges, rags, or roller brushes will cover the most area. On the small design areas, try to get the cover up on a table so that you will be more comfortable painting the smaller details. Also, do not be surprised by the overlapping strokes that can show up with these techniques. Some people have used sprayers, but these do not seem to penetrate the threads because of the water-resistant properties of treated canvas. The paint sits on the surface. Paint needs to be worked into the material. To create a very light or stained look to your designs, heavily water down the paints and apply with a sponge or light hand with the paintbrush.

Painting a Liner

The same paints used for decorating a cover can also be used to paint a liner. Crayons, permanent magic markers, and indelible inks can also be used in the process. Do not use watercolors, as they will run if the liner gets wet. If a waterproofing sealant is applied to the surface, marking pens can run or give a halo effect of yellow or greenish cast around the darker marked areas. Water repellents like Scotch Guard, which come as an aerosol spay, might be better than Behr or Thompson, which are of a heavier consistency when applied with a brush or sprayer.

Pattern designs for a liner are generally geometric, are taken from rawhide or parfleche designs, and are considered a woman's art. Other designs are of heroic or war exploits of the man. These can depict buffalo hunts, horse stealing, landscape

Eighteen-foot interior of Cheyenne lodge built by Darry Wood. Owned and decorated by Linda Holley in 1978.

Pictograph-painted inner liner depicting war exploits.

View of liner with all materials in place.

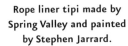

Rope liner tipi made by Spring Valley and painted by Stephen Jarrard.

views, or any pictographic designs. Not found on liners are the war bonnet design or sunburst. They are found on buffalo robes, which would be hung up behind the owner or act as a liner themselves. In the Laubins' book on tipis, such a robe is hanging behind them in color plate 7. Today, many people have painted similar designs on their liners at the lift-pole area.

Before painting a liner, research any design that you are considering. If trying to get the historic look, stay simple and geometric, with a light touch on the colors. The old rectangular liners had patterns running around the top and then in groups going from top to bottom. Designs did not follow the poles or seams as the old liners did not have vertical seams like today's liners. Some Blackfoot liners not only have a pattern running horizontally across the entire length of the top, but also three more rows evenly spaced parallel to the top row and then vertical patterns about every 2 feet. The Smithsonian and National Museum of the American Indian have several examples of tipi liners showing geometric designs.

For a placement of designs on a fitted liner, make a pattern showing all vertical seams or where the panels join. Plan your design around the fact that there will be beds, boxes, and other goods piled up around the bottom of the liner. It is not necessary to go all the way to the bottom with a pattern or down every seam or pole. The designs can also be a combination of geometric and pictographic. Drawings can be traditional or based on happenings in your world or past experiences. What goes on or in your tipi is your choice.

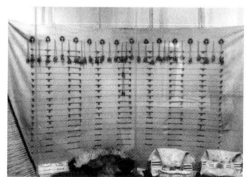 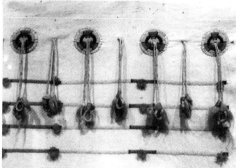

Cheyenne-beaded liner.

Beaded Liners

For the most part, beaded liners are found in Cheyenne, Arapaho, and Crow lodges. These liners are rectangular panels of muslin, with rows of horizontal, single-lane, colored beadwork inserted every so many inches with tufts of wool yarn or sheep's wool. The women who made the liners above were part of the Cheyenne Women's Quilling (Marriott 1956) or Beading Society (Coleman 1980). At the top of these panels was found a row of beaded and quilled rosettes with sheep toes and colored wool hanging from each one. These special liners were used during the summer or on special occasions. Some tipis could have two or more liners or bed curtains hanging around the full perimeter of the lodge.

Decorations or Ornaments on Tipis

Ornaments are materials added to the surface of the cover. Examples of these ornaments are quilled pendants, beaded rosettes, horsehair tassels, dewclaws of sheep and deer, and the tin tinkles of the Sioux.

Billy Maxwell of Montana, longtime Native American cultural enthusiast and interpreter for the Lewis and Clark Center, gives an overall description of where the decorations are placed as told to him: "The tipi had beaded discs at the four sides and bison tails hanging from the ear tips. Floratine Blue Thunder commented that ears with bull [bison] tails was a sign that the owner was a giving person. I know that old hide lodges would have a split tail at the top tip from the single split hide that makes the flaps."

In 1833, Prince Maximilian described a Minatare or Hidatsa tipi in his travels: "Each side of the entrance [was] finished with a stripe and rosettes of dyed porcupine quills very neatly executed" (Maximilian 1906, 61).

Details of the medallions are described by Hassrick (Hassrick 1962, 212) and Kroeber (Kroeber 1983, 60) as being made of quill and beadwork and attached to the cover in a ceremony. Hassrick takes his information from the Crows living in the 1950s while Kroeber's information from the Arapaho is fifty or more years earlier. Rosettes were usually anywhere from 4 to 8 inches in diameter and often a lock of hair or fur was inserted in the center. Four rosettes matched, but the fifth one attached at the back of the cover just below the tie point on the lift pole. It was usually bigger or of a different design and shape, trapezoidal or rectangular. Rosettes were placed in a southeast, southwest, northwest, and northeast direction if the tipi was facing east at a height of about 6 to 8 feet. This height varied with the makers. Cheyenne, Arapaho, Kiowa, Gros Ventres, Shoshone, and Ponca tribes used these and similar types of adornments. Drawn examples of the Kiowa, Cheyenne, and

Rosettes and dangles, referred to as stars, for outside of tipi. They are put on at the four directions.

Above: Decorated
Arapaho tipis at St.
Louis Fair, 1904–05.

Right: Rawhide door
and beaded Cheyenne
cover, 1910.

Sioux are shown in several sketchbooks. Photographs taken from 1880 to the 1940s also give ample evidence of their use among the tribes. Some old photographs also show a lock of hair or fur sewn to the bottom of the rosette on the sides of the tipi, rather than from the center.

Hassrick and Kroeber go on to describe the dangles or tinklers of the Sioux and Cheyenne, which are applied to the front of the lodge, smoke flaps, and door: "A well-appointed tipi required additional embellishment with 'tipi front quills.' These dangles made of short strips of rawhide wrapped with brightly colored porcupine quills to which were attached horsetails hung from their center might be attached to the tipi to the height of a man's head and at equal intervals" (Hassrick 1964, 212).

"Arapaho and Cheyenne applied these quilled pendants, arranging them in two vertical rows on the front of the tent and edge of the flaps" (Kroeber 1983, 60).

The crafting guilds for women of the Cheyenne and Arapaho, called "the Trade Guild of the Southern Cheyenne Women" (Marriott 1956, 1) or "the Cheyenne Women's Sewing Society" (Coleman 1980, 50), came about as a fulfillment of a vow to acknowledge the good deeds of the husband or other desired happening. The first written observation of this type of tipi was in 1811 (Coleman 1980, 50).

Four types of special decorative beadwork were made by the members: rosettes for the tipi cover, pillows, wall (describing a liner), bedspreads, and doors (Marriott 1956, 20). Marriott goes on to describe the beaded/quilled ornaments used on the four different styles of lodges. It is not recommended that these covers be copied, as they are still made by members of the guilds. A brief description is taken from the article:

> Tipis were of four types, again depending on the amount of work involved. The first type, which brought the least honor to the maker, had a row of vertical stripes of beading down the back, four medallions on the sides—one at each quarter—and a large medallion at the juncture of the smoke flaps. From the top of each smoke flap to the point where it joined the tipi proper were five tassels, similar to the ones on the wall, but having three buckskin strands instead of two. From the bottom of the smoke-flaps to the top of the door hung six more tassels. There was also a tassel in the center of each medallion. The tassels on the tipi were flat, so that they would not blow about and get torn. Those on the wall (liner) were round, since they hung inside. Second was made with four medallions of blue beads and no other ornament. Third type was known as the 'ghost tipi.' On this tipi the medallions were black and yellow a black ring around the yellow disk. It had no connection with the Ghost Dance, but derived its name from having once been set up to mark a burial place. The fourth type, the highest and most honorable, had four tassels, each of three buckskin strings and a cow's tail. There was a single medallion at the tipi,

bearing the design of a birth with outstretched wings. The bird was worked in red beads against a black background." (Marriott 1956, 20)

The women who made these items must have taken great pride in the beauty and craftsmanship required to become members of the guild. The woman's role in the tribe was enhanced by the meeting of these required skills. It must have been a lovely sight to see the great beaded/quilled cover amongst some of the painted lodges. Only women who had passed the required test could make the rosettes, tassels, pendants, special walls (liners), and pillows. These were not common embellishments and required special ceremonies in the making, just as in a painted lodge.

Sioux lodges also used four rosettes, but the tribes did not seem to have the women's societies, such as the Cheyenne Women's Sewing Society. The main difference between the Sioux and Cheyenne pendants is that the tinkler or dangle is attached to the bottom as a pendant. The Sioux use metal tin cones for their tinklers and the Cheyenne use a dew toe from a sheep or deer. Placement on the covers is about the same, but the designs on the medallions and dangles are different.

As the tribes visited and mixed on the Plains, the designs and materials also became mixed. Photographs and existing collected tipis of the Sioux and Cheyenne show the similarities and changes in the construction of dangles, smoke flaps, and medallions. A tipi made by a Cheyenne family or group could be gifted to a Sioux family or group and then that tipi was decorated by the new group, taking on different properties other than when it was originally made. Now it is hard to tell whether the tipi is Sioux or Cheyenne. And then there is the intermarrying of families, which also influenced tipi making. In addition, the Sioux and Northern Cheyenne often camped together, further adding to the tribal mixture.

Streamers and ribbons have been featured on the tips of many lodge poles. These are often shown in the paintings and drawings of Catlin and Alfred Jacob Miller.

Frank Blackwell Mayer made drawings of Sioux lodges in the Little Crow village in 1851, which did not show such streamers (Mayer 1906, 112). In later photos of Indian villages, the streamers are also absent. It would seem that ribbons or colored cloth on pole tips is a very optional decoration. Tribal fairs and Wild West shows become popular toward the end of the nineteenth century and tipis displayed more streamers. Streamers show wind direction in areas where there are swirling winds or variable wind directions like east of the Mississippi. Materials of red cloth or any color should be colorfast. There is nothing like a cover where ribbon, tufts of hair, and strips of leather have bled, leaving colored streaks down the sides of the cover.

Today, there are all kinds of colored ribbons, cloth, and feathers for the four directions. On occasion, horsetails on a lift pole can be seen. Anything will go and does, along with all kinds of reasons for doing them. That is OK—use whatever works for you. I use yellow steamers because they look great and complement my painted cover.

Making Dangles or Tassels for a Tipi

Dangles or tassels, as some tribes refer to them, are decorations or symbolic icons attached to tipi covers, liners, doors, and smoke flaps. They are also pictured in old-time photos and ledger drawings. In the past, they were usually seen on Cheyenne (Tsistsistas), Arapaho (Hinanina), Shoshone, Kiowa, Bannock, Hidatsa, Crow, Ute, and some Ponca tipis. Today, you can see them on almost any tipi cover.

According to traditional beliefs, as the dewclaws "clicked" together, they imitated the sound of deer or buffalo. From my own experience, the dangles make very little noise except in a big wind and that is not much of a sound.

Today's dangles seem to be just decorations. Tipi covers can have as few as ten and upwards of one hundred or so. It all depends on where you want them located. Traditional standards have dangles on set areas around the covers, doors, and linings. These areas are along the smoke flaps, the front on either side of the lacing pins, and down the back, where they are placed in two vertical columns. Another place is along the top of the door covering, which is mostly seen with Cheyenne lodges.

Materials for Dangles and Tassels

Traditional Materials

- Old strap or harness leather that is approximately 1/8 inch thick for the base. Sometimes you will see rawhide.

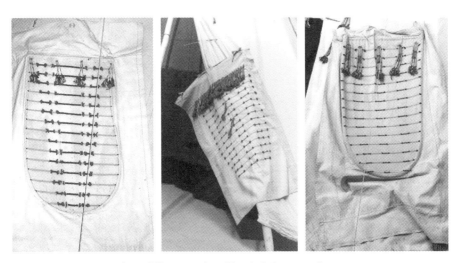

Three different styles of beaded Cheyenne doors.

- Porcupine quills, leaves of cattails, cornhusks, and sometimes bird quills.
- Colors: aniline dyes; roots of horsetail plants for the black, natural earth pigments; insects; and animal urine.
- Dewclaws of deer, sheep, elk, and buffalo. The toe itself is rarely used.
- Pieces of cloth, soft leather for ties, and sinew.
- An awl or a small piece of pointed steel or iron you can heat up to burn a hole in leather.
- Tufts of wool, horsehair, yarn, frayed cloth.

Modern Materials You Can Find Today

- Rawhide or leather harness found at a leather supply store. Some people use old milk jugs or plastic containers. The latter is not recommend as they break apart with age and develop sharp edges that cut into the covering of the lodge as it is folded for travel or storage.
- Quills, leaves of cattails, cornhusks, and my favorite, raffia (a grass-like material found in almost every craft store that comes in several pre-dyed colors).
- Colored, synthetic, artificial sinews. They come in red, green, blue, white, yellow, and natural.
- Dewclaws, or toes of deer.
- Pieces of blue or red cloth, soft leather for the ties, artificial sinew, or real animal sinew.
- Steel awl, ice pick, or a hole puncher.
- Tufts of real sheep hair (wool), horsehair, or acrylic yarn. Undyed real, natural wool does not sun fade as fast as the fake yarn, but there are exceptions to the rule. And all this depends on the dye methods used.
- Good pair of scissors and/or shears for cutting cloth and cutting heavy leather.
- Matte polyurethane available at a hardware store or art supply house.

Materials for dangles.

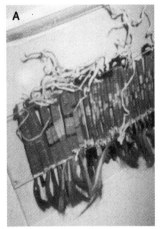
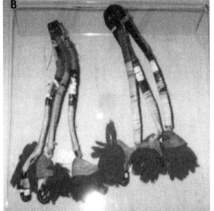

A. Sioux tinklers quill wrapped. B. Northern Cheyenne dangles with sheep toes.
C. Plant-fiber-wrapped dangle. Dangle or tinklers wrapped on harness leather or rawhide.

Colors

- Traditional dangles used very basic colors: red, white, blue to black, green, and yellow.
- The Sioux used red, yellow, purple, or faded blue.
- The Cheyenne used red, dark blue to black, white, and yellow to light orange.

The Cheyenne had special meanings for colors:
Bright red—war
Yellow—women and buffalo calves (fertility)
Black—discolored bodies of dead enemies and the night sky
Blue—power of the creator
White—snow, potential for rebirth and east direction

Dye your materials with Rit Dye, or better yet, go to an arts supply store and buy Batik dyes, which are sun and colorfast. They cost more, but do not bleed or fade as much as the Rit does. If you are using the Rit Dye, put in some vinegar or salt to the bath to help set the color. Rinse completely and then let it dry.

When coloring your own wrappings of wool or horsehair, be sure to check for colorfastness. Streaks of red or blue running down the sides of your nice white cover after a rainstorm is not good.

Construction of the Dangle/Drop

- Choose the area on the cover, door, or lining where you want the drop attached.
- Decide if the dangle will have one to three "legs" and how wide, long, and what style (Sioux, Cheyenne?) they should be. (See drawings for sizes and shapes.)
- Gather your materials. The base of the dangle can be rawhide or strap leather (or rawhide dog chews flattened out).
- Cut a template pattern for the dangle. This will save you time and material when making multiple pieces. Make the template of cardboard or heavy paper that will hold a shape for outlining several times.
- Cut out the dangle forms using heavy shears, scissors, a rotary blade, or a good knife. If you are cutting out a two- or three-leg dangle, you might want to cut out a little more of the leather in the middle of the legs to leave room for your wrapping material.
- Take a leather hole puncher or traditional pointed hot iron and put your holes at the top and bottom of your drop. Don't get too close to the edges, or when you pull your ties with toes through the opening you could break the hole open.
- Prepare the materials for wrapping the dangle. When I wrap, I like to start at the top and go to the bottom of each leg.
- See illustrations for wrapping and start your project.
- To protect my work, I use a modern convenience that makes my material last longer and gives it a "quilled" look. I dip each dangle in matte polyurethane and set each aside to dry. Build a little tower or drying rack by turning a stool over, wrapping string around the legs about 1 foot up and then your work on the stings to drip dry. Wire or paper clips can be used to dunk the leather. The urethane soaks into the wrappings and the rawhide to give it some protection from the elements. You may have to ream out the holes if they cover over, but that is easy with an awl. Also, this polyurethane covering helps cut down on any bleeding of the dyes.
- You could also use synthetic sinew to do your wrapping. This will not bleed and gives the same look. No need to protect from the elements.
- Dewclaws, or toes, should be cleaned. If you let them soak in warm water for a few hours, they are easier to clean, trim, and then drill a hole. Be careful, as any sharp edges can cut your cover when folded and stored. Some people take all the dangles off between uses. This process can create more wear and tear on the cover unless it does not go up very often.
- Attach decorative materials to the dewclaws and then attach them to the dangle with a soft lace of buckskin. My preference is brain-tanned buckskin lace, as it seems to hold up better in outside conditions. But again this is up to you.
- Lace the top ties into place on the cover, smoke flaps, liner, or door. Tie a knot only on one end, put through top hole, and then pull through. When you get them all done, you are ready to attach them to the surface of the cover, door, or liner.

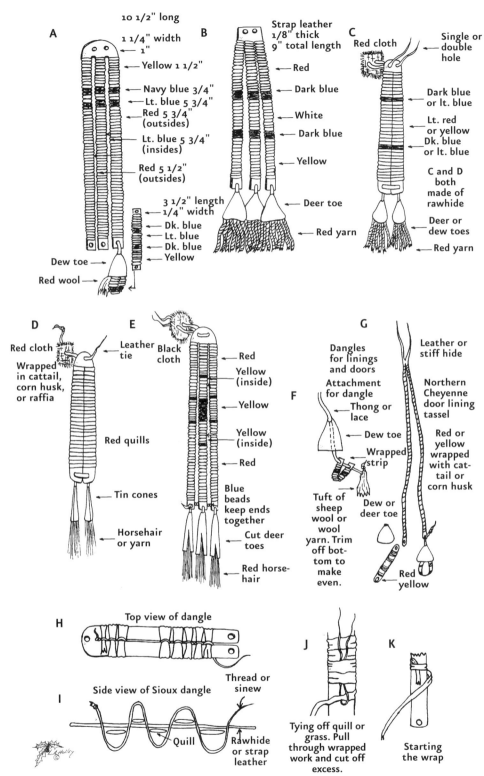

A 10 1/2" long
1 1/4" width
1"
Yellow 1 1/2"
Navy blue 3/4"
Lt. blue 5 3/4"
Red 5 3/4" (outsides)
Lt. blue 5 3/4" (insides)
Red 5 1/2" (outsides)
3 1/2" length
1/4" width
Dk. blue
Lt. blue
Dk. blue
Yellow
Dew toe
Red wool

B Strap leather 1/8" thick 9" total length
Red
Dark blue
White
Dark blue
Yellow
Deer toe
Red yarn

C Red cloth
Single or double hole
Dark blue or lt. blue
Lt. red or yellow
Dk. blue or lt. blue
C and D both made of rawhide
Deer or dew toes
Red yarn

D Red cloth
Wrapped in cattail, corn husk, or raffia
Leather tie
Red quills
Tin cones
Horsehair or yarn

E Black cloth
Red
Yellow (inside)
Yellow
Yellow (inside)
Red
Blue beads keep ends together
Cut deer toes
Red horsehair

F Dangles for linings and doors
Attachment for dangle
Thong or lace
Dew toe
Wrapped strip
Tuft of sheep wool or wool yarn. Trim off bottom to make even.
Dew or deer toe

G Leather or stiff hide
Northern Cheyenne door lining tassel
Red or yellow wrapped with cat-tail or corn husk
Red yellow

H Top view of dangle

I Side view of Sioux dangle
Thread or sinew
Quill
Rawhide or strap leather

J Tying off quill or grass. Pull through wrapped work and cut off excess.

K Starting the wrap

Directions for making dangles. A. Cheyenne. B. Northern Cheyenne. C. D. E. Sioux

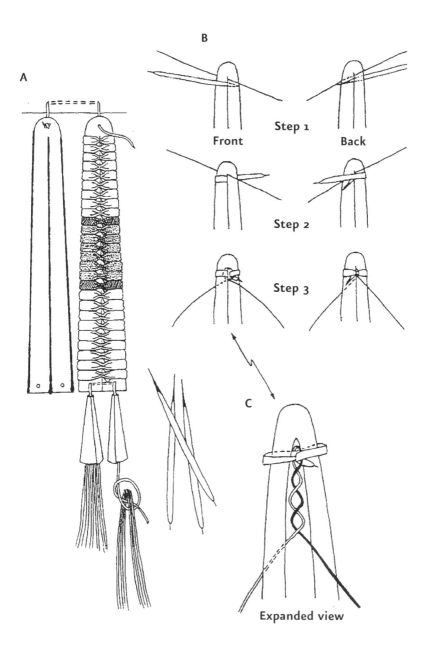

A

B

Front   Step 1   Back

Step 2

Step 3

C

Expanded view

Directions for making tinklers.

- Most dangles are attached to the cover through the canvas. This means you have to put a hole or lots of little holes in your cover. If done right, the leather lace will fill in the hole and rain will not get in. Mark where the dangle will go. Use a sharp awl to make a hole that does not tear but spreads the threads apart to place your lace through the material. Then hold a small square of cloth on the inside and go through it with the lace. This acts like a protective barrier to help keep the knot from pulling back out and tearing the cover. Use a piece of brain-tanned leather for a plug to help prevent the dangle from pulling back through the canvas.
- Once all the decorations are in place, the tipi is ready for display.
- There are other ways to make dangles. The Sioux have a decoration that is called a "tinkler." Tinklers are made of tin cones instead of dewclaws, or toes. The Dakota Tipi Tinkler is very popular for decorations on the covers of tipis, liners, and doors.

Racks for cars without rain gutters.

Transporting a Tipi

Once you get a tipi, the next big problem is taking it out of the backyard and attending a campout. How do you get your lovely, smooth, 24-foot-plus tipi poles out of the backyard? There are three choices: racks on top of the vehicle, a trailer to carry the poles, or racks plus trailer to haul all the equipment that goes with the tipi. So, which do you choose?

Here are some considerations to think about as you make your choice.

- The laws in the states you will be traveling in for carrying long items on state or county roads, the interstate, or toll roads.
- The flags or lights you will need for the overhanging poles to be in compliance with the laws.

- Your vehicle's pulling power and whether you can put a rack on the roof.
- Your vehicle's turning capacity with a trailer and poles.
- Where you can buy racks for your roof or bumper-mounted frames for racks, or how you can build them.
- Whether your pole butts are facing the front or back of vehicle.
- The weight of the poles.
- The height of your trailer or vehicle and the overhangs.
- The types of ropes or cords you will use to tie down equipment and poles.
- The wind resistance on the racks and trailer that will affect gas mileage with and without equipment.

I am not responsible for any damages or accidents you may have trying out any of these ideas! This chapter will not give any specifics on how to build a trailer or racks, but it will give you some ideas of things that have worked or not worked for me and other people

Racks

First look at the car you have in the garage. Is it sturdy enough to carry poles on top and carry the equipment that goes with the tipi? Don't forget the family and pets. I once knew a person who had an old 1969 Volkswagen Beetle, who was able

Racks for cars without rain gutters.

to put his 24-foot long tipi poles on top of the bug. He used a light luggage rack available at most department stores at that time. Poles were secured in two bundles and to the front and back bumper with ropes. Though he could not get much equipment into the Volkswagen, he was still able to transport his cover, liner, and poles. You can have your poles face whichever way works for you as long as they are balanced. I prefer that my pole butts are toward the front of the vehicle to balance the weight and reduce wind resistance.

My first tipi poles were over 30 feet long, and my mode of transportation was a small Toyota Land Cruiser. It was obvious to me that my poles were not going on top of this vehicle. So I opted for a trailer. This trailer was called Moby Dick because it was 28 feet long and approximately 3 feet wide, with a wooden box built in the middle. It looked more like a bluish green steel bridge going down the road. The poles fit great in the racks on the trailer. The only problem was turning. I had to make a very wide swing. This type of trailer was good for just parking and storing the poles with everything on it. But after a year, I deemed it too much of a problem and decided to go with a van that could carry the poles on top and all my equipment inside.

My next van had special racks built for it that were cradled in the rain gutters. The racks were made of reinforced metal rebar with a large 4 x 4 piece of wood connecting the two metal braces. I also cut my poles back from the butts to 28 feet, which made them lighter and easier to control and set up. There was a rack in the front of the van

Jim Keener from Miami, Florida. Fancy rig with bumper hitches front and back, with area for steel lock box. Walt Disney World, Orlando, Florida, Thanksgiving Camp, 2002. Racks mounted with heavy foam padding and tied to the front bumper.

and one toward the back of the van. In order to cradle each pole individually, the wood across the top had 17 V cuts. In each V cut, or U shape, was a small peg or concrete nail placed in the wood in order to hold each pole. The pole was drilled with a small 1/2-inch hole to a depth of 1 inch to fit on each peg. Then each pole was roped down in place so it would not slide forward or backward. The butts of

David Ansonia's truck in the Alps.

the poles went forward just 5 or so feet in front of the van with the tips going to the back. Even with the van there was a need for flags and lights at night. When the wood was cut for the racks, there was an angle cut in them that swept toward the back to help with wind resistance.

After my divorce, I sold my big 18-foot lodge and van. I then went to a 14-foot tipi, a Toyota Tercel, and a small trailer. Later I purchased Yakima heavy-duty canoe racks for the Tercel and built a little "do it yourself" 4 x 4-foot trailer. The built-in roof racks that came with the car were not sturdy enough to hold poles. On the canoe racks, I made the same type of wood top bracing as on the van to hold each pole. The trailer helped with the overhangs of the poles in travel. It gave me a legal overhang of 4 feet beyond the trailer edge, but I still used flags for safety.

Today (three cars and four more trailers later), I drive a Ford Explorer and pull a trailer. My tipi poles are 24 feet long for a 17-foot lodge, and I still use the rack system of the individual pole cradles in wood. And I am on my eighth trailer. Unfortunately, when I built this trailer (which happens to be 12 feet long, 5 feet wide, and 4 feet tall), I did not take into account how tall the Explorer was with the poles on top. If I hit some kind of the ditch, the poles go crashing into the trailer.

It is also difficult to make turns when they slide across the trailer top. To solve this problem, I built a taller wood support for the back rack. This makes the poles clear the trailer top by another foot. So, if you are going to have a trailer, make sure that your poles clear the trailer by at least 1 foot. Or, that the trailer is 1 foot lower than the roof of your vehicle.

A rack on top of your car is a simple and great way for carrying poles if you do not want to have a bumper system welded to the front or back. Just make sure it fits your rain gutter or has the curved bracing for those cars that no longer have them. Some of the best racks are available at the bicycle and canoe shops, which sell heavy-duty models. Cheaper racks can break or collapse under the weight of the poles. Or you can go to a welding shop and have your racks made to your specifications. But absolutely use a rack. Never tie poles directly on the top of your vehicle. A dented-in roof and broken windshield will convince you on the first bump.

You can have special rack holders welded or attached to the front and back bumper of your vehicle. Then the pole racks are bolted on when needed for travel and taken off when finished. Trucks and vans use these for carrying ladders or heavy equipment. Camper shells will need a rack that wraps around the shell. Some racks are welded under the chassis and wrap around the body, front, and rear and are connected to the main pole mounts.

The basic framework for the racks are an H or Y. Experiment to find what works best for you. I keep inventing new racks and trailers with each new car or tipi. Size makes a big difference in hauling tipis—the size of the poles, car, and equipment. Each affects the other.

If you are not using a frame that cradles each individual pole, spread out the poles or at least put them in two bundles on the outer edges. Do not put them in one bundle in the center. For best wind resistance, do not have the flat surface facing the front.

Poles sticking too far out front can make visibility difficult and can also become a problem at stop signs and when you turn corners. They might catch hotel light poles, hanging roofs, or awning covers. I've known some to hit those old neon lights in motel parking lots. Those lights may be old, but they are expensive to replace! If possible, know where you are going and know the clearance from side to side and front to back. Keep your distance from other vehicles on the road so that a sudden stop by the driver ahead of you does not result in your poles going through his vehicle.

Secure your poles. If your poles are not secured front to back, a sudden stop can send your poles flying. This is one reason I have the holding pins. Try driving and stopping in a vacant lot when you first set up your pole arrangement to see how secure they are.

Do not overload the top of your car. If it is top heavy, it will be prone to rolling over. There is nothing like being pulled out of a creek where have you landed on your side after making too sharp of a turn with the extra load. Injury, vehicle damage, and embarrassment can be avoided by paying attention to the weight you are carrying on top.

Trailers

I have bought or built eight trailers. I now know what I like best. There are the box and flatbed styles. With the box styles, materials can be out of the weather and locked. The open flatbed is only good for hauling poles until you build a box to store equipment. The best trailer is the factory aluminum with dual axles because it is lightweight and it stays level without the front being on a jack or on the hitch. Size depends on your budget and how much you carry.

If you are imaginative, you can take some of the lawn trailers and build your covered box. Or you can go to a welding shop and design your framework for size and length of a box. Small "do-it-yourself" trailers can be ordered through the mail and delivered to you for assembly.

Tipi owner Guy Pazzogna Vaudois shared his driving experiences and problems in Europe and the United States with me:

> After having spent more than twenty years driving trucks carrying poles in the Dakotas, Nebraska, Wyoming, and Montana, it appeared to me that the best way is to bundle the poles together so that they form a single longitudinal beam trailer: one end with the hitch and at the other end a shaft (the simplest possible).
>
> This setup allows for having the poles the closest to the ground. In France, where I am, toll is a function of the height of the load. Under 2 meters height, no change in toll, but 9 to 10 meters, there is a toll.
>
> In France, the load must not be wider than the vehicle by more than 20 centimeters on each side. Load can be longer up to 3 meters at the rear with signal, or 1 meter without signal. In the front, load cannot extend farther than the bumpers. Apparently in Switzerland, poles can extend by 1.5 meters both at the front and the rear.
>
> How is it in other European countries and in North America? No technical inspection is required in France for a trailer less then 500 Kg GWT; no regulation either for its construction if length is less than 12 meters (+ 1 meter or + 3 meters) between hitch and rear lights. The overall carriage (truck and trailer) shall be less than 18.75 meters total.
>
> I own a Chevy Suburban 4 x 4, 5.5 meters long. I can carry my 13-meter-long poles without any problem in a trailer less than 500 Kg. When loading the poles in the trailer and passing them over the truck roof, height limitation becomes a problem.

There are many types of cars, trucks, and vans that can carry poles. With today's rising gas prices, it may be necessary to decide which will work best for you and still let you transport your tipi. Using a vehicle alone or with a trailer is a decision you have to face. Hopefully some of the suggestions and information given here will help you make your choice.

Above: Jeff Mos (NightHawk) of Tipis from Africa with his Citroën, Xsara Picasso pulling a trailer for his 6-meter poles (16-foot tipi). Beerse in Belgium at the 2005 Beer Valley Rendezvous.

Middle and Below: Specially built steel trailer with racks on top, pulled behind a station wagon. Poles are 24 feet long. Side and back doors with covered open access on top. Linda Holley's fifth trailer for heavy-duty storage of poles and equipment. National Powwow trailer poles fit butts in the front box then going back.

Tips on the Care and Buying of a Tipi

Here are some general tips on maintenance for the tipi or tent owner:

- To increase the longevity of the canvas, keep the canvas dry.
- It is best not to ever "wash" your canvas. It takes out all the waterproofing and other protective chemicals you might have on the cover. Just keep it as clean as possible.
- If your canvas was treated and you have cleaned it with soapy water or some other chemical to get rid of mildew or dirt, you will have to re-waterproof your canvas.
- When taking down your tipi from a dusty encampment, always take a broom to the inside and swat outward to knock off the dust and dirt on the surface. It is like beating an old rug on a line. Then shake it really hard on the lift pole. Once you have beaten out the dust, you can start the takedown.
- Do not store canvas directly on a concrete floor. Concrete stores moisture and will rot the canvas or cardboard box (if in one).
- Do not take the cover down or store it away while it is wet. Moisture will cause the canvas to mildew, which will eventually lead to the canvas rotting. Never put a damp tent into storage. If you must take your tipi down when it is wet, set it back up at your home or next location as soon as possible so it can dry completely.
- Keep canvas taut at all times and smoke-flap poles snug up to the tipi. Go inside your tipi and push out any poles that have shifted in the frame. Choose poles for the smoke flaps that are smooth with no rough spots to snag the canvas (refer to Poles, Pole Care, and Pole Maintenance chapter).
- Treat the canvas with approved preservatives for cloth. Canvak and Mildex are preservative liquids specifically made for canvas. They help with waterproofing and mildew resistance of cloth materials. Behr or Olympic water seals can also be used, but read the label before application.

- UV rays from the sun are destructive and will degrade the canvas. So, if you are not going to be using your lodge, store it in a clean, dry, and critter-free area. When left up year-round, a tipi will typically last five years (depending on the climate). Storing a tipi when not in use will double its life. Some tipis can have a longer lifespan if the utmost care is taken.
- It is important to occasionally air out the tipi. To reduce the humidity inside the lodge, build a small fire as this will dry out the air. The small amount of tannic acid and other chemicals that are deposited on the canvas from a fire tend to repel mildew. This process is kind of like smoking a ham, which helps the tipi last through the winter. UV exposure also helps reduce mildew, but it will deteriorate the canvas with time.
- This is a homemade recipe for fire-retardant liquid that can be applied to canvas: 9 ounces 20 Mule Team Borax; 4 ounces boric acid; 1 gallon lukewarm water. Combine all and spray or paint onto canvas.
- In the Northeast and other locations downwind from power or industrial plants, acid rain is a problem. When it rains, diluted acid showers down on your tipi. If this happens, hose off your tipi with plain water as soon as possible. This will help dilute any acid that remains. Dry the tent well before folding and storing it.
- Do not store your ropes with your canvas. Ropes are sometimes treated with oil and they will leave a stain on the surface of the tipi.

Making Your Tipi Mildew Resistant

Mildew is one of the most common problems that can attack your canvas. Even if your tipi is made of a fabric that is mildew resistant, it will mildew if left damp. Mildew is very destructive to cotton fabrics as well as other materials. Mildew usually forms when damp tipis are put in storage. It can also start under certain conditions of humidity and temperature. If mildew has started to grow, it can be stopped from spreading by thoroughly drying the tent, preferably in the hot sun, and applying a cleaner such as IOSSO Tent & Camping Gear Cleaner. This cleaner is made to remove tough dirt and mildew stains. Afterwards, you will find it necessary to treat the tent with a water-repellent compound such as Canvak. If using another treatment, be sure to read the labels to make sure it is safe for use on canvas.

IOSSO cleaner removes tough dirt, mold, mildew, algae, most food and drink stains, and bloodstains. It is color safe and may be used on most fabrics, vinyl, plastics, canvas, carpeting, and wood. It is biodegradable, nontoxic, and does not contain bleach or chlorine products, which degrade fabric fibers.

If you get mildew on your canvas, here are some home remedies that might work. But there are always problems with any remedy.

For mildew, spray the canvas with a 50/50 mix of white vinegar and water and let it dry in the sun. This will kill the mildew but won't remove the spots.

This method is only used as a last resort! Try scrubbing with a brush and a bleach solution of 1/4 cup bleach in a 2-gallon bucket of warm water. Let the area dry completely. This will kill the mildew and stop it from spreading, but will not remove the discoloration. Make sure to use lots of water; bleach will destroy the canvas if not diluted.

In about 8 ounces of water, dissolve 2 teaspoons of salt and 2 teaspoons of concentrated lemon juice. Wash the mildewed cloth with this solution and then rinse with fresh water. Let dry in open air before using.

Do not use any product like X-14 that has a high bleach content. It will shred or disintegrate the material, which will get rid of the spots and the canvas.

If your tipi is really dirty, get a pressure washer. Set it for a very light spray; you do not want to put a hole in the canvas. Set the cover up on the poles and spray from the inside out.

Making Your Tipi Water Resistant

Canvak is an easy-to-apply canvas preservative. Its properties prolong the life of older tipis. It contains mildew retardant as well as an excellent water repellent. One gallon covers approximately one hundred square feet. Canvak is not recommended for synthetic fabrics. This product is to be used after you clean the canvas or when treating material that has not had prior waterproofing treatment. After any treatment has been applied, make sure the tent dries completely before putting it into storage.

Scotchgard is a water-repellent aerosol spray that can be bought at most house and garden stores. This is a quick repair for leaks.

Here is a homemade waterproofing formula: Mix 3 cups soybean oil with 1 1/2 cups turpentine. Paint it on your tipi and let dry. Reapply after a year or two of hard use or outdoor exposure.

After cleaning with any product, you will need to re-waterproof your canvas. Re-waterproof on the same poles you use to set up. Make sure it is a warm or very warm day and the sun is out. Warm days help to heat up the chemicals in the waterproofing materials and make application easier to apply and penetrate the canvas surface. With a garden sprayer, put the chemical application on the cover from the outside. Work from the top to the bottom. Do not do this in your yard as it kills all the grass. Put it on a driveway or a vacant lot and treat it there. Avoid blacktop as it will stain your canvas.

With heavy use, it is a good idea to re-waterproof your tipi every couple of years. All chemicals will wash or wear off in time.

Security

How do you keep people out of your tipi? The Laubins described the idea of crossed sticks over the door (Laubins 1957, 91). In the historic pictures I have seen, sticker thorn bushes, animal hides, and large wooden boxes or crates are shown.

First-Aid Kit for Tipis

Always have a first-aid kit for yourself and one for your tipi. Having been in two tornados and two floods, and being the queen of all klutzes, I am prepared for all emergencies. You need a first-aid kit for doing emergency repairs on your tipi as well. Sometimes you are camped in areas or places where getting materials is impossible. You must rely on yourself to keep your tipi in good living condition. The kit will grow or decrease as your needs change. For quick access, put materials in a nice parfleche box or some type of container.

Here are some items you should keep on hand to repair your cover, liner, or door:

- Duct tape to quickly patch a hole
- Extra pieces of canvas for patching
- Elmer's Glue, which will attach canvas to canvas
- Quick-set glue
- Real sinew
- Awl
- Extra marbles
- Long pieces of leather
- A few steel nails
- Extra ties
- Extra rain pegs
- Extra lacing pins
- Glovers (canvas) needles for sewing canvas
- Sewing needles
- Thread of various thicknesses of cotton and fake sinew
- Swiss Army knife
- Scissors
- Matches and candles and clean wipes

What to Look for in a New or Used Tipi

With all the new and used tipis for sale, you need to know which tipi fits your needs. Before making that first big buy, ask yourself these questions:

- How many people will be using your tipi or will it just be you? Consider the kids, spouse or significant other, close friends, and the dog.
- Where do you intend to camp? Rendezvous, powwow, backyard, nearby state park, private land, show or demonstration?
- Do you plan on doing long-distance driving with your tipi? This will affect the size of the tipi/poles and equipment you can take.

- Do you anticipate pitching the tipi and leaving it up for long periods of time, such as three months or a few years, or do you intend to use it for just weekend campouts?
- What state or region do you live in? Climate in your area may affect your choice of material.
- Which season do you anticipate using it the most—fall, winter, spring, or summer? These all bring different problems with them depending on where you pitch the tipi.
- Where will you store all the materials, such as poles, the tipi itself, and support gear?
- How often will your tipi be used?

Material

Generally, most tipi makers today offer their tipis in 13-ounce Sunforger, which seems to be the industry standard, although a few good quality makers still use 10-ounce Sunforger. I would get the heavier material unless you think the overall weight could be a problem. The 10-ounce is adequate for the liner. Along with the new acrylic blends of material, some makers offer an 18-ounce and even a 20-ounce highly treated canvas for long-term setups. I wouldn't want a tipi made of these materials unless I intended to pitch my lodge for several months or more. I think it would be a mistake to go with one of the cheaper canvases, such as single-fill canvas, to save money. Use the best quality canvas, even if that means a delay in purchasing the tent until more money can be saved.

Construction

Each tipi maker has their own areas of reinforcement for certain wear and stress areas of the cover. These areas can include the tie point, door, gore, smoke flaps, and smoke-flap pockets. Problems can occur later if the following areas are not properly sewn:

- Some type of binding or overlay material, flat cording, or biased seam binding of 1 inch x 12 inches, covering both sides of the tie point. It should cover over the top of the gore to help protect it from the abrasions of constant movement or wrapping around the poles.
- Smoke-flap pockets need to be at least two thicknesses of canvas. This will help prevent the smoke pole from pushing through. Heavily sewn pockets will reinforce the seam from the constant pushing of the pole.
- The corner of the smoke flap where the pocket is attached should have another piece of canvas sewn in and should be over-stitched a few times to take the stress of the smoke pole. Many tears happen where the pocket attaches to the flap.
- Door openings get the most use so they should have a biased seam binding or other type of cording sewn all around or turned several times to make a smooth, thick seam. Leather can be used for this purpose, but it doesn't last as

long with constant sun and/or moisture exposure, which leads to either cracking or not drying out, which creates mildew.

- Lacing-pin holes should be sewn so that they do not tear or spread out with use. Buttonhole styles are OK but they do not give a tight fit around the lacing pin. Some tipi makers who do not reinforce the holes use extra material inside the lacing-pin area or material that does not stretch.
- Any of the types of sewn seams will work on the cover and there appears to be no best seam for keeping out water or for durability. Straight stitch or zigzag—they all work in the give-and-take movement of the cover or liner using canvas. Since it is a one-thread stitch, the only stitch not recommended on a tipi is a "chain stitch," as it will come out if pulled. All other stitches are interlocking with a top and bottom thread.

Repairs and Warranties

In choosing a tipi maker, look for the quality of the workmanship and ask others what they like or dislike about their lodge. Ask what tore out first and how it was repaired. Some companies will fix their lodges for free while others charge a fee. This does depend on how, where, and what was damaged on the lodge. A warranty will not cover a burn hole in your cover from a lit cigarette thrown from another car into the back of your open trailer. But the damage can be repaired for a cost.

Size

Sizes of tipis also are different with each tipi maker. For an 18-foot tipi, measurements can vary by as much as 1 to 2 feet smaller or larger. When ordering a tipi ask what the finished measurement of the cover will be from the bottom back to front when pitched. It does not matter the distance from the bottom front to smoke flaps or bottom back up to the lift-pole area. Side to side should be within a foot or two of the back to front dimension. How much head room will be determined by the length of the lift and steepness of the front. If your tipi is tall, you will have good head room; if it is short, you will have less but more storage for the sides.

Used Tipis

Finding a good used tipi poses different problems than does buying a brand new one. Here are a few things to look at and question if you are considering a second-hand tipi:

- Who was the maker? It is easier to contact a company for repairs and additions than an individual who made it for his or her own personal use. But sometimes those made for personal use were done with lots of loving care, so it's a toss-up.
- How old is the canvas and how has it been stored? Dry rot can cause canvas to fall apart, so pull on it and see how it holds up. Some canvas can last thirty years if properly stored.

- What has been done to the canvas? Does it need re-waterproofing? When was the last time this procedure was done?
- Ask about usage. Where did most of the camping take place?
- Unfold the cover, liner, and door. Is there any damage, such as mildew, tears, or dirt?
- Are all ties or marbles in place? If not, can the tipi be repaired? If there are several tears around the bottom, then it is starting to rot and it will keep on tearing.
- Are lacing-pin holes intact?
- Is the door bottom intact? Has it been fixed by some reinforcement?
- Are smoke-flap pockets intact? Are there signs of popping through?
- Is the tie point or lift tab attached securely to the cover? Is the cording or rope for the lift pole in good shape or can it be replaced?
- Does the door fit the opening area and are all ties and wood in place? Is the lacing-pin area of the door torn or worn through?
- Is the liner a rope or pole setup?
- Does the liner have all ties at the top and bottom and are they long enough to tie to the rope or fit around a pole?
- Is the bottom of the liner rotting out from mildew or extreme use?
- Does the liner fit the cover? Some liners are too small or too big for the cover.
- Is the tipi decorated with paint or beadwork? Is the paint cracking? Has the cover been re-waterproofed after it was painted?
- Do you like the designs and does the overall style fit into your use? It is impossible to repaint a tipi or take paint off.
- Are the dangles and beadwork in good shape or repairable if you intend to keep them?
- Does the tipi have a door? Check on how it is placed on the cover for wear and tear. It may have to be replaced or re-waterproofed.
- Are the poles rotted or breaking apart? Stand one straight up and then shake it vigorously. Even though the poles may look good, some do not show damage until they are shaken.

A good used lodge will fit your needs and last longer than a week or two. Do not be afraid to ask questions before buying. Being an informed buyer will save you time and money.

NMLRA Western Rendezvous at Dubois, Wyoming, 1994.

Today's Tipi Encampments

There are many large tipi encampments held in the United States. They range from primitive to more modern camps. If you like dressing up to play the part of an old-time buckskinner or mountain man, then go to a rendezvous or Buffalo Days encampment. If you like to just camp, there are private encampments, powwows, or lodge owners at Disney World. Or there is your own backyard. Finally, you can get a group of people together, find a spot, and camp. Groups in every part of the United States sponsor some type of tipi camping. Look on the Internet for information or ask a company that makes tipis about

Interested cow in John Neidenthal's 14-foot tipi at the Buffalo Days Camp, 1980,
Charlie Knight Ranch.

encampments. You may want to try out a few different types of encampments
to see what you like.

Rendezvous

The National Muzzle Loading Rifles Association (NMLRA) and, later, the National
Association of Primitive Riflemen (NAPR) started the early 1960s/1970s events
that became very popular for the historically inclined tipi owner. These organizations combined their events in the late '70s and early '80s until the NAPR went
under. Today the NMLRA has formed a new group called the National
Rendezvous and Living History Foundation (NRLHF) to support primitive camping and muzzle loading. They sponsor regional encampments all over the United
States, such as the Eastern, Northeastern, Southeastern, Midwestern, and
Southwestern Rendezvous. Each of these events has its own style or regulations
for tipis, white tents, and tarps.

Blackfoot tipis at Fort Benton Fur Trade Symposium.

In the late 1970s, near Tampa, Florida, the Alafia Rendezvous was started by a group of people who wanted to camp in their tipis and have a good time shooting and cooking in the style of the nineteenth century. Today it is the largest encampment in the Southeast. It meets the third weekend in January. It has expanded in the last twenty-five years from the original two tipis to over one hundred tipis and twelve hundred other period camps and tents.

Other large rendezvous are the Rocky Mountain Nationals, the High Plains Regional, Pacific Primitive, White Oak Society, 1838 Rendezvous Association, and many others too numerous to list here. It is now possible to search for a rendezvous camp near you on the Internet. Some people travel every weekend during the spring and summer to these rendezvous, either staying a weekend or for the whole week. Rendezvous wind down during the winter and then start back up in the early spring. If you don't like going to big events, there are always the smaller ones. Always check rendezvous rules before going to an event. Many rendezvous are very strict on their camping guidelines. Some regulations specify what clothing, tents, and materials you can bring into camp while others just ask that you be discreet.

Buffalo Days Camps

Buffalo Days camps are not rendezvous. Rules are strictly enforced. Tipi encampments follow the old Native American traditional ways of the 1870s. In order to attend this event, a committee must jury/judge your equipment and then an invitation is given. They are usually held in the month of July and in a western state. The camp goes on for approximately a week and a half to two weeks. At Buffalo Days, horses are provided for a rental fee or you can bring your own. However, you and the horse must be in traditional attire. Sometimes there is even a buffalo hunt, along with raids on the cavalry and nearby settlements. Each group tries to be as authentic as possible. There is a welcoming group dinner and all participants come dressed in their best finery. These type of camps are held out West, where there is room to roam and room for the mock battles and trail rides.

Ken Weldner, Curtis Carter, and Armin in Buffalo Days tipi.

Curtis Carter Buffalo Days–style lodge.

Powwows

The basic powwows, as we know them, have been going on since the early twentieth century. Crow Fair in Montana is said to be the largest tipi encampment in the world. It is held in August along with the annual Crow Fair Rodeo. This event lasts for a week, with dance contests, a horse parade every day with participants in all their finery going through camp, and over a thousand lodges. With all the families getting together for cooking, talking, and dressing for the dance, this is definitely a spectacular eyeful. If you wish to go to this, make sure you call ahead and make arrangements. It is possible to camp there with your tipi or get a hotel room in nearby Hardin, Montana.

Spring Valley Lodge, owned and decorated by Stephen Jarrard, Orlando, Florida, powwow, 1998.

In many other powwows, today you will see tipi camps in which whole families may participate. In Oklahoma, Montana, the Dakotas, Wyoming, and other western states, people come together for the major family dances. At the larger contest dances, the emphasis is not on tipis but on dance. There used to be contests for tipis at powwows in which ribbons and prize money were awarded. Tipi contests have declined over the past thirty years. This may be due in part to the rising cost of gasoline and many people's switching to smaller, more economical cars. There are still a few small dances and the National Powwow is held every three years.

If you go to a dance, be prepared for the tourists, who might come into your lodge whether you are there or not. Tourists think the tipis are there for their enjoyment and do not realize that these are the lodgings of people who are participating in the dance. You might have to rope off your lodge, like I have many times, to keep uninvited guests from the inside of your tipi and to keep people from touching the outside of your tipi. You will be asked a myriad of questions, so, if you are so inclined, you can explain what a tipi is, how it is set up, and even give tours inside. Most of us are very proud of our lodges and do not mind showing people around. But there are horror stories of tourists just popping into a tipi when the

Above: Roy Martin's
tipi at National
Powwow.

Dance
powwow.

Interior of John
Neidenthal's lodge.
Tipi made by
Linda Holley.

people were sleeping or of tourists sitting on the portable potty. Check out a dance before you go, making sure that there is room for your tipi, if there are facilities or bathrooms, and what kind of security there is for your camp. Many dances do not have an available area for tipis or even one for camping in general, so you have to get a motel room.

Modern Day Camps and Disney World

You do not have to get dressed up for dancing or shooting to go camping. Some people have a few acres set aside and invite friends over to camp in their lodges or bring a tent. It's just good, old fun camping, cooking, and enjoying your family and friends. General campouts are held all over the United States at special times of the year like New Year's, Easter, or Thanksgiving, or for just friend or family reunions. I have held campouts at state parks, on a friend's sixty acres, and in my own small backyard.

Disney World Lodge Owners Camp in Orlando, Florida, 2004.

Thanksgiving Lodge Owners Rendezvous was started originally by John Niedenthal of South Florida. This rendezvous has been going on since 1971 for family and friends. This is the time when all types of tipi owners gather for one large encampment. The only requirement is that you have a tipi and are registered in advance because of the limited number of tipis that can attend. But you must preregister to attend. This event started out in a place called Fish Eating Creek in central Florida. Some years later it was moved to the Walt Disney World Fort Wilderness Campground complex after they opened up a primitive camping area. Now hosted by the Butler family, anyone with a tipi can share in the largest sit-down Thanksgiving family event in the Southeast. On one occasion over two hundred people sat down to twenty-five turkeys (which we cook on the site). Who knows how many pumpkin pies, dressing, baked potatoes, and desserts were cooked and eaten. This encampment lasts for an entire week and gives you the run of the Disney World camping facilities with access to the Disney World entertainment area. There are men's and women's restrooms, with showers right next to the camping area. And if you don't want to stay in camp, you can leave the Disney World complex to enjoy anything in the Orlando area. The only real planned event is the Thanksgiving day turkey dinner, which leaves you time to do anything you want for the week or days you are encamped.

Of all the events that have been listed in this chapter, probably the best one is just setting up your tipi in your backyard, building a nice fire, and looking up from your own smoke flaps and enjoying the starry sky. Invite the neighbors over for a visit. They probably have already seen the poles going up and are very curious about what you're doing. Dig a fire pit and have a barbecue or cookout in front of the tipi and enjoy the view and the company.

Tipi Competitions

When you get a number of tipis together, every so often someone wants to see who has the best tipi. But how do you judge the different styles, tribes, time periods, and groups? This is not easy even for the most knowledgeable and experienced tipi people. What you are going to look for, in most cases, is "what is the lodge owner trying to portray?" Then see if he or she has completed that task inside and out. No matter the group, there are some general guidelines that can be followed. But keep in mind that these are only guidelines, not rules. Guidelines can change and do so because of weather, ground conditions, what the committee wants, and the majority of the tipi styles present.

The next thing you need to do for a competition is pick your judges. It can be anyone from experienced tipi owners to the beginner. A checklist with ground rules is an essential item to give the judges. The checklists are located later in this chapter. Judging is a tough job. It can take most of the day if there are a lot of tipis and it is done in a thorough manner. Plan for transportation for your judges if the tipis are scattered over a large area. I've seen everything from cars to golf carts used. Of all the competitions at a powwow or rendezvous, this is the toughest task because the competitors cannot come to the judges—the judges have to go to them.

How do you judge a tipi? Some committees ask for a popular vote from the visitors and registered campers in the tipis or tents. This popular vote doesn't always pick the best tipi, however. Sometimes it just rewards the tipi owner who has the most friends or family. Visitors have a tendency to pick the most colorful but not necessarily the most accurate camp. If going this route, the following guidelines can be used:

- All registered contestants will serve as peer judges and will be asked to judge and rank each tipi in the contest, including their own.
- All tipi owners who wish to participate in the contest must be registered with the tipi camp coordinator/head judge. Each contestant will be given a registration number on a piece of cardboard. Registration numbers must be prominently placed above the tipi door the morning of the contest. Formal judging must be completed no later than noon on the given day and the rankings turned into the tipi camp coordinator/head judge.
- The tipi camp coordinator/head judge is not eligible to participate in the tipi contest.
- Tipis will be ranked on an individual sheet, then tabulated, and the top tipis will be recognized by an announcement and/or ribbons at the event activities or camp meeting.
- A suggested guide for judging the tipi will be distributed at the time of registration.
- At the start of any tipi judging, doors should be open. If doors are decorated, they may also be swung or laid to the side for viewing.
- Judges can ask questions of the tipis owners. Some questions can be about the purpose of materials in the lodge, time period portrayed, type of tipi, and so on. The judge can determine if the tipi owners understand what they are trying to portray.

Basically there are three major areas of tipi competition: Contemporary, Contemporary Traditional, and Traditional. Even if you are a Boy Scout, Buckskinner/Rendezvous, Mother Earther, Powwower, or everyday camper, you can fit into one or more of these areas. Guidelines can be adjusted to fit the time period (depending upon tribe and location) or camp.

Contemporary tipis are modern inside and out. Any tipi that doesn't quite fit into the other two categories can fit into this category. Modern accoutrements such as chairs, table, ice boxes, modern lamps, bed, and so on can be displayed. The tipis are set up to live in for the weekend or the week. They are not set up to show traditional materials. Safety, livability, and neatness are the primary concerns. Everything is fitted, including the rain covers, liner, and doors. The cover and liner can be plain or ornately painted.

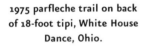

1975 parfleche trail on back
of 18-foot tipi, White House
Dance, Ohio.

Reese Tipi made tipis for *Dream
Keepers* and the TNT miniseries
Into the West.

Contemporary traditional tipis from the late 1940s to the present. Any tipi cover that does not go all the way to the ground and has a fitted liner is in this category. The liner itself is made of rectangular or trapezoidal panels carefully sewn together to match the angles of the poles. For a tailored, streamline look, a fitted liner ties on the poles/rope at the top and then to a rope/pegs or pole at the ground level. The liner has a specific underturn, or sod cloth, of about 10 to 20 inches depending on the maker. There may also be a rain cover inside. Interiors can have one to six backrests, built-up beds, robes, rawhide parfleche of folded envelopes and large boxes, hanging articles, toys, and anything else beaded or made. Outside can have a set of backrests, cooking utensils, toys, horse gear, and so on, and a covered area for shade for a complete look. This is the show tipi that most people think is the way a tipi looked in the nineteenth century, but which we now know is not true. It is the romanticized version of the tipi.

Traditional tipis represent the era from around 1840 to about 1920. They can be from any tribe or area where hide or cloth tipis were built. A cloth tipi was considered a status symbol because of the cost, lightness of material, and increase in size of the lodge. This is the time of the American Indian and his travels through the Great Plains into the reservation period. The primary purpose was to live in the tipi, not to show it off at a Wild West show or trade fair. But when on display, the tipi was shown to its finest.

There are about six or so main time periods of tipis seen in competition. Tipis are assigned to three categories for judging. Time periods listed here are approximate.

Traditional Period (1800–1860)—before the main contact of Europeans to the fur-trading times of the West. The tipis can be brain-tanned hides to canvas.

Reservation Period (1860–1890)—tribes are moved on to reservations. There are very few buffalo tipis; most covers are made of domestic cowhide, canvas, or other cloth materials.

Wild West Show Period (1880–1920)—tipis designed to show off the tipis and the Native American culture to the world.

Transitional Period (1930–1960)—Time of very few tipis, but the tipi was at the beginning of a revival. They were mostly seen at powwows.

Contemporary or Modern Period (1960?–present)—New traditional tipis and camps show interpretations of the past.

New-Traditional Period (1980–present)—going back to the old ways of the 1800s in building, setting up, and camping in a tipi.

Tipi Competition: Suggested Criteria or Guidelines

Tipi owners do not need to have the items listed in each category. These are only some of the suggested items they might have in their lodges. This is to jog the judge's memory or add to it.

Registration Number: _____

Each area is scored on a 0–25 point system. More than one point can be given if any special areas or materials are displayed.

I. Contemporary Guidelines

All tipis that do not fit into the other areas can go into this one. Any modern materials, such as chairs, tables, ice boxes, modern lamps, and beds can be used in the tipi. The tipi is set up to live in for the weekend or the week, not to show traditional materials. Safety, livability, and neatness are the primary concerns.

Tipi Setup:

_____1. Orderliness of rack three pole/four pole. Poles wrapped four times, with rope going down to a peg behind the fireplace for safety.

_____2. Tightness of cover wrinkles and evenness to ground. Usually above ground about 3 to 6 inches or more. Can see liner underneath cover from the outside.

_____3. Position of smoke flaps. Are smoke-flap poles uniform in back?

_____4. Pegs pounded in at angle or straight. Can be carved, painted, or decorated in some manner.

_____5. Lacing pins are neat and orderly. Can be decorated (painted, quilled, or beaded).

_____6. Streamers or some type of decorations on top of poles.

_____7. Inside is neat and clean.

_____8. Lining is up and neatly positioned.

_____9. Outside area is neat and clean.

_____10. Shade canopies are neatly maintained. There is no trash in area.

_____11. If there is one, fireplace is neat and ready to start.

_____12. Tipi is set up for weather conditions (closed up for rain, sides up for heat, and so on).

_____13. Smoke flaps are set for wind directions.

_____14. Door is rolled up and out of the way for easy entrance.

_____15. Bottom pins are pulled from door area for easy entry and exit as per weather conditions.

_____16. Overall, tipi is neat and clean.

Special instructions for the head judge(s) or notes to convey, if any:

_____

_____

_____

Total points_____

Registration Number: _____

Each area is scored on a 0–25 point system. More than one point can be given if any special areas or materials are displayed.

II. Contemporary Traditional Guidelines

Tipi Setup:

_____ 1. Orderliness of rack three pole/four pole. Poles wrapped four times, with rope going down to a peg behind the fireplace for safety.

_____ 2. Tightness of cover wrinkles and evenness to ground. Usually above ground about 3 to 6 inches or more. Can see liner underneath cover from the outside.

_____ 3. Position of smoke flaps. Are smoke-flap poles uniform in back?

_____ 4. Pegs pounded in at angle or straight. Can be carved, painted, or decorated in some manner.

_____ 5. Lacing pins are neat and orderly. Can be decorated (painted, quilled, or beaded).

_____ 6. Fitted lining of some type (plain, beaded, or painted).

_____ 7. Front door pole(s) out front for smoke flaps.

_____ 8. Streamers or some type of "flags" on poles (cloth, hair locks, feathers, and colorful yarns).

_____ 9. Door painted, beaded, or made of rawhide or other material.

_____ 10. Two to three sets of backrests with buffalo robes and blankets.

_____ 11. Optional tripod for men's items or medicine bundles.

_____ 12. Rawhide parfleche, boxes, and small/big trunks.

_____ 13. Decorated items hanging inside the tipi and/or around the outside for display.

_____ 14. Fire pit to fit the size of the tipi, with rocks around the perimeter.

_____ 15. Optional altar behind the fire pit or close to the lining area, either on the ground or hanging from the poles.

_____ 16. Overall, tipi is neat and clean.

Special instructions for the head judge(s) or notes to convey, if any:

_____

_____

_____

Total points _____

Registration Number: _____
Each area is scored on a 0–25 point system. More than one point can be given if any special areas or materials are displayed.

III. Traditional Guidelines
Tipis fit into the area of 1840 to 1880 and can be from any tribe or area where cloth tipis were built. This a time before the Wild West shows and big tribal fairs and lodges were on display. Primary purpose is to live in.

Tipi Setup:

_____1. Orderliness of rack three pole/four pole. Optional use of tie rope.

_____2. Cover is down to ground all the way around. If not, wood, sticks, and wood boxes can cover the areas to prevent airflow.

_____3. Set for weather. If hot, sides are up; if cold, cover is down to the ground.

_____4. No fitted liner of any type. Rectangular muslin (beaded), calico cloth, robes, blankets, shawls, and leather liners are attached at the top by rope or pole (not attached at bottom in any way except by articles placed on top of bottom underturn). Liner can be optional.

_____5. Use of smoke-flap poles optional.

_____6. No door poles out front. Smoke flaps can be tied to pegs that hold the cover down or not at all.

_____7. There can be some cloth, undecorated or lightly decorated, and streamers on poles. There can be use of feathers or hair locks.

_____8. Pegs for holding down cover are pounded in at an angle.

_____9. Door can be blankets, rawhide, beaded panels, fur hides, or framed cloth over wood sticks bent.

_____10. One or two sets of backrests with buffalo hides/blankets for beds.

_____11. Built-up beds that are off the ground with backrest for head and foot.

_____12. Clothing and most material in rawhide parfleches are pushed around inside the bottom of the tipi either holding lining in place or not. Some items can be hanging inside or displayed in lodge. Not overly done.

_____13. Cooking herbs hang from poles to the left as you go inside.

_____14. Outside cooking area can be a covered brush arbor or with blankets.

_____15. Tripods, horse gear, and traveling items can be stored outside along with children's toys.

_____16. Inside/outside can be a mess or in some disarray. No skulls unless this is a society or medicine lodge. Then it needs to be set up in this manner with all decorations and materials.

Special instructions for the head judge(s) or notes to convey, if any:

_____

Total points_____

Supplemental Tipi Contest Sheet (when not using the previous guidelines)

Tipi owners do not have to have the items listed in each category. These are only some of the suggested items they might have in their lodges. This is to jog the judges' memory or add to it.

Registration Number: _____
Name of Owner:_____
Style of Tipi/Camp:_____
Each area is scored on a 0–10 point system.

I. Tipi Setup (most important of the 4 categories)

_____1. Orderliness of rack three pole/four pole.
_____2. Tightness of cover wrinkles and evenness of ground.
_____3. Position of smoke flaps and smoke-flap poles.
_____4. Pegs.
_____5. Lacing pins.
_____6. Lining of some type can be up or down for summer or anytime.
_____7. Optional: front door pole(s) for smoke flaps.
Points_____

Sections II-IV are optional. If they display any of the materials, then they should be given points. If none of these items are shown, then no points should be given. These areas should be judged based on tribe, guild, society, time period, and group portrayed.

II. Outside Decoration of Tipi

_____1. Pole tips—streamers, dangles, hair locks, and so on.
_____2. Other decorations (beaded, painted, or plain). Does decoration fit tribal style/time period?
_____3. Peg and lacing-pin decorations.
_____ 4. Door decorations (painted, beaded, plain, blanket, fur).
Points_____

III. Outside Encampment Area of Tipi

_____1. Medicine bundles or tripods, weapons tripods, or holders.
_____2. Horse gear.
_____3. General outside living look—fire pit for cooking, cooking gear, robes or blankets on ground, shade canopies.
Points_____

IV. Interior Decorations

_____1. Backrests (carved or painted tripods), robes, blankets, beds and pillows.
_____2. Rawhide parfleche, boxes, small trunks.
_____3. Fire holes (these can be just rocks around grass or cedar shavings/sage).
_____4. Altars are individual preference.
_____5. Beaded articles, bags, clothing, blanket strips, and so on.
_____6. Linings—painted or decorated—pole or rope lining.
_____7. Women's tools, men's weapons (these could be outside for use).
_____8. Children's toys, baby carriers, and so on.
_____9. Overall impression? Neat or overdone?
Points_____ **Total Points**_____

Traditional 1800 to 1870s: What You Will Not Find in and around a Plains Tipi

The following is a list of some of the common mistakes people make when they are trying to set up a traditional tipi. If this is your intent, you might look over the list and make sure you are not committing the error of having any of these items. There are probably exceptions to every item, but don't make the exception the rule. The judges won't.

Traditional tipis should *not* have the following:

- Mandela and dream catchers. These were not part of a traditional tipi or camp. Fancy mandelas and dream catchers came out of the 1960s.
- Lawn chairs.
- Plank wood backrests.
- Modern cooking equipment.
- Leg-bone lacing pins. Lacing pins were wood and not much bigger than a #2 pencil in thickness or length.
- Very decorated pegs.
- Highly decorated streamers.
- Cow or buffalo skulls, or any skulls for that matter. The use of the buffalo skull is for the Sun Dance ceremony and not usually an everyday item in or around a tipi. Skulls are spiritual and generally not for the public view.
- Awnings attached to the front of a tipi. These are buckskinner items that came around in the last twenty years or so.
- Large rawhide boxes. The Sioux were basically the only ones who had the boxes, and these came out in the 1870s or so. Sizes were about 15 x 15 x 18 inches. There were other types of containers, but they are special rawhide items folded in the shape of a box.

- Large wrought-iron cook sets inside the tipi. Remember, you are cooking in your bedroom/living room unless it is winter and wood is scarce. You can have a small tripod for hanging pots.
- Lots of items hanging around the tipi. Unless being used, personal material should be put away.
- Medicine bundles should be put away in their containers or hung in a back area above your head. They can be hung on the top back of tipi, above the door, or on a tripod outside.
- Door pole out front.
- Fitted/tailored liner—depending on weather, a rectangular cloth tied at its top to poles or rope, around the tipi about 4 to 6 feet off the ground, or the tipi doesn't have to have a liner.

David Ansonia's Nomadics tipis in Switzerland.

Tipis Outside
the United States

Ever since the *Leatherstocking Tales* by James Fennimore Cooper in 1832, the romance and lore of the noble Indian and his way of life have enchanted the entire world. Books from this time period have enticed others to emulate the dress and living structures of the Indians. Many Europeans made their way to the Great Plains of the United States to see for themselves the animals, mountains, and Native Americans. When they returned home, they also brought back with them part of the material culture of the groups they visited, such as shirts, dresses, weapons, bags, robes, and tipis. Some items went into private collections and others into the museums for all to see.

In the early twentieth century, Indian clubs started springing up for those interested in Indian culture. This may have been because of the influence of the touring Wild West shows of Buffalo Bill, 101 Ranch, and Pawnee Bill. With the making of the Indian clothing came the desire to live or camp as the Indians once lived. Of all the many types of Indian dwellings, tipis were the structures that the clubs chose to build. The Germans and Czechoslovakians formed some of the first clubs. Then the clubs seemed to spread to the rest of Europe. Currently almost every country in the world has some type of Indian club, Powwow organization, American-Western camping, rendezvous, Indian reenactment, or tipi maker.

England and Scotland have several clubs that sponsor dances and encampments. Several tipis are always displayed at Glastonbury Festival, a large music festival. Many tipi makers advertise on the Internet with information on their different style and types.

People are transporting their tipis to other countries to participate in Indian and buckskinner camps. But you still need a large area of land for big camps, so the larger countries, like Germany, France, Poland, Czechoslovakia, and Hungary, host the big events. Russia also has a large number of Indian enthusiasts and could possibly host an event in the future.

Chakra Tipis from the Netherlands. TipiVerhuur cover is lifted into place by the smoke flaps.

Special tourist villages made for the tipi camper have sprung up all over Europe. The fascination with the American West and the spirituality of Native Americans have people going to these tipi camps to find themselves or to have a good time. Most of the tipis are highly decorated with bright paints and spiritual designs on their covers. You can stay for a few days to a week and get the Indian experience. There are also frontier villages that look like Old West towns of the mid- to late 1870s, with tipis scattered around for additional authentic character.

France and Germany hold large rendezvous or Indian camps with several hundred tipis. Different nationalities come to these events, sharing their knowledge,

Piers Conway's tipi winter setup in France.

showing off their clothing and skills, and camping in the old ways. Looking at the many Web sites and photos will give you a view of the details participants pay attention to for the sake of authenticity. The Hudson Bay Indian Trading Post sells the raw materials for reproduction work to Europe and sometimes the United States. It is also possible to buy exquisitely made beaded and quilled items crafted by highly skilled craftsmen from Germany and Czechoslovakia. Some of these works can pass for original material made with the same materials and techniques used by Native Americans of the eighteenth and nineteenth centuries.

The Czech Republic and Slovakia have some of the oldest and continuous Indian groups in Europe. Based on Seton's Woodcraft from 1902, Czech Woodcraft had their first tipi camps in 1913. Interrupted by World War II, the groups or tribes renewed their interests afterwards. When the communists took over in 1948, they strongly curtailed all activity in 1951. The Woodcraft League was forced to "voluntarily disband." It did not stop the idea and its dedicated followers. During the forty years of communist rule, Woodcraft and Scouting survived by going underground and hiding under various officially condoned organizations. After the Velvet Revolution, they were free to organize again. Woodcraft League grew to more than seven hundred members by 1998, and many who practiced woodcraft skills in various organizations flocked back to Scouting. Other than the Woodcraft groups, there are also independent enthusiasts enacting Indian camps. One of these is the Indian Corral, which has a large following on the Internet and in reenacting.

Above: Czech tipi interior.

Right: Czech Indian encampment.

Left: Czech interior of Wataglapi, 2004.

Bulgarian tipi encampment.

Lyubomir Kyumyurdjiev (or White Horse) is the founder and chairman of the Bulgarian Indian Eagle Circle Society, along with Ivailo Grozdev. They describe summer gatherings in the Bulgarian mountains with the wonderful background of secluded mountains, tipis in snow, and beautiful valley views. The seclusion is one thing I have noticed in correspondence with many groups; they like to be away from the crowd and do not let their presence be known to uninitiated people around them. Intrusions from the outside world into their camps are not welcome. This is true of most camps I have been to, even in the United States. But tipi enthusiasts are always pleased to share information with other knowing people, no matter what country they might be from.

Eagle Circle participants often dress like Native Americans, eat traditional food, make jewelry, build large tipis, and hold powwows for twenty days in the mountains in order to remember historical events and get in touch with the spirit of the Native American people across the ocean. They're very knowledgeable about the different Native American groups, though they admit that their initial interest was in the romanticized version they learned as children. Over the years, through the Internet and the exchange of information between Bulgaria and America, as well as with other Native American studies groups throughout Europe, they have learned more about the culture and history of Native Americans, and now they know a more accurate "truth."

Hungary has Indian clubs, similar to the Czech groups, that have been going on for at least forty-two years. Indian club member Krisztina Szabo describes the tipi encampments with great love. Her husband and son, Csaba, are very involved. She describes an encampment as follows:

Our camp always is in summer in July for two weeks. During this time, we live in tipis, we wear only Indian clothes this time, and we don't use technology, and we try to follow Indian traditions. We have got Lakota, Oglala, Blackfoot Blood, Siksika, Pawnee, River Crow, Mountain Crow, Wild Crow, Hidatsa, Hunkpapa, and Cheyenne tribes but we have got nine camps. And we go on the warpath against each other day and night, anytime at all. In two weeks, every tribe can fight every other tribe. This is always very exciting because another tribe can fight our tribe at two o'clock a.m. or 4 o'clock p.m. We don't know when will come somebody or when will come to steal horses. And the battles are always to be very exciting, too. I really enjoy them.

**Above left: Interior of Hungarian tipi. Above right: Hungarian spring.
Below: Hungarian winter encampment.**

Above: Russian tipi camp, 2003.

Left: Dmitriy and wife from the
Russian Indian Club.

Dmitriy from Russia has been engaged with the art and culture of the Lakota
and Cheyenne for many years during the long suppression by the Soviet Union.
All people interested in Indian culture during the communist regime had to do it
with some difficulty. They collected materials, little by little, in libraries and
schools and then practiced in the forest. His group is probably one of the oldest in
Russia. Dmitriy talks about a Russian gathering as follows:

> We tried to not be limited to the books, but to make something in prac-
> tice, to receive real experience. Our tipi, our old tipi—was one of the very
> first, which was made in Russia. My older brothers made it in 1975–79.
> We lived in it. It became simply sacred for us. We smoked in it pipes and
> were prayed many times. New tipi we have sewed recently because our
> club and our families have grown; it was necessary to move. Children
> require the special care, as well as our parents, which sometimes also will
> carry out with us time in tipi.

Many Italians are fascinated by Indians and tipis. Several people have bought property and set up their structures. Some have even learned English so they can read the Laubins' book on tipis to construct their first lodges. Conversion of feet and inches into metric units was the first hurdle; getting the sewing machines, fabric, and then an area to work were the next steps. Giorgio Strazzari thinks he was probably the first tipi owner in Italy. Other tipis followed according to the demands from his friends. His tipi survived a rare wind and hailstorm, which destroyed all the vineyards on the outskirts of his town:

> The zone was then declared subject to natural calamity. The following year, we moved to another land near to the Swiss border. We mounted a tipi of 6 meters of diameter, painting suit, furnishing and of all the comfort. In particular, we spread on the bottom a gravel layer, one of ferns, and finally one of soft and perfumed pine needles. We still remember with immense delight the beautiful evenings passed observing stars and the moon, wrapped in our sleeping bags and in the resin scent.

He then describes how his family felt staying in a tipi:

> Since the first lights of the dawn, we felt the songs of all the birds of the surrounding forest. After a pair of months of permanence in the tipis, we realized to be in complete harmony with the natural rhythms, we woke up without efforts at the sunrise and with the darkness of the night it arrived also a healthy sleep. All this did not lack to astonish various friends coming from from the city that did not succeed to explain this change and behaviour. The friends were not the only ones to visit our tipis; it was also attractive for small mices, cats, and fox during in their nocturnal wanderings.

Neta and Larry Schwartz tipi located in the Mt. Carmel mountain range, Israel, within the Roman quarry.

Japanese tipi.

From Israel, Neta and Larry Schwartz have their plain white 20-foot, 13-ounce Sunforger Nomadics set up year-round within a 2,000-year-old Roman quarry nested between the Carmel Mountain Range in the east and the Mediterranean Sea in the west. Their painted tipi is located under the large limestone rocks of the quarry that were used to build the aqueducts that brought fresh water to the Roman port of Caesarea when the Roman Empire was flourishing in that part of the world. The flowering cactus on the right in the photo on page 191 is called "the Queen of the Night" since the flower, the size of a large grapefruit, only opens at night and closes the next morning. They used bamboo poles since their original option of wood poles was difficult to find.

Australia and New Zealand have their share of Western participation with rendezvous and tipi camps. It seems that many of the tipi camps are for the New Agers or spiritual-seeking groups who want to have an "Indian experience." All over the world, the tipi is being associated with spirituality and ceremonies.

In Japan and Korea, the tipi has found a home. They are made from the Laubins' pattern out of canvas and synthetic materials. One tipi, found in Japan, was completely made from blue plastic tarps sewn together. There was even a type of hibachi fireplace inside, carefully supported a few inches above the floor. The floor was also blue plastic. The tipi appeared to be about 14 feet, or 4 meters or so, and the poles were bamboo. Another tipi, with a painted bear on the side, was made from what appeared to be a canvas material, just like tipis made in the United States. For those in "the hobby," Japan has its own tipi-making company and Indian trading posts for fur, leather, and beads.

Now the tipi has spread to South America and Africa, with the first tipi makers in those respective countries setting up shop. With the tipi being such a versatile camping medium for most types of weather, it is no wonder that it is seen around the world. Other types of tipi-style housing have been used by the nomads of Russia, Finland, Norway, and Canada. Some are made of bark, reeds, hides, or cloth. But the most romantic and widely used is the Native American cloth tipi.

Tipi made by Darry Wood from awning material, 1977, North Florida Indian Cultural Society powwow.

Modern Tipis

The tipi is an ever-evolving structure that continues to change in materials and use. With the new space-age synthetics, there is an ever-increasing interest in using these materials to prolong the life of the cover and liner against rot and mildew. Today, there are those who are trying to reinvent the tipi by making it more a permanent structure by using these synthetics. Military and civilian campers have been using red and blue striped awning material for tipi covers for a few hundred years. Sunbrella makes a synthetic or acrylic stripped material that can be made into a long-lasting and colorful cover. It also comes in solid colors. Since it is a synthetic, it does not rot, and it is mildew and UV resistant. It also does not breathe or let air pass through. Since plastics can melt in high heat, interior fires, if used, need to be watched carefully. Darry Wood was one of the first people to incorporate this new material into his tipi liners and covers. His lodges stand out at any powwow or camp, not only for the colorful covers but also for his craftsmanship.

Another experimental tipi was made by Brooke E. Demos, who took synthetic materials to a new level. Her tipi is made from processed postconsumer plastic bags, which she wove on a 36-inch, 4-harness floor loom. The tipi poles are 12-foot closet rods painted blue to highlight the blue trim of the cover.

A couple of tipi manufacturers have sewn in clear vinyl or plastic material to replace panels or sections of the cover to make "windows" to lighten up the inside of the tipi. This does let in more light, but it also presents possible problems with the plastic deteriorating before the cloth, due to UV rays. Also, constant taking down and putting up may cause the vinyl to crack and break over time.

Rainbow Tipis of Australia is not standing still in tipi design. Using solid colors of Sunbrella materials, zippers, and window screening, they bring their product designs into the twenty-first century. Keeping the basic structure, they incorporate zippered awning sides, screened windows, and clear plastic interior rain covers. This may be the ultimate tipi camp where the sides of the tipi can be raised to form sun screens and built-in mesh is used to keep the bugs out.

Tripods have always been set up with ropes tied in different variations of

Rainbow Tipis from Australia showing the use of synthetic materials, pull-out awning from cover, and screened windows on the sides.

Made from postconsumer plastic shopping bags woven on a loom for cover.

knots with the goal of keeping the lodge up for long lengths of time. Unfortunately, over time and because of wood shrinkage or expansion, the tie rope loosens up and can slip, causing the structure to fail. Arrow Tipi of Canada has come up with what it calls a Widget. The Widget bolts together the three tripod poles into an interlocking group that will not slide or break. A tipi can stay up for a few years, depending on the poles and cover material, without coming down at the tie point.

Because the 20- to 30-foot poles are sometimes hard to transport, poles may be changing too. People are coming up with ways to cut the poles in half and then join them back together using sleeves made of plastic, metal, or carbon alloy-based materials. Because wood shrinks and expands with time and weather, the problem is keeping a tight fit where the poles join. Solving this would also prevent the other problem of water going down the pole, hitting the sleeve, and dripping into the living area below. And the cut/sleeved area still needs to maintain its strength in high winds. It has been suggested that the pole be cut in half and a double screw of wood or plastic be inserted and the two poles screwed back together. This also runs into the same problem with the contraction and expansion of wood.

Widgets for setting up the tripod by Arrow Tipi, Canada.

Synthetic poles made of carbon fibers, similar to pole-vaulting material, as well as poured plastic resins over a reinforcing center core have been investigated. Unfortunately, the cost is highly prohibitive for the everyday camper for just one pole. Disney World has some of these built into their exhibits and tourist attractions.

Innovative ways of setting up a tipi cover and poles come from Froit Yurts in the Netherlands. He said he learned this method from a traveling Sioux Indian. He set the poles up in a spiral sequence on the tripod. Each pole is wrapped in place one time before the next one is set up. This is repeated for each pole. Not using a lift pole at the tie point in the cover, but using the smoke-flap poles and placing them in the smoke-flap pockets, the lightweight cover is lifted into place by two people. The cover is then pulled around the poles, as in the traditional method, and laced in the front. Froit told me that they only set their tipis up in the good weather of summer.

In the early 1930s, Ben Hunt wrote an article, with drawings, on a tipi that

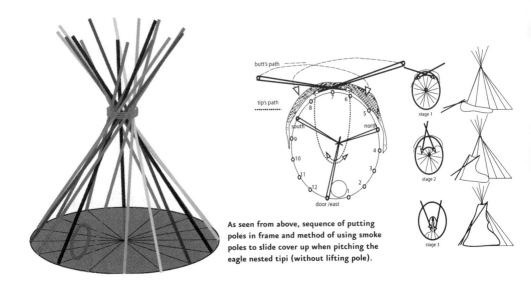

butt's path

tip's path

south   north

door /east

stage 1

stage 2

stage 3

As seen from above, sequence of putting poles in frame and method of using smoke poles to slide cover up when pitching the eagle nested tipi (without lifting pole).

Froit-Netherlands spiral-based tipi setup with smoke-flap poles.

only used three poles segmented or spliced together with a sleeve or double ferrules. The rest of the poles were replaced with ropes radiating from the tripod tie point to the ground. He called this his "three-pole tepee." Today, there are manufacturers recreating this style of tipi with one pole in the center and the ropes radiating from the center down to pegs in the ground. The cover and liner are made from lightweight or rip-stop nylon used in windsocks, jackets, and modern pop-up tents. The center pole is sleeved and a cross bar is bolted near the top to form the smoke-flap opening. This tipi is very transportable and a convenient way to enjoy tipi camping without all the poles and weighty canvas for setup.

The last major innovation I have seen comes from Fun Camp Co. of Canada. These tipis are an adaptation of the tipi design in a permanent stationary camp. A concrete platform is built inside the pole structure. The top area of poles do not use a tripod setup but an adjustable metal cap, where the main poles are bolted into the cap. The top poles of the lodge are wired and bolted to the top metal structure.

When the cover is fully extended and closed up, the metal top serves as an adjustable flue, controlled from a rope inside the lodge. This adjustable plate can be opened or closed to adjust the ventilation inside, just as smoke flaps in a traditional tipi are set for airflow.

These modern versions of a tipi also have built-in bug screens for the door. Inside are places for framed beds, a chair, and a central propane fire, if wanted.

With the new discoveries in plastics, synthetics, and UV-resistant materials, there is no stopping the imagination in adapting traditional designed tipis into more comfortable and longer-lasting lodges. But a choice may need to be made by

the tipi enthusiast as to how many of these new ideas you want to implement and what you want from tipi camping. You'll need to decide whether you're a primitive traditionalist tipi camper or a high-tech, I-want-all-my-conveniences tipi camper. You will have to make the choice on how you want to camp and in what manner. Some of these choices will depend on money, transportation, and why you chose a tipi.

Fun Camp Company of Canada. Poles fit into a top form and a concrete base pad.

Camp Stories

Darry Wood started living in a tipi with his family in the early 1970s. He lived in a tipi in rural Upstate New York for three winters, during a six-year period when the tipi was the only home his family had. He and his wife sold their suburban home and started out with a six-year-old child and a big dog. By the time they folded the tent and moved into a log house, where they now live, they had two children, a dog, and a cat.

By the time Darry decided on where their first winter's campsite would be, he and his wife had made themselves an 18-footer and moved from Tallahassee to the Catskill Mountains. They were just getting used to the significantly greater space when a Thanksgiving day snowstorm dropped a 2-foot blanket of snow on them. It was quite an eye-opener, as were the below-zero temperatures and icy winds that soon followed.

They were now using a 16-foot tipi for storing the extra gear and ever-accumulating possessions. Darry remembers sitting before a raging fire late at night while the north wind rattled the poles. The dog's water dish, frozen solid, served as one of the weights trying to seal out the draft coming in under the lining door. Darry remembers looking at his little brood, snuggled there beside him under deep piles of wool blankets, and thinking to himself, "You've got this all wrong, we should be storing our stuff in this 18-foot lodge, and living in the 16-footer." The smaller lodge was easier to heat.

Doug Rodgers relates these stories and advice about living in a tipi out in the woods:

> I have a friend who lived in his tipi for nearly two decades. The highly important thing to note is that this friend was single. He had no wife and no children whose needs he had to meet. He was/is a rugged outdoorsman type. I have another friend who lived in a tipi two years (near me, in Alabama) with a wife and four young children, two still in diapers. It was a tough experience. They had to haul water to the site. They took showers at a park a few miles away. They had some sort of privy in the woods not

far from the tipi. The wife was not the rugged outdoor type and it was hard on her. After a couple of years, they moved into a house. Despite some serious downsides to the experience, the whole family feels that it was one of the highlights of their lives—being outside, seeing wildlife, sitting by the fire at night, family togetherness, cooking outdoors, experiencing the moon and stars in a way that most people never do, and experiencing the changes in the seasons in an intimate way.

I've lived in a lodge. The only changes I'd make are to get a stove (wood burns slower and you can cook on it), extend stovepipe up through the poles/smoke hole. That way you're not flooded out. If you're going to stay in it for a few years, put in a wooden foundation on 2 x 6's on a solid base of rock or cement pillar and then floor over with 2 x 4's spaced about 1/4 inch apart. Then you can design so your lodge has a porch all around. You can get an old closet or bureau to hold your clothes under an outside shed; that way they don't get too smoky to wear to work. Just hit the laundromat once a week—then fill up the bottom of the closet with some pet bedding cedar chips, which are cheap at the store; smell of cedar keeps bugs at bay, too. Since you've got the shower figured by using a solar setup, no need to put in water system. Get rid of the apartment and you'll be able to afford a new lodge cover every couple years easily.

If you're not keen on peeling poles (who is?), plunge them into running water, a ditch, or creek. This seems to take away the sticky sap that holds the bark on so tight and they'll peel slicker than a carrot at a kitchen sink. For kitchen doings, put in a small table along one side with slide-out mouse- and bug-proof compartments. Couple coolers kept in 3-foot hole dug in between floor joists for constant-temperature root-cellar box; eggs and cheese keep well at 40 to 50 degrees; double wrap ice in grocery sack paper keeps for five days in cooler, so meat is good for week.

I use a style of cot for a bed. Get some old used carpet for floor covering in winter and keep out breezes and bugs and you're in business. I was out West so there was no problem with mildew in that dry climate. I keep a fire going to keep it fairly dried out. This is all the advice I can offer. Only downside thing is the darkness of a winter lodge. Winters are long, in the mountains. I sorely missed the luxury of having a window.

Hurricane Andrew in 1992 was a great test for living in a tipi. I had friends whose homes were completely destroyed. But they were able to salvage their tipi, liner, and few poles from the remains of their houses. They refused to live in those "green army" tents that were set up for shelters. With more poles brought in from other parts of Florida, they set up their tipi in the yard. They lived in this tipi while cleaning up what was left of their house and goods. Even in the extreme heat and rain, they chose the tipi because it was light and airy for the weather conditions. With the streamers waving above the debris that was once Homestead, Florida, we could find the tipi amongst the surrounding rubble.

From the Internet, **monkeytown99** related this story of living in his lodge:

My wife and I were drumming in our lodge and we were lost in the rhythm as can oftentimes happen. There was a rustling in the liner and something was trying to get in. It had obviously come in under the cover, which we usually keep a few inches off the ground. It moved along the wall poking and prodding. As the hypnotic effects of the drumming were wearing off, I got my wits about me and was going for a stick to beat this animal off with when it poked its head around the liner at the door opening —it was one of my dogs with a "what's all the fuss about" look on his face. I was relieved it was him, but disappointed at the same time—I was thrilled in thinking that an animal spirit was visiting our lodge . . . but nervous that it might be a bear or cougar!

The other time we had a visitor was when we weren't home. A feral domestic cat—we keep them around to put the run on skunks—had lunch, a bird, in our lodge and left the feathers and a turd as souvenirs of his adventure.

Monkeytown99 also made a point about privacy and noise in a tipi:

Another time we must have set [our tipi] up on a drain field because that night it rained and there floated my rubber ducky right beside my pillow.

Then you always have those moments where someone just can't stop snoring . . . pinching their nose doesn't help . . . you're desperately trying to get a good night's rest because next day there is dance competition and it's just not happening!

Then there was the story of the attack of the killer armadillo. Do you know that no one will help you out when you yell "Armadillo!"? We kept hearing someone yell "Armadillo!" but we thought it was just someone having a nightmare. Suddenly I heard someone yell "Fire!" and a couple of us ran into the tipi with water buckets. No fire, but one really angry, horny-plated animal that wanted out but could not find the door. It had come in from under the cover and liner but could not get back out the same way because of the underturn of the liner. It took four of us to herd it out.

Asher Rospigliosi talks of a strange critter at the Glastonbury Festival in England in 1997 when there was a heavy rain. He had to get out the spade and dig trenching around his lodge and a couple of others. A young Chinese woman who spoke no English took shelter in his lodge and stayed for three days. She was very self-contained; she slept curled up away from him and his three sons. One night, in a break from the rain, she entertained them by juggling fire clubs around the central fire; shortly after that she disappeared.

Leon Dunham was camping in his mother's pasture and after a late night of watching a movie, he came back to find this camp had been attacked by the natives. The door was torn off, a couple of stakes were pulled out of the ground, and lacing pins were missing or chewed up. From the mess inside, it was obvious at least one critter had been inside. Looking around outside with a flashlight, he found two horses standing by the barn, looking at him with a classic "what?" look. He also related: "Then there was [a time in] New Mexico where we got driven nuts by ants, but it was the big furry spider that made us spend the night in the bus instead of the tipi."

And then, in another trip to camp in their tipi for a few weeks:

On a two-week trip to Niobrara, Nebraska, we carried our tipi on our VW bus and set it up in the state park there for four days for a family reunion. It was a great hit. One of the things we noticed on this trip was many more tipis and tipi poles were being set up around the country. More than we've seen before (last major trip like this was three years ago—we are from Oregon). We did not get a close look at any of the other tipis. But my impression is that most of them were from one of the commercial manufacturers. We did not notice any that were obviously homemade or were of skins rather than canvas. Many of them were in private camp-ground/resort/lodge facilities, but an awful lot were just sitting behind somebody's house out on the range. Very nice to see . . .

We ended up sleeping in the tipi only one night of the four because of storms. One night was so bad we even drove away from our chosen camp-site to a protected place between the nearby hills. For long periods of time, lightning was so continuous you could read by it. The storm lasted four hours or so. In the morning when we went back to the tipi, [we] found it had been blown together and leaned up against the tree we had put it under.

Everything was soaked, but nothing [was] broken or torn. It appeared the rain had softened the ground enough that the wind pulled the stakes out and moved the poles together. It looked pretty funny. Had we been inside we think we would have been fine. We will be putting the stakes in better and such. We were able to squeeze inside it and simply walk the poles back out and restaked it and all was fine.

Our camp was set up on a small ledge overlooking the Niobrara River—quite exposed to the east, which is where the storm came from in the wee hours of the morning. It was quite educational—like, yes, put the stakes in good! Even if it is a beautiful day when you're setting up? And is this site really a good one? Hmmm, nice view, but . . .

One of the things we decided on was to have everyone who came to see our tipi sign the liner. I liked that a lot. Very nontraditional—but fun. On the last night, the older kids (third and fourth cousins at this point in this family) came to the tipi and had a late night together. A much nicer use than just us sleeping in it!

We did take some friendly ribbing from a couple of guys in South Dakota about the short poles we had on the bus. They definitely thought they should be 25 to 30 feet long. The poor old bus was overloaded as it was the summer of 2005.

Why People Never Camp with Me

People never camp with me because, well, let's see, I burned down my 12-foot tipi when I left a candle burning that I thought I had blown out. I went out to do my morning thing and about an hour later, I heard that horrible word, "Fire!" Being at a rendezvous I was thinking about the firing line for the muzzleloaders—not so. The smoke and flame was from my tipi, which was burning to the ground. Many of my good friends were trying to put it out. With canvas going down around me, I stupidly ran in to save my camera equipment, bedding, and clothes. It is nice to say I was OK and my personal gear was saved by my quick-thinking friends pulling the lacing pins out to get the cover down. My cover and liner were destroyed and my poles were scorched, as was my reputation.

Back in 1978, I was camped out at a powwow in White House, Ohio. Never again will I let someone tell me where to camp when I know the area is a "little" low. Well, it rained that night and now I have a 2-foot-high tide mark all around my liner. It took three days for the water to drain away and for me to take down the lodge. There is nothing like sleeping in a van full of wet buffalo robes and rawhide.

When the "First American Mobile Home" meets the "Modern American Mobile Home," there can be a clash. How about my tipi poles going through the back of one of those big travel homes that backed into my van and tipi racks? Boy, did it cost that guy some big bucks. He had to pay for half a new set of 28-foot poles, which were shortened to 20 and 14 feet. My poles went from his bedroom into the bathroom. It looked like a jousting tournament gone wrong with the splintered wood, glass, and metal. The travel home driver wanted me to pay for damages! The police said it was entirely his fault. I had lights and flags on the poles to conform to state laws. I was outside screaming my head off trying to get him to stop. He wasn't looking! Those were beautiful poles I had spent long hours and days sanding to a fine finish. You could run your hands down their entire length without a single splinter. Darn!

Then one time I set up all my poles, lining, and had the door. I had, however, forgotten the cover for my 14-foot lodge. I was kindly invited to move in with two gentlemen (thank you, Chip), who offered me half of their living area in a new 9 x 15-foot Marquee that I had just made for them. Now they were true Southern gentlemen. They even put up a curtain to divide the tent and give me privacy. For the rest of the week, and for years afterward, I have been teased by the camp.

At the NMLRA Midwestern, sometimes called the "Mud Western" after the period it was held on the Kickapoo River in Illinois, a tornado went through camp. Well, it got my small wedge tent that was set up outside my big 18-foot lodge and sent two tent poles through the side of my lodge, just missing the head of a friend, George Kuhn, who had bravely camped with me. I spent the next few hours, in the rain, trying to find equipment, supplies, and friends. As it turned out, other camps were destroyed or blown over; but no one was seriously hurt. When the sun finally came out, it looked like a disaster area. Broken wood, canvas, and clothing were all over the place. About 5 feet above the ground, my lodge had two large tears of about 25 and 36 inches long. I know because I measured them, as I needed to find the extra canvas to repair the damage and find something to stand on while making repairs.

This is when I found the value of having a tipi repair kit, with extra canvas, Elmer's Glue, and sewing needles. I was very upset fixing the tears and hoping that I would get it done before the next big storm hit. If the winds had gotten into the tears, it would have ripped my whole tipi apart as these rips got bigger going up the side. I must say I was very proud of myself because some years later that same tipi survived another tornado and the patchwork held together.

Well, a few years later I had that same tipi in Tampa, Florida, and our camp was hit by another tornado. This was the big Alafia Rendezvous and I had set up my 18-foot lodge with everything in it. I had buffalo robes, parfleches, beaded robes, bedding, backrests . . . everything. I had also set up a 9 x 15-foot Marquee tent for shade, storage, and cooking for the week. While I went back home, friends of mine were going to watch my camp until I came back in a few days.

When I returned a few days later to camp on a starry night, the camp looked unpopulated and abandoned. Coming over the bend and up the small hill that overlooked my tipi, I was horrified to see that I had no camp. All the other tipis and tents were there, but not mine, not even my Marquee tent. And where were my friends and all the people? I could see candles and campfires in the area . . . and then I saw my fire pit, with my rocks surrounding the pit . . . but no tipi. Out of the dark stepped a friend who said, "Guess what? You know the old fairy tales where once upon a time something happens . . . or as we say in the buckskinning way, 'This ain't no s—t?' Well, this tornado came down and took the tipis on the hill, some tents in the second camp, and then came down and sucked up your tipi and Marquee out of the middle of all these tipis." I stood there dumfounded and could only say, "OK . . . joke's over, now where did you guys hide my tipi?" which I said several times in complete disbelief. I really thought they had moved my camp just for a big laugh. But no, it was sucked up by a tornado. Now the other people in camp came out of the shadows to tell me the story about what had happened and how they had saved my equipment. Many people volunteered to help me put the tipi back up the next day.

Looking at my cover neatly rolled up and dried out, I decided to put the tipi back up that night. Some people let me borrow a few more poles to replace those that were broken. A few hours later all was back up, and I spent the rest of the night in my fluffy, warm bed. In the daylight, I was amazed that the cover was not more damaged. A few marble ties were torn at the bottom of the lining, which was ripped in a couple of places. Eight other tipis were not so lucky. They were torn to pieces by the wind and their poles were smashed. In my case, because the soil was sandier, the wind had just sucked the tipi up and moved it about 50 feet into another lodge where it slid down on its side. The tipi might have survived intact if my pegs had been longer to go into the soft soil or it might have been saved because it pulled out so easy. As for my Marquee tent, it was found in the lake and pulled out to dry. Thank goodness for friends at rendezvous and powwows; whether you know them or not, they all pull together in a disaster.

In another camp, I woke up one morning to find a cow halfway in my tipi door. Someone had left a gate open and the cows had come back to their pasture in which several tipis were now camped. Horns do not go well with canvas . . . canvas loses every time.

While I was at home, I found another use for tipi poles. A hot-air balloon crashed or slowly landed in my swimming pool. And do not believe that old story about getting to drink champagne and eat strawberries after they land. My tipi poles were used to help support the envelope from sinking farther into the deep end while we scurried to retrieve the basket part.

It is never a good idea to carry watermelons in the back of your car next to the windows, especially several days before pitching your tipi. As in my case, they have a tendency as they get hot to explode all over your blankets, cover, and you when you are trying to open up the side door. There is nothing like the smell of fermented melon all over you and your blankets, clothing, and tipi. And I didn't get to eat the melon after traveling all that way.

Make sure you take a long, heavy bat with you when using the outhouses in Florida. I was using the facilities around 2:00 a.m. when I tried to open the door to get out. It just would not budge as I kept banging on something outside. Then I started hearing a hissing and a low growl. I knew I was in trouble. Being that Florida is a very water-oriented state, I realized that on the other side of the door was one big, mean, angry alligator. They do not like being hit on the head or snout with anything. My only recourse was to stay in the rather smelly outhouse or yell for help. So, knowing that you get more of a response yelling "Fire!" rather than "Armadillo!" or "Alligator!" I yelled "Fire!" Were those guys ever surprised when they came running.

Questions

Questions about living in a tipi, and what you need to think about before taking the plunge.

Is it possible that living in a tipi is a cheaper way of living?
It is if you like camping. You will need an area for the human waste and garbage.

Where will your water and electricity come from?
If you have a power pole near you, it is possible to run an extension line to the lodge. Or use a car battery or other devices like generators to run lights and other appliances. Water can be brought in or you can set up a water station nearby for running water. You need water for sanitary purposes, drinking, and cooking daily. But most people just live in the tipi as a primitive lifestyle. Why not? One of the greatest pleasures of having a lodge is its lack of modern conveniences.

Do you use the fire pit in your tipi during the summer months? If so, how do you keep from getting too hot?

You can have a fire in the summer, but the heat can run you out. Cooking is done in an outdoor arbor or shaded area. The tipi sides are rolled up or opened up in the front. It is like spreading your wings to let the air pass through. At night, you might have a little smoky fire to keep the biting bugs at bay.

How do you keep cool in the summer?

Do not use a liner. The cover goes all the way to the ground except when rolled up during the day to catch the breeze. There are portable air conditioners that you can put in the lodge, but you need electricity to run them. If you have electricity, you can also use a portable fan.

Do you have a problem with rodents coming and living with you?

No matter where you camp, you are going to have some type of little critter who comes to visit you. The only way to help prevent this is to build your tipi up on platform with the cover going all the way to the ground. The lining must be sealed all the way around and to the door.

What do you use for bedding?

Anything you want or that can fit in a tipi. Some people use air mattresses and others use foam padding. The primitive groups just use sleep pallets of blankets and buffalo robes. Whatever you use, put it on some type of waterproof tarp. You do not want to wake up in a flooded, water-soaked bed.

What do a husband and wife or anyone do about the intimacy issue?

You can put curtains in but keep the sound down. Otherwise, how big is the car? Today we are far more modest. I have been in that situation . . . so it was under the buffalo robes and very quiet. It was fun, and exciting too, if you get my meaning.

Where do you store all of your clothing since there are no closets?

Usually in another tipi since I have two tipis. I have a smaller one for cooking and storage. For cooking and when the weather is bad, I put up a big awning to cover the tables, chairs, and fire pit.

What about cooking? Do you cook right over the fire, or do you have to invest in special camp kitchen stuff?

Depending on what you want to call cooking, you can do it over the open fire and Dutch ovens. I love the Dutch oven pots. My entire kitchen is in a special storage box built to hold food items. Then there is a long extension cord for electricity use. I dug a trench in the ground to hide the cord for my microwave. OK, OK, it is not that completely primitive, but I like my TV and computer. Batteries can also work for some items.

Do you feel safe at night when you sleep in a tipi?

Very much so. Especially with Mr. Smith, Mr. Wesson, and sometimes Mr. Browning (small handguns) right next to me. I have had some unexpected guests, human and animal, and some big bugs. In this day and age, do what you think will offer protection.

Appendix

Documenting the Historic Tipi

Seton, Ernest Thompson. *Two Little Savages*. New York: Doubleday Page & Co., 1903, 64-76.

"You make ten Oak pins a foot long and an inch square, Sam. I've a notion how to fix them." Then Yan cut ten pieces of the rope, each two feet long, and made a hole about every three feet around the base of the cover above the rope in the outer seam. He passed one end of each short rope through this and knotted it to the other end. Thus he had ten peg-loops, and the teepee was fastened down and looked like a glorious success.

Caleb came over and nodded . . . "Got yer teepee, I see? Not bad, but what did ye face her to the west fur?"

"Fronting the creek," explained Yan.

"I forgot to tell ye," said Caleb, "an Injun teepee always fronts the east; first, that gives the morning sun inside; next, the most wind is from the west, so the smoke is bound to draw."

"And what if the wind is right due east?" asked Sam, "which it surely will be when it rains?"

"And when the wind's east," continued Caleb, addressing no one in particular, and not as though in answer to a question, "ye lap the flaps across each other tight in front, so," and he crossed his hands over his chest. "That leaves the east side high and shuts out the rain; if it don't draw then, ye raise the bottom of the cover under the door just a little—that always fetches her. An' when you change her round don't put her in under them trees. Trees is dangerous; in a storm they draw lightning, an' branches fall from them, an' after rain they keep on dripping for an hour. Ye need all the sun ye kin get on a teepee."

Sam and Yan did so, and when it was finished Raften said: "Now, fetch that little canvas I told yer ma to put in; that's to fasten to the poles for an inner tent over the bed."

"Indians don't have them that I ever heard of," said Little Beaver.

"Yan, did ye iver hear of a teepee linin' or a dew-cloth?"

"Oh, I remember reading about it now, and they are like that, and it's on them that the Indians paint their records. Isn't that bully," as he saw Raften add two long inner stakes which held the dew-cloth like a canopy. . . .

The shower grew heavier instead of ending. Caleb went out and dug a trench all round the teepee to catch the rain, then a leader to take it away. . . . "Where's your anchor rope?" asked the Trapper.

Sam produced the loose end; the other was fastened properly to the poles above. It had never been used, for so far the weather had been fine; but now Caleb sunk a heavy stake, lashed the anchor rope to that, then went out and drove all the pegs a little deeper. . . . The smoke hung heavy in the top of the teepee and kept crowding down until it became unpleasant.

"Lift the teepee cover on the windward side, Yan. There, that's it—but hold on," as a great gust came in, driving the smoke and ashes around in whirlwinds. "You had ought to have a lining. Give me that canvas: that'll do." Taking great care not to touch the teepee cover, Caleb fastened the lining across three pole spaces so that the opening under the canvas was behind it. This turned the draught from their backs and, sending it over their heads, quickly cleared the teepee of smoke as well as kept off what little rain entered by the smoke hole."

Fletcher, Alice C., and Francis La Flesche. *The Omaha Tribe*. Lincoln: University of Nebraska Press, 1972, 285–87.

Included in this book is "An Average Day in Camp Among the Sioux," written in 1885, which is from Alice Fletcher's journals.

On the day designated for a journey every one is astir, while the stars are still shining. Those who sleep late are wakened by the crackling of the leaping blaze. Shadowy forms are moving about the entrance to the lodge, and the boiling kettle warns the sleepy one that he had better be up and ready for breakfast. To slip out into the cool morning air, to dash the water over the face and hands, and dry them on the tall grass, is the work of a moment; and, with a little shaking together, every one is ready for the morning meal. This is portioned out by the wife, and each one silently eats his share. The baby still sleeps on its cradle-board, but the older children are relishing their broth with the vigor of young life. As each one finishes, he passes his dish to the matron, springs up, and leaves the tent. When the mother has eaten, she too goes out, and, with rapid steps and bent form, passes around the outside of the tent, pulling up the tent-pins used to hold the tent-cloth taut, and throwing down the poles which support the smoke-flaps. If there is an adult female companion, she takes out the round, slender sticks which fasten the tent-cloth together in front. The two women then fold back the cloth in plaits on each side, bringing it together in two long plaits at the back pole; and this is now tipped backward, and allowed to fall to the ground. The cloth is loosened from the upper part of the pole, and rapidly doubled up into a compact bundle. The baby, who has wakened and lain cooing to the rattle of blue beads dangling from the bow over its cradle-board, gives a shout as the sunlight falls in its face, and watches the quick motions of the mother throwing down the tent-poles, thus leaving the circle free of access. It is the leader's tent which first falls as a signal to all the others.

Meanwhile the boys are off with many a whoop, and snatch of song, gathering together the ponies. The men are busy looking after the wagons, or else sit in groups and discuss the journey and the routine of the intended visits, or attend to the packing of the gifts to be bestowed. All visitors are expected to bring presents to their hosts. The younger children run here and there, undisturbed in their play by the commotion. Soon the boys come riding in, swinging the ends of their lariats in wide circles, and driving before them a motley herd of ponies, some frisking and galloping, and others in a dogged trot, none following a path, or keeping a straight line, but spreading out on each side in the onward movement. As they come abreast with the dismantled tent, the women, without any break in their talk, make a dash at a pony, and generally capture him. The animal may, if he is good-natured, at once submit to be packed, two poles on each side, the packs containing the gala dress: bass filled with meat and corn are adjusted like panniers. Between the poles, which trail behind, a skin or blanket is fastened; and here the young children and the puppy have a comfortable time together as they journey. There are enough ponies for all the men and women to ride, and colts running along beside.

If wagons are to be used in traveling, the tent-poles are tied on each side of the wagon box. The harness is dragged along by a woman, who slings the mass of straps and buckles on the pony's back, he giving a light start as the load drops on him. The buckling is quickly done by the women, and the stores packed in the bottom of the wagon. Finally the kettle and coffee pot are picked up; and nothing is left of the camp but circles of trampled grass, each one with a pile of ashes in its centre.

The delight of being 'off' affects every one, the older people enjoying it sedately: the young men dash about up on the hills, where they stand silhouetted against the cloudless sky. Now and then they drop from their ponies, and lie flat on the ground, while the animal nibbles unconcernedly. The women ride with the stores in the bottom of the wagon, and the men on the seat, driving. It is hard, teeth-chattering work to travel in the bottom of a springless wagon, and no fun to ford a rapid river full of quicksands; for down will go one wheel, and the water come swirling in, wetting every thing and every body. At such times the bags of provisions are held high aloft in the hands: all else must take its chance. Those on the ponies fare better; for, with the feet on the horse's neck, all goes well, unless the little fellow gets into a very bad hole, and topples over into the water. Sometimes the men take off leggings and moccasins, roll them in a bundle, tie them on the head or back of the neck, and wade over, leaving the pony to follow. Such persons generally have time enough to lie down on the bank to dry off, and from their vantage-point watch the struggles of the loaded wagon as the men spring from their seat into the stream, and tug at the wheels to save the vehicle from sinking.

All day we ride over the prairie-trails, starting up the birds, seeing the flash of the antelope, or catching sight of the retreating wolf. If location serves, about three o'clock we camp, always near a stream and timber. It is the work of a few moments to set up the tents, while the men and boys scatter with the ponies. The young girls go laughing to the creek for water, the older women cut and gather the dry wood, and in less than an hour the thin blue smoke is curling through the tent-flaps, and the kettle hanging on its crotch-stick over the fire. Each bundle of bedding is thrown down in the place its owner is to occupy, and it will be untied and spread when needed.

There is a fascination in lying on the grass after a hard day's ride, and watching the settling of a camp. The old men gather in groups, and smoke the pipe. The young men lie at full length, resting on their elbows, their ornaments glistening in the sunlight as these gallants keep watch through the swaying grass of tents where coy maidens are on household cares intent. It is not unlikely that more than one youth is planning how he can best gain access to his sweetheart, and speak a few words to her when she goes for water to the creek in the early morning; and it is equally possible that similar thoughts are flitting through the girl's head. The creek or the spring is the trysting-place for lovers, but the chances for a word are hard to gain.

It is against etiquette for a young woman to speak to any man in public who is not a near relation; and such a one, by the law of the gentes, can never be a lover. But young hearts are stronger than society restrictions; and so when the girl, accompanied by her mother or aunt, goes for water in the early morning, she will sometimes drop behind her chaperone, and the young man, who has lain hid in the grass, darts forward, swiftly and silently, and secures the favored moment. Should the mother turn, he as instantly drops in the grass; while the girl demurely walks on, keeping her secret.

The small boys have already fallen into games, and are shooting arrows of barbed grass. From within the cone-shaped tents comes the sound of the chatter of the women, broken now and then by loud laughter. This might arise from the practical joking of the mother's brother. Such a relative is privileged in the home, and the source of many sports. While the women are cutting up the meat for the evening meal, and preparing the corn-cake, the young man, lounging in the shadows of the tent, has improvised a drum, captured his small nephew, and breaking into song, bids the little fellow dance for his supper. He obeys with a zest, his scalp-lock, and the flaps of his breechcloth, snapping to the tune. The little sister, having secured a premature bite from the mother, stands diligently eating, as she watches her brother's antics, stimulated by the mischief-loving uncle.

There are shiftless folly among Indians, persons who are always borrowing from their more forehanded relatives; but not all borrowers are of this class. A custom prevails concerning borrowing a kettle susceptible of easy misconstruction by our own tidy housewives; that is, that it is expected, when a borrowed kettle is returned, that there will be a small portion of the food which has been cooked in the kettle remaining in the bottom of the pot. The language has a particular word to designate this remnant. Should this custom be disregarded by any one, that person would never be able to borrow again, as the owner must always know what was cooked in her kettle.

Great indignation was the result of the action of a white woman, who returned a scoured kettle. She meant to teach a lesson in cleanliness; but her act was much talked over, and interpreted as fresh evidence of the meanness of white folk!

Soon the savory odors give token that supper is ready. Dishes are set in the traditional places occupied by the members of the family, and the food ladled out, and portioned to each person. The little girl is sent out to call the men in. There is no formality about the family meal. If the father is a religious man, he may take a bit of his food, lift it up, and drop it in the fire; the act is without ostentation, and apparently unobserved by the others. Sometimes the children take their supper together outside the tent. The mother seldom eats until all are fully served. She may join her children with her portion; or if she has female companions in the tent, they will draw together, and gossip over the meal. Every one falls to with zest, and the pot is generally emptied.

After eating, all lie down, stretching out in the tent, or going outside if the day is fine, and resting in the long slanting sunlight. As the air cools, a fire is kindled; and here grouped about the companionable blaze we watch the stars come out. Some persons doze, some discuss the journey, or recount reminiscences of former times: the women gather together and complete the story of the day; while the children chase the fireflies, or subside into drowsy listeners. Across the hum of voices is borne the song of a young man, who, hidden in the grass, lies on his back drumming on his breast as he sings. There are no urgent demands upon any one. The matron has no dishes or linen to wash, or scrubbing to do; there is nothing to clear away after the evening meal. The single pot is emptied, and set to one side. No transitory fashions perplex the fancy of the maiden; no lessons to learn harass the child. The men talk or sing, unconscious of money making or losing, or questions in science or art. To the people, no great disasters are probable, no great successes possible. The stars above silently hold their secrets, the unmarred prairie tells no tales and the silence of uninquisitive ignorance shuts down upon our little life.

To one thrust from the midst of civilization into so strange a camp-circle, the summer days hardly bring a realizing sense of the great estrangement between the two orders of society. It is only when the frozen calm of winter obliterates every touch of color and individuality of outline in the landscape that it becomes possible to gauge fully the mental poverty of aboriginal life. The cold nights when the tent freezes hard so that it sounds like a drum, and the frost lies thick on the bedrobes, make one dread to rise early; and the sun is often up before the fire is kindled, and the kettle bubbles with the morning meal. After looking to what comfort it is possible to give the ponies, and having gathered in the wood, the outdoor work of the day is over.

In winter the tent is made warmer by putting a lining around to half the height of the tent-cloth, and by banking without and within, stuffing with grass the space between the lower edge of the tent-cloth and the ground to keep out the wind. This done, and with plenty of wood to feed the fire, one can be passably comfortable. During the day the women are busy making clothes, mending moccasins, or embroidering gala garments with porcupine quills or beads: the men, if not out trapping, are engaged in fashioning pipes and clubs, or shaping spoons on the ball of the foot. The winter is the season for story-telling, and many hours of the evening are spent in this enjoyment.

The cold season brings pleasures to the children, snowballing, sliding down bill on blocks of ice, or standing on a flat stick and coasting swiftly, balancing with a pole. The glow on the faces of the little ones as they run in breathless from their sport to meet the welcome of the group within the tent, is about the only zest the days bring.

Indian good manners just the reverse of ours, never speak to the person by name when present, no word of courtesy, silence, never good morning or good night, come silently, go silently.

In the tent the wife's place is by the door at the left hand as you enter, husband next, guest at the rear opposite the door. Other members of the family on the right.

We built our fire in the tent, cooked and sat by it. Smoke made the eyes smart, the lower one sits the less smoke. Indians lie down in tent—sensible. I did so. Straw and hay in the bottom of the tent. The floor was all muddy, clay. No grass under the trees. . . .

Fletcher, Alice C., and Francis La Flesche. *The Omaha Tribe*. Lincoln: University of Nebraska Press, 1972, 95–97.

The earth lodge and the tipi (tent) were the only types of dwelling used by the Omaha during the last few centuries. The tipi (pl. 17 and fig. 16) was a conical tent. Formerly the cover was made of 9 to 12 buffalo skins tanned on both sides. To cut and sew this cover so that it would fit well and be shapely when stretched over the circular framework of poles required skillful workmanship the result of training and of accurate measurements. The cover was cut semicircular. To the straight edges, which were to form the front of the tent, were added at the top triangular flaps. These were to be adjusted by poles according to the directions from whirls the wind blew so as to guide the smoke from the central fire out of the tent. These smoke-flaps were called *ti'hugabtli"tha* (from *ti*, "tent or house;" *hugabtli"tha*, "to twist"). At intervals from about 3 feet above the bottom up to the smoke-flaps holes were made and worked in the straight edges. Through these holes pins (sticks) about 8 inches long, well shaped and often ornamented, were thrust to fasten the tent together, when the two edges lapped in front or were laced together with a thong. This front lap of the tent was called *ti'mo"thule* (from *ti*, "tent"; *mo"thuhe*, "breast"). The term refers to this part of the hide forming the lap. The tent poles were 14 to 16 feet long. Straight young cedar poles were preferred. The bark was removed and the poles were rubbed smooth. The setting up of a tent was always a woman's task. She first took four poles, laid them together on the ground, and then tied them firmly with a thong about 3 feet from one end. She then raised the poles and spread their free ends apart and thrust them firmly into the ground. These four tied poles formed the true frame-work of the tent. Other poles—10 to 20 in number, according to the size of the tent—were arranged in a circle, one end pressed well into the ground, the other end laid in the forks made by the tied ends of the four poles. There was a definite order in setting up the poles so that they would lock one another, and when they were all in place they constituted an elastic hut firm frame, which could resist a fairly heavy wind. There was no name for the fundamental four poles, nor for any other pole except the one at the back, to which the tent cover was tied. This pole was called *teçi'deugashke*, "the one to which the buffalo tail was tied." The name tells that the back part of the tent cover was a whole hide, the tail indicating the center line. When the poles were all set, this back pole was laid on the ground and the tent cover brought. This had been folded so as to be ready to be tied and opened. The front edges had been rolled or folded over and over back to the line indicating the middle of the cover; on this line thongs had been sewed at the top and bottom of the cover; the cover was laid on the ground in such manner that this back line was parallel to the pole, which was then securely tried to the cover by the thongs. When this was done, the pole, the folded tent cover were grasped firmly together, and set in place. Then, if there were two women doing the work, one took one fold of the cover and the other the other fold, and walked with her side around the framework of poles. The two straight edges were then lapped over each other and the wooden pins were put in or the thong was threaded. Each of the lower ends of the straight edges had a loop sewed to it, and through both loops a stake was thrust into the ground. The oval opening formed the door, which was called *tizhe'be*. Over this opening a skin was hung. A stick fastened across from one foreleg to the other, and another stick running from one hind leg to the other, held this covering taut, so that it could be easily tipped to one side when a person stooped to enter the oval door open-ing. It was always an interesting sight to watch the rapid and precise movements of the women and their deftness in setting up a tent. On a journey, no matter how dark the evening might be when the tent was pitched the opening was generally so arranged as to face the east. In the village, or in a camping place likely to be used for some time, a band of willow withes was bound around the frame of poles about midway their height to give addi-tional stability.

Page, Elizabeth M. *In Camp and Tepee: An Indian Mission Story.* **New York: Fleming H. Revell Co., 1915, 76, 100.**

Page 76

The Mohonk Lodge, like every other new institution among Indians, had to begin slowly. Mrs. Roe's first idea had been that the actual work of the "Indian House" would fall to the Indian women, that they would prepare for any festivities or clear away afterwards, that they would keep it clean and in order, as the best of them did their tepees in camp. But a few weeks' experience showed the necessity for modifying this plan. Housekeeping in a tepee was a very different science from that in a white man's house. If anything spilled on an Indian woman's pounded earth floor, her method was to let it soak in as speedily as might be and when any given area became soaked to the point of saturation so that odors were intolerable even to a camp-trained nose, then she moved her tepee to a new spot, leaving the sunshine, the rain and Nature's scavengers to do a more thorough house-cleaning than she could ever hope to accomplish. Presented with the problem of a non-porous floor and an immovable structure the Indian's method affected nothing but a glaring failure. The missionaries visited tepee after tepee, some comparatively neat, others disgusting in their dirt and unsightliness, everywhere to be greeted with friendliness.

Page 100

Nearby was a wagon that had just come to a standstill and the man was leading away the horses while the woman, her baby on her back, was pulling the long poles out from behind. Near her the old grandmother, her white hair blown in elf-locks across her face, and her tattered blanket whipped about her bent, shriveled form, was rooting up the grass with a queer bone instrument and pounding the earth down hard and smooth with a stone to make the tepee-floor. Just beyond them a young girl, evidently a bride, judging from her new equipment, had already raised the formidable tripod of sixteen-foot poles, and Mrs. Roe watched with interest the slender girlish figure as, holding the long rope that tied her three main props, she raised pole after pole, setting them in position and then with a quick turn of her wrist sending a loop whirling up the rope to settle over the pointed end and tie it fast. Every movement was easy, assured and graceful, and the brown face, framed in its wings of glossy black hair, that she turned to her mother who cackled approval from the wagon-seat, was radiant with winsome happiness. The two last poles to which the spotless new tepee cloth was fastened were put in place, the cloth was pinned securely together save for the low doorway at the bottom, the lower edge was staked down close on the sunny side but pushed up a little on the other to catch the breeze, before the mother descended from her perch to light the fire in the hole in the centre of the tepee's floor.

Lowie, Robert H. *The Crow Indians.* **New York: Rinehart, 1935, 33–36.**

Everything connected with the tipi belonged to the women's sphere of influence. Desiring extra long poles, they were bound not only to strip the bark but to pare down the logs to a suitable diameter, since a forty-foot pine would be far too thick at the base for a lodge pole. To prevent slipping on the ground they pointed the butts. Like the Blackfoot and Shoshone but in contrast to their Dakota and Cheyenne sisters, the Crow women invariably set up four—not three—poles as a foundation for the rest. It takes a pair to pitch the tipi, one woman raising the crossed foundation-poles above her head, her assistant pulling on a guy rope. The poles are then separated so that the butts form an oblong. Naturally the last pole set up carries the cover, which is brought around the framework and pinned in front. In making this adjustment a woman mounts on rungs made to cross between the two front poles or nowadays uses a regular ladder. Outside the framework are put two special poles, which when moved back and forth open or shut the smoke-hole. For greater safety in stormy weather an inside guy-rope is tied to a peg near the fireplace while outside guys are fastened to a peg on a tree. It took an expert to design a cover, and the housewife employing her would pay her four different kinds of property. The designer had as many as twenty collaborators, whom she instructed in the requisite sewing together of skins and whom the tipi owner remunerated with a feast. A whole day was spent on making the sinew thread. Work on the cover was considered particularly appropriate to the fall of the year. When the lodge was put up, the people burnt sagebrush and weeds inside and as the smoke appeared through the hides they said, "This will keep out the rain," and opened the smoke-vent. The housewife's husband invited old men to smoke with him; the guests recited coups and said, "In the spring this will be a very good tipi from which to make bags and moccasins." The fireplace was approximately in the center of the lodge, and the rear (*aco', aco'ria*) was the place of honor. It was there that chief Rotten-belly received Maximilian, bidding the Prince seat himself at his left. On either side of the entrance was an *aro'kape*, and between it and the rear the *icgyewatsu'a*. In the latter were spread the robes for sleeping, and a husband and wife were likely to rest there when not receiving visitors. The bottom of the cover was pegged to the ground; according to Bear-crane, rocks formerly weighted it down, but another informant restricts this custom to the winter season. Against draft the Crow used a hide screen (*bitä'ricia*), on which the owner often had his deeds depicted. Bedsteads were lacking; the Indian slept on several hides and covered themselves with skin robes. But they had backrests of willows strung with sinew, which were suspended from tripods and covered with buffalo skins.

Hassrick, Royal B. *The Sioux: Life and Customs of a Warrior Society*. Norman: University of Oklahoma Press, 1964, 212–13.

... fifteen to twenty feet high, and extremely heavy, the poles must be well secured in case of wind and storm. Three main poles were first set up as foundation, usually secured with a guy rope to a stake driven into the earth at a point approximately in the center of the tipi. The remaining poles were then placed in the crotch formed by the junction of the main poles. The exact position of the poles was adjusted after the cover was placed, forming an ellipse rather than a perfect circle so that the front of the tipi was steeper than the rear ...

Beds of folded buffalo robes were placed away from the door at intervals around the perimeter of the tipi. The place of honor opposite the door at the back of the lodge was sometimes reserved for the master, although often he and wife slept nearer the entrance to the south. Back rests of willow rods supported by tripods were placed at the head and foot of the owner's bed. Parfleches and soft leather storage bags containing foods, utensils, and clothing were stacked along the dew cloth between the beds. On a forked pole to the left of the door hung the water bag. Firewood was stored just outside the door. From the tipi poles, or from tripods supporting the back rests, the man might hang his painted bonnet case and his medicine pouch. Shield was hung from a forked pole a the rear or the tipi ...

... some families tied cut deer hoofs and later tine bells to the tipi tightening rope. When the wind blew, music filled the tipi ...

Decorated on the exterior with its four medallions and rows of quilled pendants paralleling the entrance, frequently painted with bold symbols and animal figures belonging to the husband, and topped by a spiral of graceful lodge poles extending from the apex often tipped with long white or red deerskin streamers or a scalp which airily fluttered in the breeze.... The dew cloth embroidered in horizontal stripes of quilling served as a handsome background for the painted back rests and decorated packing cases ...

The flaps, for example, were "woman's arms."

Humfreville, J. Lee. *Twenty Years Among Our Hostile Indians.* **New York: Hunter and Co., 1899, 75, 101-4.**

Page 75

There was no regularity in setting the lodges of an Indian camp. No one, not even the chief, had supervision over the manner of place where the lodges were to be set. They were erected in such places as best suited each individual owner. There were no streets or walks, neither did the owner of lodge claim the space around it which he kept clean, and no sanitary precautions whatever were taken. Dirt, bones, and filth of every description were strewn everywhere, and the stench was frequently unendurable to any . . .

Page 101–4

Indian women did all the tanning for the family requirements and the work was done in various ways. When it was intended that a shin should be very soft and pliable, only the brain of the animal and clear fresh water were used. Shins tanned in this way were made into dresses, leggings, moccasins, and other articles of personal and wearing apparel.

The shins used for the lodge covers, and hides used for horse equipment and coarser articles of home and camp life were tanned in a different way and with much less care. They were simply thrown into the water and allowed to remain until their hair fell off, when they were stretched tight on the ground by driving sticks through holes cut in the edges while the hide was wet and soft. Scraping knives made from the horn of the elk were generally used. The women would get down on their hands and knees on the hide and scrape off all the flesh and pulpy matter. After the hide had dried it was put through a process of softening before it was in condition to be used as a lodge cover. The hide used for this purpose was usually that of a buffalo bull, as it was much thicker and more serviceable than that of a buffalo cow. Lodge covers were made by the women, who sewed them together with thongs. From ten to twenty hides were required for the covering of each lodge according to its size.

Poles for the lodges were difficult to obtain by the Indians of the plains, where wood was scarce and good straight poles hard to find, and they were accordingly highly valued. They were procured and finished by the women, and were necessarily of sound, straight young trees, generally of pine, birch or other light but strong wood. They were from one and one-half to three inches in diameter, and from fifteen to twenty-five feet in length. The bark and every small knot or growth was carefully removed from them and they were made perfectly smooth. In putting up a lodge from fifteen to twenty-five of these poles were used. The covering was drawn over them and fastened with skewers or sticks where the edges of the covering met. At the top of the lodge was a large flap in the corner of which the end of a pole was inserted. When this flap was closed it kept the heat in and the cold out, and unless opened when the fire was built the interior would soon be filled with smoke. The lower edge of the lodge covering was fastened to the ground by long pegs driven deep into the earth. The pegs prevented the lodge from being blown over by high winds. The entrance was the only hole of any size, except the top, in the entire covering. This entrance was covered by a hide, drawn over a hoop made from a small branch and hung over the hole. The opening was rarely closed, except in cold weather or to keep the dogs out.

Even the best of these lodges afforded but slight protection against severe storms or bitter cold. Rain found its way into them and the snow blew through the holes underneath the covering, half-filling the interior, making it exceedingly uncomfortable. During the severe rainstorms the beds and sometimes the lodges were flooded, and the occupants were compelled to flee to higher ground with such effects as they could carry.

Lodge fires were necessarily built on the ground and around them the women and children huddled to keep warm. During winter storms when the Indians were compelled to go about their camps in the performance of necessary duties they frequently did so barefoot, as their moccasins and leggings became saturated with water or snow in a short time, and when in that condition were cold and disagreeable to the wearer. They preferred to keep their footwear dry even at the expense of temporary discomfort. Both men and women frequently carried their moccasins and leggings in their hands after having been caught in a cold rain or snowstorm. Sometimes during the cold weather they wore sandals made from the flint hides of some animal as a protection to the soles of the feet. During the prolonged cold storm or blizzard, which was frequent in the far north, the Indians and their animals, including their dogs, were great sufferers.

Lodges of this description were probably the best habitations that could be used by these nomads; for, being continually on the move, it was necessary to transport their entire camp equipment from place to place. They were easily and quickly put up and taken down, and it was a rare thing, even in the severest wind storm, for one of them to be blown down, although it sometimes occurred.

Frequently the coverings were fantastically painted with figures outlined in different colors, red and blue being the favorite. These figures represented different scenes, some depicting a warrior seated on his horse in deadly combat with a hostile brave; an Indian fighting a bear with his spear; an Indian on foot killing a man with his bow and arrow, tomahawk, knife, or lance; or some other prodigious deed of valor. Sometimes the entire lodge covering was decorated with these rude drawings. They generally commemorated some great event in the career of the occupant of the lodge or hairbreadth escape of himself or some of the male members of his family. These drawings were usually made by the men, some of them showing considerable artistic ability. Some of the women also possessed no little skill. Nearly all Indians were fond of decorating their lodge covers in this manner, using the brightest colors they could obtain, and some of their imaginary or real deeds of valor were portrayed in the most picturesque style, though they were often more glaring than artistic.

When the wild Indians retired to sleep they wrapped themselves in the robes or blankets they had worn during the day. The beds were more a name than a reality; these consisted of the dried hides of buffalo, horses, or other animals, laid upon the ground to keep out the dampness. Occasionally they placed an additional buffalo robe or two on top. For pillows they used skins, or any bulky soft stuff which they might have at hand. The interior arrangement of an Indian lodge was a series of such beds arranged in a circle, leaving a space in the center for the fire on which the cooking was done, and it also served to some extent to warm the lodge in winter.

Page 107

People of today little realize how long it took the Indians to acquire or accumulate the small amount of stuff they had in their keeping. Beads, porcupine work, Iroquois shells, claws and teeth of bears and mountain lions, arrowheads, lances, shield, pipes and stems, bows and arrows, and horse equipments largely made up their possessions. These were handed down from generation to generation, and were much prized as having been the property of their forefathers. As they never cleaned or washed their effects, their dirty condition can be readily imagined. All their habitations were foul-smelling from the unutterably filthy condition of their entire belongings.

The Liner or Lining

[i] I have a copy of Ella Deloria's papers and in them she refers to the lining by the Lakota term *ozan* (there is a nasal n and the o is slightly separated from the z). Then I checked with all the language instructors here and they came back with the same translation, a curtain or liner that hangs down.

A dew-curtain, called an *oza*, was hung all around and was long enough to be tucked under the carpet. This was made in matched pieces, with strings attached for tying them together and to the tipi poles. Many an oza (ozan) was elaborately decorated at about 2 to 4 feet intervals, with vertical bands of fancy work in patterns of bright colors—or so painted. This dew-curtain, which was tied to the poles at a height of perhaps 4 feet, and the sloping tipi wall, together formed a little circular alleyway, like a lean-to in shape. And there all surplus foods and robes were stored, as well as extra personal belongings of the family, all packed in proper containers. This storage area was an insulation as we, and the inside of the tipi was always noticeably warmer because of it. The dew-curtain was usually of either doe or calfskin.

This summer curtain was purely for decoration and was hung only across the back of the *ticatku* (place of honor). If anything, this was more elaborate than the winter curtain, the primary purpose of which was to protect against extreme cold.

Again nowhere could we come up with any word for the addition as I refer to it.

I now think that Laubin was confused when translating terms in regard to the lodge and since that is the only book so far, it became the correct term. Again in Lakota language the word ozan translates as something that hangs down (i.e., a curtain in Western terms; *ozanpi* translates to "bed curtains"). Therefore, no relationship to what Laubin describes and I call a canopy. Thus, the term would be more appropriately used for the so-called liner or liners or robes used to hang from the poles. Pete Gibbs, past curator of the British museum and now teacher at the University of South Dakota, supplied this information in e-mail and personal contact.

[ii] As well, Buechel gives *oza(n)* as a curtain, and *oza(n)pi* as bed curtains—probably vertically rigged curtain to give privacy to sleepers. I think *ozan* also refers to the general liner—but that would have to be verified. I know that Eastman called the interior rain ceiling/heat retained an "ozan"—enforcing the meaning of it being a curtain (of any kind).

Undoubtedly all tribes had their own terminology for such riggings for the interiors of tipis. Rather than to establish Lakota terminology as the norm, perhaps the appropriate, corresponding English terms could/should be used. English speakers have enough trouble pronouncing foreign words correctly. I hear Lakota and other words poorly uttered frequently. *Parfletch* (for parfleche)—"sh" sound at the end, not "etch!" (*chaNUMBpa*—the second syllable like English "numb!" Oj vej!

I think the Laubins got it a bit wrong. Milford Chandler actually told them about the ceiling or temporary rain shield, which they called "ozan." They didn't believe him at first, and then didn't credit him as an informant for it. I think Mr. Chandler got his info from Dr. Charles Eastman, a close personal friend of his.

In Lakota, an ozan is a curtain, and the Lakota term for what most people call the liner or dew cloth. At times the liner would be left to hang straight down to reduce the area to be heated inside the lodge. The term evidently derives from *oyu'zan*, "to spread out, as a curtain" (according to Buechel). He translates *ozan* as a curtain (not a ceiling). He gives bed curtains as *ozanpi*. Again, the "a" is nasalized. These are curtains that are hung from ropes stretched across a lodge to give sleeping couples privacy.

I think Chandler used *ozan* for the liner, dividers (*ozanpi*), and a temporary rain shield that could be rigged as a semicircular ceiling toward the back of the inside a tipi, behind the fire. Probably no one ever cut a separate half circle to make a permanent ceiling. In extremely cold weather, the partial ceiling could also serve to trap heat from the fire, making a snug compartment in the back of the lodge. This is what most people now think of as an ozan. Another misconception!

Benson Lanford, noted authority on Native American material and author, supplied this information to me in personal phone calls and letters.

Glossary

Terms Used in the Making of a Tipi

Bevel: Putting an angle on a blade to make it sharp.

Brain-tanned: Using the brains of an animal to break down the fibers of an animal hide to make it soft.

Daguerreotypes: Photographic process developed on tin in the 1830s.

Drawknife: Double-handled blade used for removing surface bark or wood.

Gore: Triangular piece of material that gives extra stretch and strength in going around tie point of poles.

Lockstitch: Stitching on the sewing machine that gives even tension to the top needle and bottom thread bobbin for a strong meeting of the two threads in the middle of the cloth.

Ozan: Liner inside the tipi used to insulate against the weather.

Radius point: A measurement used to find the circumference of the tipi.

Rebar: Concrete reinforcing bar made of steel or iron.

Travois: Poles lashed on either side of a horse or dog. At the base of two or more poles are lashed smaller poles at a right angle, which help form a platform used for carrying camp gear or materials.

Canvas Terms

Duck: The name derives from a trademark of a duck stenciled on heavy sail cloth imported from Europe around 1840. The term applies to a broad range of heavy, plain, flat, woven fabrics. Cotton duck breathes, or lets air pass through the fibers.

Army Duck: Two or more plied yarns in both warp and filling produce a cloth of high tensile strength that meet U.S. Army standards.

Single-Fill (Ounce) Duck: Fabric made with coarse, single-ply yarn. There are two warp yarns for each fill yarn. The warp yarns are woven in pairs, side by side, sized, and are predominant over the filling yarns. Untreated single-fill duck can shrink as much as 7 percent. This much shrinkage has the same effect as cutting 12 inches from the bottom of an 18-foot tipi. In other words, your 18-foot tipi may end up a 17-foot tipi if you don't choose the right fabric. Also, single-fill fabrics, when wet, have a tendency to leak if touched. (This is due to the looseness of the weave and of the yarns.) This shrinkage will also occur when painting a cover.

12-Ounce Natural Canvas: The 12-ounce per square yard, single-filled material. The natural water-repellent qualities of the fabric provide a nice dry tent, especially after it has shrunk up a bit. The material is breathable and has good insulating qualities compared to lighter weight fabrics.

14.90-Ounce Natural Canvas: 14.9-ounce per square yard, 100-percent cotton duck, single-filled material is a popular tent material and for good reason. It is tough, water repellent, and warm. Because it has 20 percent more cotton woven in it than the 12-ounce material, it has superior insulating qualities. The additional cotton also provides a tighter, more water-repellent, and more durable fabric. Although the untreated canvas is susceptible to the harmful effects of sun and moisture, it is an inexpensive alternative for arid to semiarid climates.

Marine: Product description for Marine Finish—a finish specifically designed as the best available in water repellence and mildew resistance. Do not confuse this with Marine Duck, a term often used for any duck sold to the marine trade. Sunforger Marine Finish Boat Shrunk is the original finish to offer the best in weathering qualities. Originally the same kind of process was called Vivatex, but this finish was discontinued some years ago, though some of it is still around.

9.5-Ounce Marine-Treated Army Duck: Quality fabric that is tightly woven, lightweight, and durable. It has a dry treatment that aids in mildew resistance and water repellence.

10.10-Ounce. Marine-Treated Army Duck: A premium cotton fabric more tightly woven than the single-filled variety, creating excellent strength and durability in a lighter weight base fabric. Shrinkage is greatly reduced with this fabric.

Sunforger Marine Finish Boat Shrunk: This finish comes in both 10-ounce and 13-ounce weights. It contains a special added compound that gives two to three times greater water repellence and mildew resistance than other "marine" finishes. The marine- (mineral-) treated army duck is a firm, high-thread-count, plain-woven fabric made with plied (twisted) yarns in both warp and filling. There are at least two yarns in each strand. The 10.10-ounce weight and 12.65-ounce weight refer to the ounces of thread per square yard of material. It is highly recommended if you live in an area of high humidity or rain, such as the Great Lakes area or Southeastern United States, that you use only treated material.

Sunforger Fire Resistant: This product has the treatment for water repellence and mildew resistance and an additional flame-retardant quality that meets the flammability standards of CPAI-84, an industry-wide standard. Many states now require that all tents and tipis or any camping dwelling be fire resistant. It is not the same as being fireproof.

Synthetic Canvases and Treatments

Acrylic-Coated Vinyls, 100-percent synthetic materials, are much heavier, have a problem with condensation, and can be flammable. They also lack the ability of cotton to expand when wet.

15-Ounce Starfire: This fabric is the equivalent to "all weather" ducks that are available. This is a 45 percent polyester/55 percent cotton base fabric pigmented with an acrylic topcoat. Each application is heat sealed onto the base fabric for added strength. It is water, mildew, and fire resistant. It meets Title 19, CPIA-84 (section 6), and FMVSS-302 fire requirements. It is soft, flexible, and easily cleaned. It will last a long time, but cannot be painted.

Polaris: 50 percent cotton/50 percent polyester blend. This fabric is sturdy and long lasting. It is UV resistant, breathable, mildew resistant, water repellent, and flame retardant. Polaris is flexible in extreme temperatures and recommended for tipis that will be set up for extended periods of time. It is very well suited to customization with acrylic paints or exterior latex house paints.

Sunbrella: This material is technically not canvas (which I think of as being natural fiber) but is canvas-like. It is made in 46- and 60-inch widths in an amazing array of colors, including many bold stripe patterns. Acrylic material has the advantage of being very strong and extremely decay resistant, and does not change dimension when wet. It cannot be painted. Sunbrella is used on the bottom extension for liners and some tipis.

Bibliography

Included works were written about a specific time period and based on first-person observations or artistic/photographic material.

1832—Maximilian, Prince of Wied. "Travels in the Interior of North America 1832–1834." *Early Western Travels*. Edited by Reuben G. Thawaites. Cleveland, OH: Arthur H. Clark Company, 1906.

1838—Catlin, George. *Letters and Notes of the Manners and Customs and Conditions of the Native American Indians* 2. New York: Dover Press, 1973.

1844—Carleton, Lt. James H. *The Prairie Logbooks: Dragoon Campaigns to the Pawnee Villages in 1844, and to the Rocky Mountains in 1845*. Chicago: The Caxton Club, 1943.

1849—Eastman, Mary H. *Dahcotah-Life and Legends of the Sioux Around Fort Snelling*. Minneapolis, MN: Ross & Haines, Inc., 1962.

1851—Mayer, Frank Blackwell. *With Pen and Pencil on the Frontier in 1851*. St. Paul, MN: Minnesota Historical Society, 1932.

1852—Kurz, Rudolph Friederich. *An Account of His Experiences Among Fur Traders and American Indians on the Mississippi and the Upper Missouri Rivers During the Years 1846 to 1852*. Washington D.C.: U.S. Government Printing Office, 1937.

1862—Wakefield, Sarah. *Six Weeks in the Sioux Tepees*. Falcon, 2003.

1873—Kavanagh, Thomas W. *Domestic Architecture in the Comanche Village on Medicine Creek, Indian Territory, Winter 1873*. Self published at http://php.indiana.edu/~tkavanag/asoule.html. 1990.

1874—Coleman, Winfield. *Feeding Scalps to Thunder: Shamanic Symbolism in the Art of the Cheyenne Berdache*. Vol. 1. People of the Buffalo. Dietmar Kuegler, Germany: Tatanka Press, 2003.

1876—Viola, Herman J. *Warrior Artists: Historic Cheyenne and Kiowa Indian Ledger Art*. Washington, D.C.: National Geographic Society, 1998.

1880—McCoy, Ronald. *Kiowa Memories: Images from Indian Territory 1880*. Santa Fe: Morning Star Gallery, 1987.

1885—Hamilton, Henry and Jean. *The Sioux of the Rosebud: A History in Pictures*. Norman: University of Oklahoma Press, 1981.

1898—Miller, Fred E. *Photographer of the Crows*. Missoula, MT: University of Montana: Carnan Vidfilm, Inc., 1985.

1890—Grinnell, George Bird. *The Cheyenne Indians, Their History and Ways of Life, I and II*. Lincoln: University of Nebraska Press, 1923.

1892—Mooney, James. *The Ghost: Dance, Religion, and the Sioux Outbreak of 1890–1892*. Washington D.C.: Government Printing Office, 1896.

1896—McClintock, Walter. *Old Indian Trails*. New York: Houghton Mifflin Co., 1923.

1896—McClintock, Walter. *Painted Tipis and Picture Writing of the Blackfoot Indians*. Southwest Museum Leaflet, no. 6 (1936).

1898—Ewers, John C. *Murals in the Round: Painted Tipis of the Kiowa and Kiowa-Apache Indians*. Washington D.C.: Smithsonian Institution Press, 1978.

1899—Humfreville, J. Lee. *Twenty Years Among Our Hostile Indians*. New York: Hunter and Co., 1899.

1902—Albright, Peggy. *Crow Indian Photographer: The Work of Richard Throssel*. Albuquerque: University of New Mexico Press, 1997.

1902—Kroeber, Alfred L. *The Arapaho*. Lincoln: University of Nebraska Press, 1983.

1903—Brownstone, Arni. *Bear Chief's War Deed Tipi*. Vol. 2. People of the Buffalo. Dietmar Kuegler, Germany: Tatanka Press, 2005.

1903—Seton, Ernest Thompson. *Two Little Savages*. New York: Doubleday Page & Co., 1903.

1905—Tibbles, Thomas Henry. *Buckskin and Blanket Days: Memoirs of a Friend of the Indians.* A Bison Book, 1905.

1906—Aadland, Dan. *Women and Warriors of the Plains—The Pioneer Photography of Julia E. Tuell.* New York: MacMillan, 1996.

1909—Wilson, Gilbert L. *The Horse and the Dog in Hidatsa Culture.* Anthropological Papers of the American Museum of Natural History XV, Part II. New York: American Museum Press, 1924.

1910—McClintock, Walter. *The Old North Trail: Life, Legends and Religion of the Blackfeet Indians.* London: MacMillan, 1910.

1911—Fletcher, Alice C., and Francis La Flesche. *The Omaha Tribe.* Lincoln: University of Nebraska Press, 1972.

1912—Seton, Ernest Thompson. *The Book of Woodcraft.* Garden City: Garden City Publishing, 1912.

1915—Page, Elizabeth M. *In Camp and Tepee.* New York: Fleming H. Revell Co., 1915.

1916—Durkin, Peter. "Cane Windbreaks for Tipis." *Whispering Wind* 34, no. 6 (2005).

1916—Jennings, Vanessa Paukeigope. "Kiowa Battle Tipi." *Whispering Wind* 34, no. 6 (2005).

1917—Campbell, Stanley (Vestal). "The Cheyenne Tipi." *American Anthropologist,* 1915. Vol. 17, 685–94.

1927—Campbell, Stanley (Vestal). "Tipis of the Crow Indians." *American Anthropologist,* January–March 1927.

1928—Salomon, Julian Harris. *The Book of Indian Crafts and Indian Lore.* New York: Harper and Row, 1928.

1931—Douglas, Fredrick H., ed. *The Plain Indian Tipi.* Denver Art Museum, Leaflet no. 19 (April 1931).

1932—Seton, Ernest Thompson. "Tipis: Habitations of the Indians." *The Totem Board-Woodcraft Indian Service.* Vol., 2. no 2. Seton Village, Santa Fe: University of New Mexico Press, Alberquerque, NM, February 1932, 62.

1935—Lowie, Robert H. *The Crow Indians.* New York: Rinehart, 1935.

1936—McClintock, Walter. *Blackfoot Tipi.* Southwest Museum Leaflet, no. 5, 1936.

1937—Marriott, Alice. "The Trade Guild of the Southern Cheyenne Women." *Bulletin of the Oklahoma Anthropological Society,* 4 April 1956.

1937—Pohrt, Richard A. *A Gros Ventre Painted Lodge.* Vol. 1. People of the Buffalo. Dietmar Kuegler, Germany: Tatanka Press, 2003.

1940—Lyford, Carrie A. *Quill and Beadwork of the Western Sioux.* Boulder, CO: Johnson Books, 1982.

1945—Ewers, John C. *Blackfeet Crafts.* United States Department of the Interior. Washington, D.C.: Stevens Pint: Schneider, 1945.

1954—Hunt, W. Ben. *Indian Crafts and Lore.* New York: Golden Press-West Publishing, 1954.

1954—Lowie, Robert H. *Indians of the Plains.* American Museum of Natural History, 1954.

1955—Ewers, John C. *Horse in Blackfoot Indian Culture,* Washington, D.C.: Smithsonian Institution Press, 1955.

1957—Laubin, Reginald and Gladys. *The Indian Tipi: Its History, Construction, and Use.* Norman: University of Oklahoma Press, 1957.

1960—Thulin, William D., and Thomas Thulin. *Tipi Life.* Self-published, 1960.

1961—Denig, Edwin Thompson. *Five Indian Tribes of the Upper Missouri.* Norman: University of Oklahoma Press, 1961.

1962—Grinnell, George Bird. *Blackfoot Lodge Tales.* Lincoln: University of Nebraska Press, 1962.

1964—Hassrick, Royal B. *The Sioux: Life and Customs of a Warrior Society.* Norman: University of Oklahoma Press, 1964.

1967—Bad Heart Bull, Amos. *A Pictographic History of the Oglala Sioux.* Lincoln: University of Nebraska Press, 1967.

1967—Hiller, Carl. *From Teepees to Towers: A Photographic History of American Architecture.* Boston: Little Brown & Company, 1967.

1969—Powell, Peter J. *Sweet Medicine: Volume One.* Norman: University of Oklahoma Press, 1969.

1970—*Mother Earth News.* "The Plains Indian Tipi, Build it and Move In." Vol. 1, no. 1 (January 1970): 29–40.

1971—Peterson, Helmut and Wolfgang de Bruyn. *Indianishe Zeltbemalun.* Leipzig, Germany: Prisma-Verlag, 1990.

1972—Hungry, Adolf Wolf. *Tipi Life.* Good Medicine Book, 1972.

1972—Mails, Thomas E. *Mystic Warriors of the Plains.* Garden City, NY: Doubleday, 1972.

1972—Wood, Guy (Darry). "The All American, Do It Yourself, Portable Shelter." *Aquarian Angel,* 1972.

1973—Capps, Benjamin. *The Indians (the Old West).* New York: Time-Life Books, 1973.

1973—Hunt, W. Ben. *The Complete How-To Book of Indiancraft.* Racine, WI: Macmillan Publishing Co., 1973.

1973—Past, Earl. "The Indian Tipi 'Castle of the Plains.'" *American Indian Crafts and Culture* 7, no. 2 (February 1973): 8–11, 15.

1973—Raleigh, Steve, and Paul Alexander. "Tipi-Making." *Woodstock Craftsman's Manual* 2, New York: Praeger, 1973.

1973—United States Department of the Interior. *Painted Tipis by Contemporary Plain Indian Artists,* 1973.

1974—Moore, John. "A Study of Religious Symbolism Among the Cheyenne Indians." PhD diss., New York University, 1974.

1974—Neidenthal, John. "Cheyenne Decorations." *Florida Indian Hobbyist Assoc. Newsletter,* 1974.

1974—Robinson, Peter D. "Tipi on the Tundra." *Alaska,* October 1974.

1975—Lodge Owners Society, Lodge Owners Quarterly, or Lodge Owners. Self-published newsletter/small magazine out of SD and then TN, 1975.

1975—*Women's Quilting Society.* The Old West Series. New York: Time-Life Books, 1975.

1978—Maurer, Evan M. *Visions of the People: American Indian Art.* New York: Doubleday, 1978.

1979—Blair, Neal. "The Incomparable Tipi." *Wyoming Wildlife,* March 1979.

1979—Brasser, Ted J. "The Pedigree of the Hugging Bear Tipi in the Blackfoot Camp." *American Indian Art* (Winter 1979).

1979—Hatton, E. M. *The Tent Book.* Itasca, IL: Houghton Mifflin, 1979.

1979—Holley, Linda A. *North Fla. Indian Culture Society. Whispering Wind.* Vol. 12, no. 5 (1979): 16–17.

1979—Kolk, Glenn and Jacalyn. "Tipi Tips." *Camping Journal,* April 1979, 33–52.

1979—*Mother Earth News.* "That Good Ol' Tipi Living," May/June 1979.

1979—Neale, Gay. "The Ultimate Mobile Home." *The Indian Trader* 10, no. 10 (1979): 1–4

1980—Coleman, Winfield. "The Cheyenne Women's Sewing Society." Conference on Design Symbology and Decoration at the Buffalo Bill Historical Center in Cody, WY, 1980.

1980—Glenn, George. "The Lodge." *Track of the Wolf.* Book of Buckskinning I. Texarkana, TX: Rebel Publishing Co., 1980: 53–73.

1980—Kiowa Indian News. *Painted Tipis of the Kiowa and Kiowa-Apache Indians,* September 1980.

1980—Walter, Bill. "Tipi Know-How." *Track of the Wolf.* Book of Buckskinning I., Texarkana, TX: Rebel Publishing Co., 1980.

1980—Walter, Bill and Lila. "Flap Facts." *The Buckskin Report,* June 1980.

1981—Horse Capture, George P. "The Timeless Tipi Symbol of the Great Circle of Life." *The American West,* March/April 1981.

1982—Brasser, Ted J. "The Tipi as an Element in the Emergence of Historical Plains Indian Nomadism." *Plains Indian Anthropologist* 1 (1982): 27–98.

1982—Finnigan, James T. *Tipi Rings and Plains Prehistory: A Reassessment of Their Archaeological Potential.* National Museums of Canada,1982.

1982—Jackson, Jaime. *The Canvas Tipi.* Lafayette, CA: Lodgepole Press, 1982.

1982—Thomson, Scott. "A Tipi Dedication." *Whispering Wind.* Vol. 15, no. 3 (1982): 22–23.

1984—Engages. "Canvas Tipi." *The Museum of the Fur Trade Quarterly* 20, no. 3 (1984): 13–14.

1984—Lorenz, Ray. "A Shelter for All Seasons." *Sports Afield,* October 1984, 66–69, 108–112.

1984—Yue, David and Charlotte. *The Tipi: A Center of Native American Life.* New York: Knopf Books for Young Readers, 1984.

1985—Lynch, "Owl" Lanny Winterin. "Tipi Furnishings." *Buckskin Report* (Spring 1985).

1986—Wuellner, Lance H. "The Indian Tipi." *Muzzle Blasts,* November 1986.

1987—O'Meara, Jim. "The Terrible Tipi." *Muzzleloader,* November/December 1987.

1987—Whitefield, Patrick. *Tipi Living. Simple Living.* East Meon, Hampshire, UK: Permanent Publications, 1987.

1988—Peterson, Karen Daniels. *American Pictographic Images: Historical Works on Paper by the Plains Indians.* Alexander Gallery-New York and Morning Star Gallery-Santa Fe, New Mexico. Princeton Polychrome Press, New York, 1988.

1989—Warcloud, Paul. *Dakotah Sioux Indian Dictionary.* Tekakwith Fine Arts Center, Sisseton, SD.

1990—Nabokov, Peter, and Robert Eastern. *Native American Architecture.* New York: Oxford University Press, 1990.

1990—Peterson, Helmut and Wolfgang de Bruyn. *Indianishe Zeltbemalun.* Leipzig, Germany: Prisma-Verlag, 1990.

1990—Reese, Frank Pond. *The 20th Century Indian Tipi: How to Choose and Use a Tipi Today.* Reese Tipis Publication, 1990.

1990—Scriver, Bob. *The Blackfeet: Artist of the Northern Plains, The Scriver Collection of Blackfeet Indian Artifacts and Related Objects, 1894–1990.* Kansas City: Lowell Press, Inc., 1990.

1993—Atwill, Lionel. "Tepee: The Ultimate Hunting Lodge." *Sports Afield,* October 1993, 74–80.

1993—Brewer, Kathy. "A Brief Discussion of 19th Century Plains Women's Roles." *Whispering Wind* 26, no. 2 (1993): 20–23.

1993—"The Buffalo Hunters." The American Indians Series. Alexandria, VA: Time-Life Books, 1993.

1993—Goble, Paul. *Her Seven Brothers.* New York: Bradbury Press, 1988.

1993—Lewellyn, Dixie. *A Plains Indian's Talking Tipi.* Beverly Hills, FL: Rhythm & Reading Resources, 1993.

1994—Kaye, Dena. "Taming a Tepee: A Western Fantasy in Aspen." *Architectural Digest,* August 1994, 72–75, 139–141.

1994—Szabo, Joyce M. *Howling Wolf and the History of Ledger Art.* Albuquerque: University of New Mexico Press, 1994.

1994—Taylor, Colin F. *The Plains Indian.* New York: Crescent Books, 1994.

1994—*This is My Tipi: A Gallery Guide to Dreams and Dusty Stars: Blackfeet Lodge Decoration.* Pamphlet, High Desert Museum, Bend, OR, September 1993–July 10, 1994.

1995—Blue Evening Star. *Tipis & Yurts: Authentic Design for Circular Shelters.* Ashville, NC: Lark Books, 1995.

1995—Durkin, Peter. "Black Feet Tipis." *Whispering Wind* 30, no. 6 (1995): 38–39.

1995—Durkin, Peter. "Carrying Tipi Poles: You can get there from here.'" *Whispering Wind* 30, no. 5 (1995): 36.

1995—*Tribes of the Southern Plains: The American Indians.* Alexandria, VA: Time-Life Books, 1995.

1996—Durkin, Peter. "Cheyenne Tipi Beds." *Whispering Wind* 34, no. 2 (2004).

1996—Durkin, Peter. "Cheyenne Tipi Guilds." Unpublished article, 1996.

1996—Durkin, Peter. "Miniature Tipis and James Mooney." *Whispering Wind* 28, no. 2 (1996): 40–43.

1996—Durkin, Peter. "Rawhide Tipi Doors." *Whispering Wind* 27, no. 5 (1996): 39–41.

1996—Jennys, Susan. "The Tipi in the Early 1800s." *Muzzleloader,* January/February 1996. 45–49.

1996—McCoy, Ron. "Searching for Clues in Kiowa Ledger Drawings." *American Indian Art Magazine* (Summer 1996): 54–61.

1996—Redfern, Patrick. *The Tipi-Construction and Use.* Self-published booklet, Book Publishing Co., 1996.

1997—Durkin, Peter. "The Hide Tipis" *Whispering Wind* 29, no. 1 (1997): 38–39.

1997—Durkin, Peter. "Tipi Camps." *Whispering Wind* 28, no. 5 (1997): 30–33.

1997—Ewers, John C. *Plains Indian History and Culture: Essays on Continuity and Change.* Norman: University of Oklahoma Press, 1997

1997—Housler, Wes. "Mountaineers and Hide Lodges." *Rendezvous,* October/December 1997.

1997—Jennys, Susan. "Ladies Living History: Portraying the Plains Indian Woman Part II." *Muzzle Blasts Magazine,* May 1997, 43–45.

1997—Miller, Preston E., and Carolyn Corey. *The Four Winds Guide to Indian Artifacts.* Atglen, PA: Schiffer Publishing Ltd., 1997.

1998—Chronister, Allen. "Chief Washakie and an Eastern Shoshone Camp." *Whispering Wind* 29, no. 3 (1998): 21–23.

1998—Chronister, Allen. "Nez Perce Camp, Rawhide Tipis and Hats." *Whispering Wind* 29, no. 6 (1998): 24–26.

1998—Durkin, Peter. "Plains Indian Encampment." *Whispering Wind* 29, no. 4 (1998): 38–39.

1999—Garcia, Louis. "Tipi Tinklers." *Whispering Wind* 130, no. 2 (1999): 4–11.

1999—Hunter, Tony A. "Short Visit to a Tipi: Parts One and Two." *Muzzleloader,* January/February 1999, 26–30.

1999—Jones, James E. *Make Your Own Tipi.* Living History Publishers, Inc., 1999.

1999—Living History Publishers, Inc., *Tipi Living Magazine.* 5 issues, (July 1999–Winter 2001).

1999—Terry, Mike. *Daily Life in a Plains Indian Village 1868.* New York: Clarion Books, 1999.

2000—Adams, Kimberly L. and Dawson Kurnizki. *Tipi (Native American Homes):* New York: Rourke Publishing, 2000.

2000—Berry, Charlotte. "Tipi." *Cowboys and Indians* (Fall 2000).

2000—Chronister, Allen. "Cloth Tipi Covers." *Museum of the Fur Trade Quarterly* 36, no. 3 (2000): 13–14.

2000—Durkin, Peter. "Southern Cheyenne Hide Tipi." *Whispering Wind* 30, no. 6 (2000): 44–45.

2000—Roller, Pete. "Winter Tipi Camping." *Whispering Wind* 30, no.6 (2000): 22–25.

2001—Durkin, Peter. "Tipi Interiors." *Whispering Wind* 31, no. 3 (2001): 42.

2001—Goble, Paul. *Her Seven Brothers.* Reprint ed. London: Aladdin Books, 1993.

2001—Greene, Candace S. *Silver Horn: Master Illustrator of the Kiowas.* Norman: University of Oklahoma Press, 2001.

2001—Pearson, David. *Yurts, Tipis and Benders or Circle Houses: Yurts, Tipis and Benders.* White River Junction, VT: Chelsea Green Publishing, 2001.

2002—Geissal, Dynah. "Tipi." *Backwoods Home Magazine,* July/August 2002, 17–23.

2002—Macek, Jiri. *Taborime V Tipi.* Liga lesni moudrosti., 2002.

2003—Bruno, Isabelle. *Yourtes et Tipis.* France: HoÄ«beke, 2003.

2003—Cannavaro, Brian. *How to Set up a Blackfoot Lodge.* Kalispell, MT: Fort Selish Spice and Trading Co., Inc., 2003.

2003—Cortez, Javier and Dyanne Fry. *Tipi: A Modern How-To Guide.* Austin, TX: Dos Puertas Publishing, 2003.

2003—Hunt, Heidi. "Tipis and Yurts." *Mother Earth News,* December/January 2003, 56–59.

2003—Price, Dan. "Living Free." *Mother Earth News*, December/January 2003.

2004—Durkin, Peter. "Cheyenne Tipi Beds." *Whispering Wind* 34, no. 2 (2004): 26–27.

2005—Durkin, Peter. "Cane Windbreaks for Tipis." *Whispering Wind* 34, no. 6 (2005): 32–35.

2005—Helland, Mary Arnoux. *Picking Up Ewers' Trail of the Fort Peck Reservation Assiniboines.* Vol. 2. People of the Buffalo. Dietmar Kuegler, Germany: Tatanka Press, 2005.

2005—Jennings, Vanessa Paukeigope. "Kiowa Battle Tipi." *Whispering Wind* 34, no. 6 (2005): 16–18.

2006— Belitz, Larry. *The Buffalo Hide Tipi of the Sioux.* Sioux Falls, SD: Pine Hill Press, 2006.

2006—Hungry, Adolf Wolf. *The Tipi: Traditional Native American Shelter*. Summertown, TN: Native Voices, 2006.

Resources

U.S. Tipi Makers

AH~KI Tipi
510.268.8779
hometown.aol.com/redpath/earth.html

Anchor TeePees
PO Box 3477
Evansville, IN 47733
800.322.8368
www.anchorinc.com/teepees.html

Buffalo Days Tipi
R.D. 1, Box 70
Galway, NY 12074
578.882.9997
www.portalmarket.com/buffalodaystipi.html

The Colorado Tent Company
6489 E. 39th Ave
Denver, CO 80203
800.354.8368
303.294.0924
www.coloradotent.net

The Colorado Yurt Company or
Earthworks Tipis
28 W. S. 4th St.
Montrose, CO 81402
800.288.3190
www.coloradoyurt.com

Conneautville Canvas
Conneaut Ville, PA
814.587.2755

Dave Ellis Canvas Products
387 CR. 234
Durango, CO 81301
877.259.2059
www.cowboycamp.net

DeadBird Tipis
33905 RCR 43A
Steamboat Springs, CO 80487
970.879.0314
www.deadbirdtipi.com/index.php
hertzog@springsips.com

Don Strinz Tipi
2325 'O' St. Rd.
Milford, NE 68405
800.525.8474 (TIPI)
www.strinztipi.com

Dreaming Buffalo Tipi
PO Box 9285
Santa Fe, NM 87504
505.424.8626
www.dreamingbuffalo.com

Fabricon
806 W. Spruce
Missoula, MT 59801
406.728.8300
fabricon.com

Four Directions Tribal Dwellings
1801 Old Greensprings Hwy.
Ashland, OR 97520
541.601.6997
541.821.0400
www.roguedwellings.com

Four Seasons Tentmasters
4221 Livesay Rd.
Sand Creek, MI 49279
517.436.6245
www.geocities.com/tentmasters

Fox River Traders
110 Ombre Rose Dr.
Combined Locks, WI 54113
920.759.2347
www.foxrivertraders.com

Goodwin Cole
8320 Belvedere Ave.
Sacramento, CA 95826
800.752.4477
goodwincole.com

Harris Canvas & Camping
501 30th Ave. SE
Minneapolis, MN 55414
612.331.1321
800.397.5026
www.harriscanvascamp.com

The High Desert Trading Post
Tularosa, NM
www.highdeserttradingpost.com
sales@highdeserttradingpost.com

Idaho Canvas Products
195 Northgate Mile
PO Box 50856
Idaho Falls, ID 83405
888.395.7999
www.idahocanvas.com/id50.htm

Jesse Salcedo Tipis
PO Box 620834
Woodside, CA 94062
650.369-0383
www.salcedocustomtipi.com/jesse.html

Kinney's Tents and Tepees
1407 N. Custer Ave.
Hardin, MT 59034
406.665.3422
888.523.3422
www.forevermontana.com/tepees.htm

Konza Tipi
785.494.2797
barchery@kansas.net
www.kansas.net/~barchery
   /ol'ebuff.html/konza_tipi.htm

M BAR M
2970 Texas Ave.
Grand Junction, CO 81504
970.263.4599
www.teepees4u.com

Manataka Tipis
PO Box 476
Hot Springs Reservation, AR 71902
501.627.0555
www.manataka.org/page39.html

Montana Canvas
Box 390
Belgrade, MT 59714
406.388.1225
www.montanacanvas.com

Nomadics Tipi Makers
17671 Snow Creek Rd.
Bend, OR 97701
541.389.3980
www.tipi.com

Northwest Tipis
2001 S. Main St. Rd.
Horicon, WI 53032
920.485.4744

Old West Enterprises
RR 1 Box 11
Lapwai, ID 83540
www.angelfire.com/id/tipimaker
tipi_maker@yahoo.com

Panther Primitives
PO Box 32
Normantown, WV 25267
304.462.7718
www.pantherprimitives.com

R. K. Lodges
PO Box 58
Hackensack, MN 56452
218.675.5630
www.rklodges.com

Real Goods Solar, Wind & Hydro Web site
for an Ecologically Sustainable Future
www.realgoods.com

Reese Tipis, Inc.
2291-J Waynoka Rd.
Colorado Springs, CO 80915
719.265.6519
866.890.8474 (TIPI)
www.reesetipis.com

Red Cloud Tipis
PO Box 518
Pine Ridge, SD 57770
605.887.2810
indianyouth.org/redcloud.html

Red Hawk Trading
321 N. 5400 W.
Malad, ID 83252
800.403.4295 (HAWK)
www.redhawk-trading.com

Reliable Tent and Tipi
120 N. 18th St.
Billings, MT 59101
406.252.4689
800.544.1039
www.reliabletent.com

Sagebrush Tipi Works
PO Box 1811
Priest River, ID 83856
877.993.1155
www.sandpoint.net/sagebrush/index.html

Sheridan Tent and Awning
PO Box 998
128 N. Brooks
Sheridan, WY 82801
800.310.6313
www.sheridantent.com

Sky Lodge Tipis
247 Granite St.
Ashland, OR
888.488.8127
541.488.7737
www.skylodgetipis.com

Spirit Tipis
PO Box 262
Skull Valley, Arizona 86338
928.442.3225
www.spirittipis.com

Spring Valley Lodges
N. 3515 Hwy. F
Brodhead, WI 53520
608.897.8474 (TIPI)

Straw Bale Tipis
PO Box 126
Moyie Springs, ID 83845
208.267.1086
www.strawbaletradingpost.homestead.com/
    Tipis.html

Sweetwater Tipis and Canvas
PO Box 262
Hayesville, NC 28904
828.389.4028
www.main.nc.us/openstudio/sweetwater/
    canvas.html

Tent Smiths
PO Box 1748
Conway, NH 03818
603.447.2344
www.tentsmiths.com

Thunder Mountain Tent & Canvas
107 McClure Ave.
Nampa, ID 83651
208.467.3109
800.925.9175
www.idfishnhunt.com/thunder.html

Tomahawk Lodge
Evolution to single pole–style tipi
www.portalmarket.com/teepee.html

Trapline Lodges
PO Box 14
Whitehall, MT 59759
406.287.3580
www.trapline.com

Warren "Two Bears" Billiter
6800 Englewood
Raytown, MO 64133
816.353.6264

Western Canvas Supply & Repair
PO Box 1382
Cody, WY 82414
800.587.6707
www.westerncanvas.com

White Buffalo Lodges
PO Box 1382
Livingston, MT 59047
866.358.8547
www.whitebuffalolodges.com

Willow Winds
962 F-30
Mikado, MI 48745
989.736.3487
www.jmwillowwinds.com/index.shtml

Wrights Canvas
41 Independence Way
Cashmere WA 98814
509.782.3932

Yakima Tent
PO Box 391
Yakima, WA 98907
800.447.6169
www.yakimatent.com

Tipi Makers Around the World

Australia

OneMoon Tipis
PO Box 27
Kinglake Vic 3763
Tel. (61)+3+57 861 629
www.onemoon.com

Rainbow Tipis
3/2 Brigantine St.
Byron Bay, NSW. 2480
Arts & Industry Estate
Tel. (+61) 02 66 855895
www.RainbowTipis.com.au

The Tipi Company
PO Box 555
Tipi Farm
Dereham, Norfolk NR20 5PZ
Tel. 00 44 (0)1362 680074
www.thetipico.com

Tipis by Don O'Connor
Gentle Earth Walking
PO Box 395
Daylesford, AU 3460
Tel. 03 5348 7506
users.netconnect.com.au/
   ~sueandon/index.html

United Earth Tipis
Tel. 02 95643991
www.unitedearth.com.au

Belgium

Tymmyt Tents
9320 Nieuwerkerken
www.tymmyt.com/home.htm

Canada

Arrow Tipi
Box 115
Burton BC
VOG-1EO
Tel. 866.902.3399
www.arrowtipi.com

Bushwhacker
6517 Concession 7
Tosorontio, R.R.#1
Everett, ON L0M 1J0
Tel. 705.435.1211
www.bushwhacker.ca

Fun Camp Company
Box 7
Oro, ON L0L 2X0
Tel. 888.297.5551
www.funcampco.ca/Tipi.htm

Labis Moon Canvas Dwellings
BC
labiscreations.com
gitta@labiscreations.com

Murray Tent and Awning
Tel. 800.774.0442
www.murraytentandawning.com/
   html/teepee.html

Porcupine Canvas
33 First Ave.
Schumacher, ON P0N 1GO
Tel. 800.461.1045
www.porcupinecanvas.com

Quappelle Tipi Maker
Box 1754
Ft. Qu'Appelle
SK, SoG-1So
Tel. 306.332.4524
www.quappelletipimaker.com

Sun Maker Arts
Terry Wild
Box 159
Cumberland, BC, Vor 150
Tel. 1.250.2070
www.dwayneedwardrourke.com/
   Pages/Sunmaker/Pages/
   TipisByTerry.html

Teepee Tseiwei
640 Atironta
Wendake, QC G0A 4V0
Tel. 418.842.0157
www.tipiquebec.com

Traditional Villages
Box 655
Biggar, Saskatchewan
SOK OMO
Tel. 306.948.3832
crazyhorse_193@hotmail.com

Wi Tents and Tipis
Charlevoix, QC
Tel. 418.240.0295
www.witentes.com

Wikwemikong Tipis
81 Yellek Trail
North Bay, ON
Tel. 705.472.2577
www.wikwemikongtipicompany.com

Wolfchild Tipis and Tents
96 Mill Rd.
Cardiff Echoes, AB
Tel. 780.939.3866
members.shaw.ca/wolfchildinc/tipi.htm

Czech Republic

Delta tents
V.Toman - DELTA International
Smilovského 20
120 00 Prague 2
www.ares.cz/tents/index_uk.htm delta@ares.cz

France

Atelier de Sellerie Jean Lehman
2 rue de la garde
67 390 Saasenheim
Tel. 03 88 57 76 59
www.tipi-tente.com
jean.lehmann3@wanadoo.fr

Germany/Austria

Fam West
GmbH, Rannetsreit 3 $^1/_3$
94535 Eging am See
BRD, Germany
Tel. +49.(0)8544 – 9180878
www.naturzelte.de/eng

Red Fox
Delitzscher Straße 34
04129 Leipzig, Germany
Tel. 0341/ 9 11 35 16
www.redfox-indianstore.de

TiBo - Tipi am Bodensee
Bernaumühle 2
D-88099 Neukirch
Tel. 0 75 28 - 95 16 40
www.tipi-bodensee.de

Tipi-Werkstatt
A-8554 Soboth 155
Austria
Tel. +43 3460 259
www.tipi.at/e/1st.html

Tipi Zelte
Prälat-Sommer Str. 46
D-76846 Hauenstein/Pfalz
Tel. 06392-2390
www.tipi-zelte.de

Great Britain/Scotland

Albion Canvas
Unit 6, Barkingdon Business Park
Staverton
Totnes
Devon
TQ9 6AN UK
Tel. + 44 (0) 1803 762230
www.albioncanvas.co.uk

Grays Marquees
Southbank, Blackwater Rd.
Newport, Isle of Wight
PO30 3BG
Tel. 01983 525221
tipi-tents.co.uk/index.html
info@tipi-tents.co.uk

Hearthworks Tipis
Mr. Tara Weightman
Bushy Combe Farm
Bulwarks Ln.
Glastonbury BA6 8JT
Tel. 01749 860 708
www.hearthworks.co.uk/tipis.html

Lassana Tipis
The Linnet, Wrigglebrook Ln.
Kings Thorn, Hereford, HR2 8AW
Tel. 01981 541076
www.lassanatipis.com

Manataka Tipis
Every Hill, Shells Ln.
Colyford, Devon
EX24 6QE
Tel. +(44)(0) 1297 553456
www.manatakatipis.co.uk

Past Tents
New Farm, Main St,
Walesby, Newark
Nottinghamshire, England
NG22 9NJ
Tel. 00 44 (0)1623 862480
www.past-tents.demon.co.uk

Shelters Unlimited
Rhiw'r Gwreiddyn
Ceinws
Machynlleth Powys
SY20 9EX
Tel. 01654 761720
www.tipis.co.uk

Thunderbird Tipi
Tel. +44 (0)1505 842103
www.piloto.u-net.com

Timberline Tipis
The Old Pottery
Bull Lane
Warminster, Wiltshire BA12 8AY
Tel. O7979 420153
www.timberlinetipis.co.uk

Wigwamsam Tipis
The Strawbale Barn
The Yarner Trust
Welcombe Barton
Welcombe
Devon EX39 6HF
Tel: 0044 (0)1288 352316
www.wigwamsam.co.uk

Wolf Glen Tipis
Williamhope Cottage
Clovenfords
Galashiels
TD1 3LL
Tel. 01896 850390
www.wolfglentipis.co.uk

Woodland Yurts
80 Coleridge Vale Rd. S.
Clevedon

North Somerset
BS21 6PG
Tel. 01275 879705
www.woodlandyurts.co.uk

World Tents
Redfield
Buckingham Rd.
Winslow
Bucks
MK18 3LZ
Tel. 01296 714555
www.worldtents.co.uk

India

Canvas Emprium
283, Azad Market
Delhi-11006
Tel. +091 11 23628696
www.canvashome.com

Italy

Giorgio Strazzari Tipis
Tel. 0039031807957
www.tepee.it
lontrastrazz@libero.it

Japan

Gfield Tipis
www.joy.hi-ho.ne.jp/gfield

Netherlands/Holland

ATELIER ANNELIES
postcode 1054(ergens in
Amsterdam Centrum) naar
Atelier Annelies in 7831 AV
Nieuw Weerdinge
Tel. 0591-521018
www16.brinkster.com

Bosjuweel Tipis
Koopvaardijweg 3, 6541 BR
Nijmegen, 024-3776086
www.bosjuweel.nl/tentenevenementen/
    index.htm

Tipi Verhuur
dhr. Ben Acket
Nieuwemaastrichtsebaan 11
5126 NS Gilze
06- 51899830,
www.tipiverhuur.nl

Womime Wakan Tipis
Grindweg 216 8483 JL
Scherpenzeel (Friesland)
Vanuit Nederland: 0561481405
www.womime-wakan.com

New Zealand

Jaia Tipis
PO Box 93,
Takaka
Golden Bay
Tel. 03 525 9102
www.jaiatipis.com

Poland

Hau Kola Tipis
www.tipi-tent.com
kola@tipi.com.pl

South Africa

Sacred Arrow Tipis
www.icon.co.za/~tipi
tipi@icon.co.za

Tipis from Africa
PO.Box 1750
Nelspruit 1200
Tel. +27 (0)13 7440124
home.wanadoo.nl/jeff.mos/
    TipisFromAfrica

South America

Bacab – Nomad Art Movement
Argentina, Brazil, Chile, Peru, Bolivia
Tel. 00.54.11.4.779.0721
www.bacab-nam.org
bacabnam@hotmail.com

Spain

Tipiwakan
Tel. (00-34) 639.689.879
www.tipiwakan.org/page04_e.htm
info@tipiwakan.org

Switzerland

FAM ZELTWELT
FAM ZELTWELT GmbH
Grossholz / Postfach 158
8253 Diessenhofen TG
Schweiz

Tel. ++41/52/657 5858
www.zeltwelt.ch/deutsch/tipi/index_deutsch
    _tipi.htm

PEDDIG-KEEL
Bastelartikel +
Tipivermietung
Bachstrasse 4
9113 Degersheim
Tel. 071 371 14 44
www.peddig-keel.ch

Tipi Pole Suppliers

Buffalo Tipi Pole Co.
Idaho
208.263.6953

Chris Jenkins
Canada
250.489.5141
jenkins.chris@shaw.ca

Noisy Creek Adventures
Jeff Everson
Wisconsin
715.362.3903
noisycreekadv@hotmail.com

Nomadics Tipi Makers
Washington
541.389.3980

Pole Specialties
Montana
406.491.4966

Reese Tipis
Colorado
866.890.8474
info@reesetipis.com

Rembrandt Leather
Iowa
712.286.6321

Willow Winds
Jim Miller
Michigan
517.736.3487

Canvas Suppliers

Astrup Co.
Dealers all over the United States
Cleveland, OH
800.786.7601
www.astrup.com

Claredon Textiles, Inc.
7630 Southrail Road, Unit A
North Charleston, SC 29420
800.752.1332
www.claredontextiles.com
info@claredontextiles.com

Itex, Inc.
PO Box 5187
Englewood, CO 80155
800.525.7058
sales@banwear.com

John Boyle & Co.
Dealers all over the United States
Statesville, NC
800.438.1061
www.johnboyle.com

Buffalo Hide Tipi Makers

Larry Belitz (SS&A TRADERS)
7537 E. Belleview St.
Scottsdale, AZ 85257
480.970.4854
www.buffalorobe.com

Wes Housler
22 Bell Canyon Rd.
Cloudcroft, NM 88317
505.687.3267
wes@pvtnetworks.net

Mike Bad Hand Terry
541.964.3184
www.warriorsplus.com
badhand@badhand.org

"The Whirlwind" Ken Weidner
www.ibco.net/whirlwind/index.htm
whirlwind@ucom.net

Museum and Gallery Sites

Type in the word *tipi, tipis,* or *teepees* on many of these sites, and you will find hundreds of photos and drawings of lodges.

Beinecke Library Digital Collection, Yale University
beinecke.library.yale.edu/dl_crosscollex/ default.htm

Biographical Dictionary of the Mandan, Hidatsa, and Arikara
lib.fbcc.bia.edu/fortberthold/TATBIO.htm

The British Museum
www.thebritishmuseum.ac.uk/compass

Camping with the Sioux: Fieldwork Diary of Alice Cunningham Fletcher, Smithsonian
www.nmnh.si.edu/naa/fletcher/fletcher.htm

Canadian Museum of Civilization
www.ottawakiosk.com/civilization.html

Colorado Springs Pioneers Museum
www.cspm.org

Colorado State University Libraries
digital.library.colostate.edu

Curtis Collection
www.curtiscollection.com

Division of Anthropology, American Museum of Natural History
anthro.amnh.org

Division of Anthropology, University of Nebraska State Museum
www-museum.unl.edu/research/ anthropology/anthro.html

Domestic Architecture at the Comanche Village on Medicine Creek
php.indiana.edu/~tkavanag/asoule.html

Gallery of the Open Frontier, University of Nebraska Press
gallery.unl.edu/Gallery.html

Glenbow Archives
www.glenbow.org

Glenbow Museum
www.glenbow.org/lasearch/searmenu.htm

Indian Congress Photo Gallery, Omaha Public Library
www.omahapubliclibrary.org

The Lewis Henry Morgan Collection, New York State Museum
www.nysm.nysed.gov/morgan

Library of Congress, American Memory Collection
memory.loc.gov/ammem/amtitle.html
lcweb2.loc.gov/ammem/daghtml/daghome.html
memory.loc.gov/ammem/index.html

Library of Western Fur Trade Historical Source Documents
www.xmission.com/~drudy/mtman/mmarch.html

Mathers Museum Collections, The Wanamaker Collection
www.indiana.edu/~mathers/collections/photos/wanamake.html

Minnesota Historical Society Library and Collections
www.mnhs.org/library/index.html

Museum of Anthropology, University of Missouri-Columbia
coas.missouri.edu/AnthroMuseum/default.shtm

National Gallery of Art
www.nga.gov/cgi-bin

National Museum of the American Indian
www.nmai.si.edu

The New York Public Library
digital.nypl.org/mmpco

The Old North Trail by Walter McClintock
www.1st-hand history.org/ONT/album1.html

PBS, The West
www.pbs.org/weta/thewest/resources/archives/one/61_16.htm

Peabody Museum, Yale University
www.peabody.yale.edu/databases

Pikes Peak Library District
library.ppld.org/SpecialCollections/Project/admin/photosearch.asp?fields=subject&terms=Tipis

Plains Indian Drawings
www.tribalarts.com/feature/plains/index.html#7

Princeton University Library Western Americana photographs collection
diglib.princeton.edu

Rudolph Friederich Kurz's Sketchbook
www.xmission.com/~drudy/mtman/gif/kurz/kurz.html

Smithsonian Institution Research Information System (SIRIS)
www.siris.si.edu

Smithsonian's Collections of Kiowa Drawings
www.nmnh.si.edu/naa/kiowa/mooney.htm

Smithsonian, The Horse in Blackfoot Indian Culture by John C. Ewers
www.sil.si.edu/DigitalCollections/BAE/Bulletin159

South Dakota State Historical Society
www.sdhistory.org

Spurlock Museum at the University of Illinois Housing the Laubin Collection
www.spurlock.unuc.edu

Trans Mississippi & International Exposition
www.omaha.lib.ne.us/transmiss

University of Oklahoma Western History Collection
libraries.ou.edu/etc/westhist/intro

University of Washington Libraries Digital Collections
content.lib.washington.edu/aipnw/index.html

Western Americana Collection, Princeton University
www.princeton.edu/~rbsc/department/western

Photo and Drawing Credits

Page ii: Photo by Linda A. Holley.
Page vii: Photo by Wayne McDowell ("Weird Wayne").
Page 1: Courtesy of the Denver Public Library, Western History Collections. Photo by W. S. Soule, Call Number X-32133.
Page 5: Buffalo Bill Museum in Cody, Wyoming. 1998 photo by Linda A. Holley.
Page 8: Tallmadge Elwell Daguerreotype-Bridge Sq. Minneapolis, MN. Photo courtesy of the Minneapolis Public Library, Minneapolis Collection.
Page 9: Courtesy of Denver Public Library, Western History Collection.
Page 12: Pine Ridge Agency, S. D., Jan. 17, 1891. Private collection.
Page 13: Photo from Linda A. Holley collection.
Page 19: Gilbert L. Wilson, "Horse and Dog in Hidatsa Culture," *Anthropological Papers of the American Museum of natural History,* Vol. XV, Part II, New York, 1924.
Page 20: Postcard collection of Linda A. Holley.
Page 22: Seton design from his book *Little Savages* and Salomon/Ben Hunt-style redrawn from their craft/woodland articles, ca 1932.
Page 25: Illustrations from *The Indian Tipi: Construction and Use,* by Reginald and Gladys Laubin. Copyright 1957, 1977 by the University of Oklahoma Press, Norman. Reprinted with permission of the publisher. All rights reserved.
Page 30: Wes Housler buffalo-hide tipi, Custer Battlefield Museum, Garry Owen, MT. Permission from Put Thompson.
Page 31: Courtesy of the Western History Collection, University of Oklahoma Library.
Page 32: Drawings by Linda A. Holley.
Page 33: Drawings by Linda A. Holley.
Page 34–35: Drawings by Linda A. Holley with the permission of Brian Cannavaro.

Page 37: Drawings by Linda A. Holley.
Page 38: Southern Cheyenne 1907 tipi, 4 feet tall, from Freya's by permission.
Page 39: Drawings by Linda A. Holley.
Page 43 (above): Drawing by Linda A. Holley.
Page 43 (below): Photo by Linda A. Holley.
Page 44: Photo by Linda A. Holley.
Page 50: Photo by Jan Kisteek.
Page 51: Drawings by Linda A. Holley.
Page 52: Drawings by Linda A. Holley.
Page 53: Drawings by Linda A. Holley.
Page 54: Drawings by Linda A. Holley.
Page 55: Drawings by Linda A. Holley.
Page 56: Drawings by Linda A. Holley.
Page 57: Drawings by Linda A. Holley.
Page 58: Drawings by Linda A. Holley.
Page 59: Drawings by Linda A. Holley.
Page 60: Drawings by Linda A. Holley.
Page 61: Photos by Wayne McDowell.
Page 62: Photos by Wayne McDowell.
Page 63: Photos by Linda A. Holley.
Page 64: Drawings by Linda A. Holley.
Page 66: Drawings by Linda A. Holley.
Page 67: Drawings by Linda A. Holley.
Page 68: Drawings by Linda A. Holley.
Page 69: Postcard from Linda A. Holley collection.
Page 70–71: Drawings by Linda A. Holley.
Page 72: Photos by Wayne McDowell.
Page 73: Drawings by Linda A. Holley.
Page 74: Drawings by Linda A. Holley.
Page 75: Photos by Wayne McDowell.
Page 76: Drawings by Linda A. Holley.
Page 77: Liner made by Mike Terry. Photo by Mike Terry.
Page 78: Benson Lanford collection.
Page 79: Permission from the Western History Collections, University of Oklahoma Libraries, and Interior of Crow Lodge. Photographed by Richard Throssel.
Page 82: Drawings by Linda A. Holley.
Page 83: Drawings by Linda A. Holley.
Page 84: Drawing by Linda A. Holley.

Page 85: Drawing by Linda A. Holley.

Page 86: Photos by Wayne McDowell.

Page 87: Drawings by Linda A. Holley.

Page 88: Photos by Linda A. Holley.

Page 89: Permission from Guy Pazzogna Vaudois, France.

Page 90: Permission from Guy Pazzogna Vaudois, France.

Page 91: Permission from Atelier de Sellerie.

Page 92: Drawings A, B, and C by Linda A. Holley. D from Jaia Tipis of New Zealand.

Page 94: Photo from Rainbow Tipis in Australia.

Page 96: Photo by Linda A. Holley.

Page 98: Photo by Linda A. Holley.

Page 99: Photo by Linda A. Holley.

Page 100: Photo by Linda A. Holley.

Page 101: Photos by Linda A. Holley.

Page 102: Photo by Linda A. Holley.

Page 103: Photo by Linda A. Holley.

Page 105: Drawings Linda A. Holley.

Page 106: Drawings Linda A. Holley.

Page 108: Drawings by Linda A. Holley.

Page 109: Photos by Wayne McDowell.

Page 111: Drawings by Linda A. Holley.

Page 112: Drawing by Linda A. Holley.

Page 113: Drawings by Linda A. Holley.

Page 114: Drawings by Dr. Eweres.

Page 116: Courtesy of Benson Lanford collection.

Page 117: Drawings by Linda A. Holley.

Page 118 (left): Photo by Linda A. Holley.

Page 118 (right): Drawing by Linda A. Holley.

Page 120: Drawings by Linda A. Holley.

Page 121: Drawings and photo from Chicago Field Museum. Photo taken by Linda A. Holley.

Page 127: Photos by Louis Beergeron.

Page 129: Photo by Linda A. Holley.

Page 131 (above right and left): Photos by Linda A. Holley.

Page 131 (middle): James Jones.

Page 131 (below): Permission Nomadics Tipis.

Page 132 (above left, above right, middle, and below left): Photos by Linda A. Holley

Page 132 (below right): Photo by Brewers.

Page 134: Photo by Linda A. Holley.

Page 135: Photo by Linda A. Holley.

Page 137 (above and below): Photos by Jim Creighton.

Page 138 (above): Photo by Carolyn Corey, Four Winds Trading Co.

Page 138 (below): Denver Art Museum. Photo by Linda A. Holley.

Page 139: Lodge made by Darry Wood. Owned and decorated by Linda A. Holley.

Page 140 (above and middle): Photos by Kathy Brewer.

Page 140 (below): Photo by Linda A. Holley.

Page 141: Buffalo Bill Museum. Photos by Linda Holley.

Page 142: Photo by Linda A. Holley.

Page 143 (above): Courtesy of Western History Collections, University of Oklahoma Libraries.

Page 143 (below): Collection of Linda A. Holley.

Page 146: Photos by Linda A. Holley.

Page 147: Photo by Linda A. Holley.

Page 148: Photos by Linda A. Holley.

Page 150: Drawings by Linda A. Holley.

Page 151: Drawings by Mike Cowdrey.

Page 153: Photo by Linda A. Holley.

Page 154: Photo by Linda A. Holley.

Page 155: Photos by Linda A. Holley.

Page 156: Photo by David Ansonia.

Page 159 (above): Photo by Jeff Mos.

Page 159 (middle and below): Photos by Linda A. Holley Arts.

Page 167: Photo by Linda A. Holley.

Page 168: Photo by Linda A. Holley.

Page 169: Photo by Steve Gill.

Page 170: Photos by Ken Weinder.

Page 171: Photo by Linda A. Holley.

Page 172: Photos by Linda A. Holley.

Page 173: Photo by Linda A. Holley.

Page 176 (left): Photo by Linda A. Holley.

Page 176 (right): Photo by Richard Reese.

Page 184: Tipi decorated by David Ansonia and made by Nomadics Tipis. Photo by David Ansonia.

Page 185: Photo by Chakra Tipis.

Page 186: Photo by Piers Conway.

Page 187 (above): Preston Miller collection.

Page 187 (middle and below): Photos by Jan Kisteck.

Page 188: Photo by "White Horse."

Page 189: Photos by Kriztina Szabo.

Page 190: Dmitri collection.

Page 191: Photo by Larry Schwartz.

Page 192: Private collection.

Page 193: Photo by Linda A. Holley.

Page 194 (left two photos): Photos by Rainbow Tipis.

Page 194 (right): Photo by Brook E. Demos of Chicago.

Page 195: Photos by Arrows Tipis.

Page 196: Drawings by Froit Tipis and Yurts, #148

Page 197: Permission of Fun Camp Co. of Canada.

Color Insert Credits

Page 1: Drawings by Linda A. Holley.

Page 2 (above): Putt Thompson.

Page 2 (below): Photo by Linda A. Holley.

Page 3 (above): Back of Linda A. Holley's tipi.

Page 3 (below): Photos by Linda A. Holley.

Page 4 (above): David Ansonia.

Page 4 (below): Photo by Linda A. Holley.

Page 5 (above): Photo by Kriztina Szabo.

Page 5 (below): Photo by Jan Kisteck.

Page 6: Photo by the Brewers.

Page 7 (above): Mount Carmel tipi by Schawartz.

Page 7 (below): Photo by Ken Weidner.

Page 8 (above): From Linda A. Holley collection.

Page 8 (below): Photo by Linda A. Holley.

Index